LONGITUDINAL RESEARCH

Longitudinal Research in the Behavioral, Social, and Medical Sciences

An International Series

Editor:

SARNOFF A. MEDNICK
University of Southern California and
Psykologisk Institut, Copenhagen

Longitudinal Research

Methods and Uses in Behavioral Science

EDITED BY

Fini Schulsinger
Sarnoff A. Mednick
Joachim Knop

Martinus Nijhoff Publishing

BOSTON/THE HAGUE/LONDON

DISTRIBUTORS FOR NORTH AMERICA:
Martinus Nijhoff Publishing
Kluwer Boston, Inc.
190 Old Derby Street
Hingham, Massachusetts 02043, U.S.A.

DISTRIBUTORS OUTSIDE NORTH AMERICA:
Kluwer Academic Publishers Group
Distribution Centre
P.O. Box 322
3300 AH Dordrecht, The Netherlands

Library of Congress Cataloging in Publication Data

Main entry under title:
Longitudinal research, methods and uses in behavioral science.

(Longitudinal research in the behavioral, social, and medical sciences;   1)
Bibliography: p.
Includes index.
1. Psychological research — Longitudinal studies. 2. Social sciences — Longitudinal studies. 3. Longitudinal method. I. Schulsinger, Fini. II. Mednick, Sarnoff A. III. Knop, Joachim. IV. Series.
BF76.5.L67   300'.72   80-26885

ISBN 0-89838-056-1

CONTENTS

PREFACE

This volume is the product of a course on longitudinal prospective research arranged by the three editors in Arhus, Denmark, in 1978. The course was supported by the *Nordisk Kulturfond* for young researchers from the Nordic countries, who had planned or had simply involved themselves in longitudinal prospective research projects of various kinds. The twenty-six participants represented a wide range of professions: statisticians, psychologists, psychiatrists, nutritionists, and public health researchers. The teachers came from many countries and represented many disciplines.

The course was very successful, especially from the point of view of the quality and investment of the teachers. We felt also that the course met a strong need in this relatively new field of research. Therefore, we asked the teachers to prepare written versions of their lectures so that they could have wider dissemination; they agreed to do so.

The present book is composed of these contributions. The first chapter, after outlining some of the problems with traditional strategies in mental health research, goes on to suggest some of the possible preventive applications of longitudinal research methods. Included in Parts II and III are papers on design problems and on the tools of long-term research, such as genetics and classification, biological measurements, epidemiological guidelines, statistical models, disease registers, and developmental psychology. Part IV includes chapters describing experiences and results of a number of ongoing and well-known longitudinal projects using different types of samples — birth cohorts, school cohorts, and clinical cohorts. Part V continues this theme, its papers focusing on cohorts of individuals at high risk. Finally, Part VI considers the implications of long-term research and offers some recommendations for the design and conduct of such investigations.

The studies in this volume present a picture of longitudinal research as a method involving large populations and complex statistics. Despite the fact that the concerns of this type of work often involve clinical populations, examples of the idiographic or single-case study are not represented among these papers. This does not mean, however, that the editors find this approach less useful. Rather, it is a reflection of the fact that these methods find their way into our work in informal ways; the idiographic approach primarily inspires hypothesis formation in our discussions. Much longitudinal research effort is enriched by including the contributions of clinicians with a deep knowledge and understanding of mental patients and their lives. Several of the projects described in this volume are conducted by research teams that include clinicians.

It is our hope that these pages will serve as an appetizer and introduction for students and young researchers. While the volume is heavily behaviorally oriented, the problems and solutions described are present in social and physical health research as well.

Copenhagen   F.S.
September 1980   S.A.M.
                                                            J.K.

I INTRODUCTION: *Longitudinal Research and Intervention*

1 PROBLEMS WITH TRADITIONAL STRATEGIES IN MENTAL HEALTH RESEARCH

Sarnoff A. Mednick, John J. Griffith, and Birgitte R. Mednick

When we consider the prodigious efforts that have been made to understand the etiology of the variety of psychiatric and social deviance that humans exhibit, it can prove depressing for a researcher to assess the yield. Some have responded to this apparent lack of progress by searching for mystical sources of understanding or for magical, often poetic, treatments. Others have responded with nihilistic humor. One observer has characterized the growing mountain of writings on the etiology of mental illness as having produced an "independent problem of waste disposal." J. N. Morris (1975, p. 218), the English epidemiologist, has rather dryly commented on schizophrenia research: "Up to now, unhappily, this activity has yielded few new facts; a deficiency somewhat obscured by the communicativeness of psychiatrists and social scientists."

Perhaps one reason for the impatience with research efforts in this field is that the more "physical" illnesses have apparently yielded their secrets more readily. There is value in considering some of the reasons for this fact. Statements of etiology are statements of causes. It is difficult to construct causal statements without the benefit of experimental manipulation. This is the method of choice in attempts to understand the causes of disease. We can inject a laboratory animal with a suspect virus

3

and observe directly whether it develops a given illness. With proper controls and assuming that the animal succumbs to the illness, we can unequivocally conclude that we have established at least one partial cause of that illness. By analogy, to conduct traditional experimental-manipulative research into the causes of psychoses or recidivistic delinquency properly, we would have systematically to inflict upon children those suspect life circumstances (biochemical, physiological, social-en-vironmental) that we hypothesize to be etiologically important and observe the outcome. Of course, we will not and cannot do this research; the standard experimental-manipulative method is not available to us in research into the causes of mental illness or social deviance.

As a further elaboration of the relatively disadvantageous position of etiological research in the area of mental illness, the following related point should be made: for the more physical illnesses, organ systems sufficiently similar to those of humans may be found in laboratory animals. Therefore, findings from experimental-manipulative research using laboratory animals as subjects may, with some confidence, be generalized to diseases involving the same physical organs in humans. The organ system under most serious suspicion in *mental* illness, however, may not be considered sufficiently similar to that of other animals. Thus, in this area we are prevented from generalizing from animal research to the human situation.

In conclusion, we are forced to ignore our most powerful methods for understanding the causes of human deviance. This is very likely a larger part of the reason for our poor progress than are stupidity, laziness, or scientific ineptitude. We are hampered simply because our subjects are human. Because their illnesses are peculiarly human, we are barred from using our most effective tools. Instead, we have struggled to elaborate empirical correlates of human deviance and on this basis to construct theories that we cannot test directly.

PRIMARY PREVENTION RESEARCH — AN EXPERIMENTAL-MANIPULATIVE APPROACH

One way exists in which clinical research can exploit the efficiency and clarity of the experimental-manipulative method. The same humane code that inhibits us from experimentally manipulating the lives of children in an attempt to make them mentally ill encourages and supports careful and well-founded attempts at experimental manipulations aimed at preventing mental illness. Let us hasten to make clear that even if such preventive attempts were effective, they would not point directly to etiology; but let us not be discouraged by this fact. The history of medicine clearly documents that prevention of an affliction can precede full understanding of its cause. Moreover, the types of interventive manipulations that help to prevent mental illness may suggest where we might most profitably search for causes. For these reasons, research on the primary prevention of human deviance suggests itself as a method for consideration.

There are other reasons for a shifting emphasis toward research on prevention. As pointed out by Gruenberg (1976), the medical profession has historically given highest priority to research and development in the area of treatment technology. One effect of the great advancements made within this area has been that the proportion of chronically ill people has been steadily growing in Western societies. To be able to meet the practical demands created by this growing proportion of patients in continuous need of treatment, it has been necessary to allocate progressively more effort and resources to the continued search for improvement of treatment methods. Thus the original emphasis on treatment may be seen as having created a self-perpetuating process. One by-product of this course of events has been that relatively fewer resources and less effort have been spent in the area of prevention. It is, however, quite clear that the devotion of an increasing portion of society's resources to research on prevention may help to reduce human suffering as well as the expenditure of society's resources.

It perhaps should be pointed out that no matter what the causes of mental illness might be, an emphasis on prevention will very likely be more useful than an emphasis on treatment. If the causes are biochemical or neurophysiological, these conditions may not prove to be readily reversible. It is even more likely that the learned reactions to such biological deficiencies or environmental inadequacies may become extremely difficult to change by the time the condition is recognized. Even if the original cause of a mental or social deviance is removed, the fixed habits of response to such deviance may be resistant to treatment. Primary prevention is likely to cost less and to reduce suffering.

In order to proceed with a prevention research strategy, however, the following conditions are essential: (1) well-founded hypotheses relating possible causal and contributory factors to specific intervention techniques, and (2) methods for the early detection of individuals in the population who have a high probability of becoming deviant. The need for early detection methods arises because planned interventions may be temporally and psychologically intrusive and therefore inappropriate for administration on an unselected population-wide basis. In these cases attention will be focused on high-risk groups — that is, groups in which the expected incidence of deviance is higher than in the general population.

It is to provide data necessary for the development of etiological hypotheses and early detection techniques that longitudinal research projects are conducted as part of a primary prevention program. The approach involves assessment of a population and following that population until some significant portion evidences deviance. At that point, it is possible to analyze the data of the initial assessment and to attempt to find reliable characteristics that distinguish the eventual deviants. Such distinguishing characteristics may be useful in early detection programs and may provide hypotheses regarding intervention techniques. It is clear that the prospective longitudinal method is central to this approach.

RATIONALE FOR THE USE OF LONGITUDINAL METHODOLOGIES

Before discussing various longitudinal methods, we will first point out some of the problems involved in the use of the most obvious alternative approach: the cross-sectional comparison of a group of deviants with controls.

In the typical contrasted-groups design, researchers generally recognize that their research design involves some biased selection of deviant cases. An attempt is often made to overcome this bias by observing control groups matched for "relevant" factors. But do we really know what factors are relevant? We must begin to face the fact that almost any control group we select will be biased in some respects. For example, for valid generalization the number of patients and controls in a study should be in proportion to their numbers in the population to which we wish to generalize. Otherwise, generalization is likely to be highly fallacious. This often-repeated fallacy in research design is well known in epidemiological research: it is called *Berkson's Fallacy*. To quote Berkson (1955), "If the subpopulation . . . of a group X and its control not-X is not representative in the ratio of the marginal totals of X and not-X . . . in the general population, then association will appear even if it does not exist in the general population from which the study population is drawn." We might add that associations that do exist in the parent population may also be masked by control groups not representative of the not-X population. This also means that another investigation drawing a small sample from the same control population in the same manner is very likely to select a population biased in some other way. No doubt this problem is at the root of many failures to replicate research results in the fields of mental illness and asocial behavior. In a high-risk study, the Berkson's Fallacy problem applies as well to comparisons of high- versus low-risk groups. However, results of comparisons of eventual schizophrenics within the high-risk group (perhaps 10–16 percent of the high-risk group) with the nonschizophrenics in the high-risk group (84– 90 percent) may be generalized to other populations of high-risk subjects.

The impossibility of obtaining appropriate control subjects is most dramatically evident in the case of research in schizophrenia. The be- havior of schizophrenics is unquestionably markedly altered as a conse- quence of the illness. The schizophrenic experiences educational, economic, and social failure; prehospital, hospital, and posthospital drug regimens, long-term institutionalization; chronic illness; and sheer mis- ery. It is clear that appropriate control groups are not easily available. Consequently, in comparisons of controls and schizophrenics it is often difficult to judge what portion of the reported differences has unique relevance to the etiology of schizophrenia and what portion is a function of the consequences of schizophrenia. For example, a study by Silverman (1964) demonstrated critical differences between acute and chronic schizophrenics on a perceptual task. In 1966 Silverman, Berg, and Kantor repeated the same tasks with long-term and short-term nonpsychiatric *prisoners*. They found that the differences observed in these tasks among the normals and "acute" and "chronic" prison inmates were almost precisely the same as those observed among the normals and acute and chronic schizophrenics. The actual scores for the imprisoned and the hospitalized were highly similar at equal levels of institutionalization. The original differences observed were interpreted as the result of insti- tutionalization. Any differences found between schizophrenics and con- trols can be related to the consequences of the illness as well as to the causes. In effect, schizophrenics may be so contaminated by the conse- quences of their illness that they usually are not suitable subjects for research into the causes of their own illness. The same conclusions may be drawn at least to some degree with respect to conditions of social deviance and for less serious conditions of mental illness.

Studies of the families of schizophrenics have often been based on the etiological assumption that disturbed family processes have a role in the development of schizophrenia. It is, however, just as reasonable to as- sume the obverse of this assumption: that the presence of a schizophrenic child or adolescent plays a role in the development of family disturbance.

There is evidence for the latter assumption: studies of families with children with severe physical illnesses found them to be similar to families with schizophrenic offspring. Note that this does not imply that family variables are not involved in the etiology of schizophrenia. The study of families in which one member is already schizophrenic is simply not an excellent way to investigate this question.

All these objections to the cross-sectional study of the correlates of mental illness or social deviance, or the differences between deviants and controls, are not to suggest that these methods are bankrupt and should be abandoned. Rather, the point is that in addition to such research strategies, carefully controlled prospective longitudinal study is required.

A variety of strategies are possible in planning a longitudinal study. In the remainder of this chapter we describe longitudinal research designs and discuss some advantages and problems associated with each type.

TYPES OF LONGITUDINAL METHODOLOGIES AND THEIR ADVANTAGES

The basic definition of a longitudinal project requires some assessment of the subjects at a minimum of two points in their lives. The points of measurement should be relatively widely spaced (months or years rather than minutes or hours). Several methods for classification of longitudinal research have been suggested in the literature, including grouping by type of design and nature of subject population (Wall and Williams, 1970). The classification system outlined below is organized according to type of design and, within each design, by nature of subject population.

Among longitudinal methodologies, one can differentiate between those based on normal, unselected, representative populations and those utilizing nonrepresentative, specially selected, or deviant groups. Included in the second category are studies that use rather small normal birth cohorts but study them intensively.

Normal Representative Populations

The normal representative populations tend to be large (in the thousands). As listed in Table 1.1, several types of normal representative populations have been employed in prospective longitudinal research.

Table 1.1. Classification of Longitudinal Research.

I. Correlative Longitudinal Research

    A. Studies of Normal Representative Populations
       1. Prospective birth cohorts
       2. Prospective school-age cohorts
       3. Prospective adult cohorts
       4. Prospective community cohorts

    B. Studies of Nonrepresentative Populations
       1. Normal birth cohorts
       2. Specialized cohorts
          a. Twin cohorts
          b. Adoptee cohorts
          c. First-cousin cohorts
          d. Birth difficulty/neonatal brain damage groups
          e. Follow-up studies of deviants
          f. Studies of children at risk

II. Experimental-Manipulative Research

Birth Cohorts. A representative birth cohort ideally includes all births taking place in a given geographical area within a given time period. The British national birth cohorts are examples of such populations (Butler and Alberman, 1969; Chamberlain et al., 1975).

School and Adult Cohorts. School and adult cohorts include all individuals of a given age who are living in a given geographical area at a given time. Studies by Magnusson and Dunér (1980) and Thomae (1980) are examples of research using these two types of population.

Community Cohorts. As opposed to the previously described cohort types, community cohorts include all persons living in a given area, thus covering the entire age range. Hagnell (1980) describes a research project involving a community cohort.

This large-project design involving normal representative populations is the ideal method for most research purposes. It is ideal for a number of reasons:

1. *Representativeness.* One profound advantage of this design is the generalizability of the obtained results. For example, investigators have

established a relationship between certain autonomic nervous system factors and antisocial behavior (Siddle, 1977). These findings have been noted in a variety of highly selected abnormal populations. Their applicability to a general population could justifiably be questioned. Wadsworth (1976) presents a demonstration of the existence of a similar relationship in the 1946 British birth cohort. This one statement from a representative population supports the generalizability of the previously published work.

2. *Multipurposeness.* The large population cohorts have a great advantage in that they can be multipurpose. The oldest of these studies, the 1946 British birth cohort, has been quite successful in developing a multipurpose stance over the years. Since the populations are large, they can be used to determine early signs of later deviance for almost any social or medical condition that has a prevalence of more than 1 percent in the population. This fact suggests that in the planning stages of a new project, a cross-disciplinary group of scientists (and perhaps funding agencies) should be involved. It is important that research councils keep in mind and encourage this possible multidisciplinary utilization of birth cohorts. It can result in great economies (which will please the funding agencies) and in important opportunities to study the interaction of disparate variables (which will please the scientists).

A corollary of this multipurposeness is the possibility that a project can be utilized for studies totally unforeseen at its inception. For example, the study by Mednick (1977), based on the Danish Perinatal Project, demonstrates the usefulness of neonatal neurological signs in predicting preadolescent behavioral and neurological difficulties. This utilization was unforeseen at the inception of the project.

3. *Complete sampling.* A great advantage of longitudinal projects, especially the large birth cohorts, is that they identify a total population. Those individuals who later become institutionalized or who die have already been identified in the original population. It is possible to be aware of their absence in any subsequent assessment of the population. In contrast, these individuals would simply be overlooked in a typical cross-sectional study. This could lead to some disabling biases in the results and conclusions of such studies.

4. *Incidence and prevalence.* The representative cohorts are clearly ideal for the development of incidence and prevalence rates for almost all the attainments and afflictions of humans.

5. *Social changes.* A study by Voorhees-Rosen and Rosen (1980) illustrates the use of community longitudinal projects in evaluating the effects of social change: The Shetland Islands, a relatively sheltered area

of Scotland, are being changed by the introduction of a large oil industry. The effects on the mental health of the population can be evaluated by this project. An ongoing longitudinal project can evaluate both the effect of changes in educational systems and the effect of introducing health or social welfare plans.

Nonrepresentative Populations

Table 1.1 lists two categories of nonrepresentative populations: normal birth cohorts and specialized cohorts.

Normal Birth Cohorts.   The normal birth cohorts typically consist of a comparatively small number of subjects who are described in great detail in terms of their development of physical growth, cognitive functioning, and personality behavior. Because of the smaller size of the cohorts, it is possible for the researcher to undertake extremely intensive and re-peated assessments. Studies of normal birth cohorts are especially well adapted for disclosing discontinuities and plateaus in growth curves of physical and mental processes. Unfortunately, the smaller size of the samples studied in these birth cohorts restricts the yield of psychiatric or social deviants. Because of the intensity of assessments, however, such studies might be very useful for generating hypotheses regarding factors predisposing to adult outcomes. The Berkeley growth study (Bayley, 1964) and the longitudinal study of Thomas, Chess, and Birch (1968) constitute examples of research using normal birth cohorts.

Specialized Cohorts.   The specialized cohorts tend to be aimed very specifically at answering certain questions. The primary purpose of es-tablishing *twin cohorts* is, of course, the estimation of the heritability of traits or conditions. The longitudinal following of twins can yield a variety of special comparisons not otherwise available. If monozygotic twins are discordant for an abnormality, the data on their life circumstances can yield information on predispositional environmental factors. The findings of such a study would be completely unbiased by genetic factors. Hauge's (1980) study of Danish twins is an example of a twin cohort study.

Much the same may be said for the *adoptee cohorts* as for the twin cohorts. They are also mainly developed to explore genetic hypotheses. The following of adoptees can reveal relationships between deviant be-havior and early separation from the biological parents and foundling home experience relatively independent of (or in interaction with) genetic background. Cross-fostering designs can compare the influence of genetic and certain environmental conditions on later deviance. Adoptee cohort studies may be exemplified by the study of Hutchings and Mednick (1974).

First cousin cohorts help to illustrate whether the possible inheritance of a condition is Mendelian or not.

Perinatal damage cohorts may be of special interest since they frequently demonstrate long-term consequences of neonatal anomalies. Studies of such cohorts can lead to work on the primary prevention of the perinatal damage and/or intervention to reduce the probability of negative long-term consequences. The study of long-term consequences of asphyxia (Graham et al., 1962) is an example of the use of perinatal damage cohorts.

Long-term study of groups of *identified patients or antisocial individuals* can provide information on outcomes, changes in diagnosis, and recidivism. If the patients or clients have been assigned to a variety of treatments, the follow-up might hint at the long-term differential effects of these treatments (taking into consideration the problems of differential assignment to treatments). If the patients are intensively examined early, the relationship between these early symptoms and signs and follow-up status can suggest methods of prognosis. The report by West and Farrington (1977) illustrates a study of antisocial individuals.

Longitudinal prospective studies of *children at risk* have certain advantages. Such children may be at risk because of parental deviance or because of some deviant early experience. They are typically studied in childhood or early adolescence before they themselves evidence deviance. These early assessments are only minimally contaminated by the consequences of the abnormality. Children of schizophrenic parents have a 10–15 percent risk of becoming schizophrenic themselves; but they have not yet experienced the drugs, hospitalization, misery, and failure often associated with being schizophrenic. Consequently assessments of these children and reports by observers are not influenced by these factors or by the knowledge that the individuals have been diagnosed. Young children of alcoholics, some of whom later will themselves become alcoholic, do not have the physiological damage that will very likely accompany their future heavy drinking. When some of these high-risk individuals succumb to alcoholism or schizophrenia, childhood characteristics that distinguish them from their more fortunate fellow high-risk individuals cannot be attributed to the *effects* of heavy drinking. These characteristics may be useful in early detection of future alcoholics. These "predisposing" characteristics may suggest hypotheses relating to etiology. The only advantage of the risk design over the study of normal representative populations is the higher yield of deviant individuals in the study. This means that to obtain eventually a sample of alcoholics or schizophrenics of a given size, one can begin with a smaller total cohort. This advantage can be of great importance if time-consuming assessments are envisioned.

PROBLEM AREAS IN LONGITUDINAL RESEARCH

In addition to the strengths and advantages that we have mentioned, there are a number of potential problem areas requiring particular attention in the context of a longitudinal project:

1. *Cost*. The largest cost in a longitudinal project is the initial assessment of the subjects. If apparatus is to be used, it will be purchased at this initial stage. The initial assessment will typically encompass the largest number of individuals in the cohort. It will also require the longest and most expensive training period for the staff. In the simplest form of longitudinal project, the assessment of final outcome (mental illness, criminality, school performance, socioeconomic level, personality characteristics, and so on) is the only required additional step. If only the initial and outcome assessments are made, costs per year can be very modest. More frequently, however, assessments of the population can be profitably undertaken at intermediate stages of the research.

If, in the planning of the project, the work is multidisciplinary so that information relating to a large number of social and medical deviances can be obtained, then the basic cost for each of these subareas can be substantially reduced. In any case, when one compares the cost of gathering this information and its potential use in prevention with the suffering involved and the cost of the care, feeding, and treatment of deviant populations, it is likely that such research costs will be a very good investment.

2. *Obsolescence*. One serious problem to which all longitudinal research is subject is that measures and theories that seem important at the inception of the project may seem dated and misdirected twenty years later. It is good to advise individuals intending to begin longitudinal research to keep their theory fairly general and their choice of measures fairly eclectic and not to allow themselves to be totally dominated by any specific theoretical orientation. Researchers are wise if they record raw data from their subjects. That is to say, they should record actual ver-

balizations rather than just coding attitudes and opinions; they should record raw physiological data on magnetic tape rather than only complex derivatives of these measures. The basic raw data are more likely to be meaningful or rescorable twenty years hence.

3. *Problems in non–age-specific interpretations.* In the 1946 British cohort study, Atkins et al. (1980) report that the experience of the child (age 0–2 years) in breathing polluted air did not result in significantly more coughing or bronchitis in later adolescence. At age 25, however, those who had been subjected to highly polluted air in childhood did evidence significantly more coughing and bronchitis (personal communication). This is an instance of a sleeper effect — that is, the effect of an antecedent factor did not show itself until a later period of life. Conclusions regarding the influence of a childhood factor in a longitudinal study should not be made in an absolute manner. The report from the British birth cohort study shows us that such conclusions should be restricted to their age-specific period. As another example, there is reason to suspect that delinquency may not have the same origins as adult criminality. It is possible, therefore, that factors relating to delinquency may be different from those relating to adult criminality. Thus, if an antecedent factor is not associated with an increase in the probability of delinquency, this fact does not mean that it will be unrelated to adult criminal behavior in the same population.

4. *Population flux.* After some years of population shifts, it is possible that a large birth or school cohort may become unrepresentative of a current population. For example, in northern Europe the recent and large-scale influx of guest workers from the south could be rendering a birth cohort that began in the early 1940s unrepresentative of the current population. Of course, the cohort would still be representative of the 1940 native birth population. The cohort could also be supplemented by judicious sampling of the new immigrants.

5. *Publication.* One frequently mentioned problem of longitudinal research projects is the difficulty of achieving publication of their findings. Some reasons are fairly clear: the exciting payoff for most of these projects comes only when the subjects have reached adult age, have attained or failed to attain certain life goals, or have manifested or not manifested certain deviance. However, the longitudinal researcher can explore the possibility of exploiting certain short-term goals. For example, a longitudinal researcher interested in criminality might take delinquency as a short-term goal, and one interested in mental illness might take adjustment in school as a short-term goal.

6. *Repeated measures.* In some longitudinal projects the same mea-

sures are administered repeatedly to the subjects. This practice, of course, entails a risk that the measurement itself will change the subject. Typically, however, the risk is minimal. When we observe the difficulty of noting a significant effect of years of psychotherapy with schizophrenics, it seems unlikely that our one, two, three, or four interviews in a lifetime will significantly alter our subject populations.

CONCLUSION

Longitudinal research methods have applicability far beyond their traditional use in the study of developmental processes. We have suggested that they have special value when used within a primary prevention framework. Prospective longitudinal designs can be used to detect patterns of covariance between pathological outcome and antecedent conditions. Such findings can serve two functions: (1) they can contribute to the development of methods of early detection of populations at risk, and (2) they might suggest causal hypotheses that also would be useful in planning interventive research.

II METHODOLOGICAL BASES OF LONGITUDINAL RESEARCH:
Design and Planning

2 SOME PROBLEMS OF LONGITUDINAL RESEARCH IN THE SOCIAL SCIENCES

Carl-Gunnar Janson

This chapter has five sections. First are some comments on the term *longitudinal*. Second, formal relations among age, period, and cohort effects are discussed. The third section deals with attempts to shorten the period of data collection. Documentary procedures are considered as alternatives to retrospective approaches. Then, the problem of keeping the theoretical relevance of a protracted research project is posed. Finally, the possibilities of longitudinal studies as compared with those of other approaches are outlined. A preliminary version of the chapter forms most of a research report from Project Metropolitan (Janson, 1978, pp. 7–52; for a presentation of Project Metropolitan, see Janson, 1975).

WHAT IS A "LONGITUDINAL STUDY?"

Usage of the Term Longitudinal

In the social sciences the usage of a term is often somewhat ambiguous. The term is employed in more than one meaning, the meanings being more or less related. The term *longitudinal* is no exception. Usually it is applied to relationships; to perspectives, approaches, models, and designs involving longitudinal relations; to studies and research projects concerning such relations or constructs; and to data measuring, describing, or indicating longitudinal relations. Mostly it is used in a methodological or research-technical context.

By a "longitudinal" relationship one may mean a relationship between phenomena over time, if the time sequence between the phenomena is essential. Thus the relationship is *diachronous* as opposed to *synchronous*. Something more may also be implied in it — namely, a process of change over a period of time. The relationship can also be called *dynamic* as opposed to *static* (see Riley, 1963, p. 18). For instance, Emerson has presented a behavioristic exchange model with three concepts: a class of actions x by an organism A, an environmental situation S, and a reinforcing stimulus y. He assumes y to be contingent upon S and x and the recurrence of x to be contingent upon y. Then he says: "This three-cornered conceptual unit is entirely empirical-descriptive, and it describes a longitudinal organism-environment interactive relation." The contingency of x upon y must entail feedback. "Such feedback can be described only through longitudinal data, and this three-cornered conceptual unit therefore entails a longitudinally conceived set of relationships" (Emerson, 1969, p. 387). Emerson (1969, p. 405) also refers to "longitudinal experimentation."

A "longitudinal study" may be any diachronous study or study of a process of change. Usually, however, two limiting conditions are added. First, the study must contain diachronous data on the same individuals (or other units); and second, it must use data on "several" units. Discussing research methods in sociology, one may set "longitudinal studies" against *cross-sectional* studies (see Riley and Foner, 1968, pp. 7f.; Riley, Johnson, and Foner, 1972, p. 47). Theodorson and Theodorson (1969, p. 236) define a longitudinal study as a "study of individuals over a period of time or at successive stages." By the longitudinal method the researcher can "study trends or the effect of a stimulus, training, event, or experience with 'before' and 'after' observations." Bühler, Keith-Spiegel, and Thomas (1973, pp. 864f.) write that in developmental psychology there are three common approaches, one of which is the longitudinal. The two others are the cross-sectional and the *clinical*. "The longitudinal method consists of measuring the same individuals at different intervals over a period of time. Some longitudinal studies are relatively short-term, whereas others are impressively long-term: thirty or more years." In social ecology the units of a longitudinal study may be neighborhoods or urban areas, in organizational sociology they may be formal organizations, in family sociology families, and so on; in each case there is presumably more than one unit. (For illustrations of the usage of the term within the behavioral sciences, see the proceedings from the 1974 conference on longitudinal research in Stockholm.)

Sometimes "longitudinal analysis" is treated as synonymous with *cohort analysis,* perhaps especially in demography (cf. Henry, 1976, p. 45), in which "cohort" has a very wide meaning of any subpopulation of individuals (or other units) with a common characteristic. "Cohort analysis" then is "the study of a number of people with some common characteristic over a long period of time" (Theodorson and Theodorson, 1969, p. 58). Svalastoga (1976) prefers the term *sequential* to "longitudinal," possibly without excluding single-unit designs. The only objection to this usage of "sequential" is that "sequential analysis" already has a specific and highly technical meaning as a kind of *statistical* analysis (e.g., Mood, 1950, chap. 15).

It seems fairly clear that to use the term *longitudinal* for research projects is to exclude case studies. On the other hand, it seems somewhat arbitrary to restrict perspectives, data, and the like, in a more methodological and less research-technical context to those involving several units. The quotations from Emerson do not do so, but admittedly the term *longitudinal* is seldom found in operant psychology. It may be worth noticing that, writing from another psychological perspective, Dollard (1949, p. 4) describes the *life history* as "the long-section view of culture."

Research-Technical Usage

It seems that for methodological perspectives and the like, *longitudinal* can be taken in a wide sense as emphasizing development and change of a unit or units. In a technical context, for research projects, their type and design, a corresponding wide meaning is a summary category of studies of variation of units over time. However, several such kinds of studies have labels of their own. In a more restricted sense the term *longitudinal study* refers to a special type of such diachronous studies. In distinguishing between these types of studies one should note that they are not mutually exclusive. Some have overlapping connotations, and others are defined in terms of different aspects of the research process and may be combined.

In an attempt to clarify the restricted usage somewhat, one may start by classifying studies according to the formal character of the units they are concerned with. Some diachronous studies use their time periods or points in time — that is, their temporal units — as their analytical ("statistical") units. Often the theoretical, or substantive, unit described by the variable is on macrolevel, such as a nation or a region or a system of interacting nations or regions. There may also be a category of substantive macro-units. Sometimes, however, the substantive unit is on microlevel, such as a person, a family, or a neighborhood, or there are several such micro-units in each statistical unit. With substantive micro-units the macro-entities may be seen as populations, from which the substantive units are sampled.

Time-series analyses of macro-units are practically never called longitudinal, and those of micro-units are sometimes but not often so called. Clearly they are not what is usually referred to as longitudinal studies. The term *time-series analyses* is preferred for these studies. If we turn to diachronous studies that are not time-series analyses, we again find that studies of macro-units are rarely said to be longitudinal.

Among studies of micro-units we may distinguish three categories. In the first category different units are observed at different periods. If a unit happens to be observed on more than one occasion, it is treated as a different unit each time. Such a study is built as a series of cross-sectional substudies of unrelated samples. If a variable is recorded over time, its over-time variance can be partitioned in a between-periods component and a within-periods component. Clearly this kind of study is not longitudinal.

In the second category the same units are observed at different times, but they are not, or cannot be, individually compared over time — for example, because they have not been recorded in a way that permits identification over time. Different characteristics of the same unit at a given time may or may not be individually linked to make cross-sectional analysis possible. Variance over time can be partitioned as for the first category. If the units can be classified according to age at given times, this category of studies permits the special kind of cohort analysis that is called *external* in the next section but not the kind of analysis that is there called *internal*. Thus, studies of over-time variation of this category may be longitudinal in a limited meaning, if one accepts external analysis as a kind of longitudinal analysis that is made by category instead of by individual units as the usual longitudinal analysis. For cohorts other than birth cohorts, information on the cohort characteristic is evidently needed in addition to age for an external analysis. Note that the category-based analysis is assumed to cover a "long" period. If it does not, it is not even partially "longitudinal" in the narrow sense and probably not so even in the summary sense.

In the third category the same analytical units are observed over time and their characteristics are individually compared over time. Now the within-periods component of a variable's over-time variance can be further partitioned in a between-units component and a within-units component, from which a residual component may be separated, when observations are replicated. However, observations at different time units of a diachronous micro-unit study may well refer to different variables, so that a variable has no between-periods component of variance. In this category we find the studies that are longitudinal in the usual sense. Here we may note that units can be compared over time as to *irreversible* characteristics, even if they are not individually identified. Diachronous data on irreversible microcharacteristics thus can always be individually compared over time, as long as we do not want to correlate different characteristics.

Both the second and the third category can be further divided into subcategories according to the length of the period of observation. Examples of short-time studies are most *panel studies* and most *laboratory experiments* with a before-and-after design. Mostly they fall into the third category. Of course, what is considered a "short" period of observation depends on the context. Methodologically and in the wide research-technical sense such short-time studies may be said to be longitudinal, but in a research-technical discussion one may also prefer to limit the class of longitudinal studies to certain long-time studies. Of long-time studies of the third category some lack a period of observation in a strict sense — that is, when their time units are few and so far apart that they do not "cover" any period. Research-technically such studies are called *follow-up studies* rather than longitudinal in the strict sense, although the difference may be neither clear nor important. Thus, there remain *long-time studies of micro-units, individually compared over time and with observations covering a period.*

Longitudinal studies in this meaning and *cohort studies* strongly overlap, but their extensions are not completely identical. First, cohort studies also include external analyses on data that are not individually linked. Admittedly, however, many demographic and epidemiological external analyses concern irreversible characteristics. Second, the longitudinal category includes studies of total populations and random samples of populations. A famous example would be the Lundby psychiatric project that deals with 2,550 persons who constituted the registered population of the Lundby municipality in southern Sweden on July 1, 1947 (cf. Hagnell, 1966; Hagnell and Kreitman, 1974; Hagnell and Rorsman, 1978). To be precise, one can see such a longitudinal study as a cohort study only by viewing populations as subpopulations or by extending the wide concept of "cohort" further to include random samples and total populations. However, perhaps one can see no point in being that precise. Probably in most situations a longitudinal study and a cohort study can be said to be the same thing.

Finally, one should keep in mind that both panels and experiments may be extended over a "long" period of time and that (short) experimental studies may be prolonged to pursue long-time effects, thus becoming longitudinal in the narrow sense just defined. This concept will be further discussed in the section on the possibilities of longitudinal studies.

The discussion on the question of what is meant by a longitudinal study can be briefly summarized as in Table 2.1. In the following discussion, "longitudinal study" will be taken in the research-technical, narrow sense. Having made this specification, I now turn to some design problems of longitudinal studies, starting with problems concerning the relation among age, cohort, and period.

AGE, COHORT, AND PERIOD

Conceptual Linkage

Suppose a variable is recorded for a cohort[1] at a certain time, when the cohort members have reached a given age. The general level — that is, the average of the variable — may then depend on, among other factors, the age of the cohort members at the time of the measurement. It may also depend on conditions prevailing at that particular time. Here the effects of age and time period are obviously confounded, as age varies completely with period, if the measurement is repeated at later times. Similarly the way a variable is distributed in the cohort or covaries with another variable may be specific to the age or the period. Again age and period effects cannot be separated, since age and period covary completely.

To separate the effects, one needs another cohort, so that a given age is reached at different times and cohort members of different ages can be observed in a given period. An analysis of the variation and covariation of a variable over the categories of age, period, and cohort, or of age and

Table 2.1.   Extension of Longitudinal Study.

A. *METHODOLOGICAL CONTEXT*
Study of same unit(s) over time as to essentially time-oriented relation(s)

B. *RESEARCH-TECHNICAL CONTEXT*

Denotation				*Summary Definition*	*Narrow Definition*
a. Case Study				No	No
b. Time-Series Analysis					
Macro-units				Yes	No
Micro-units				Yes	Perhaps
c. Other Diachronous Study of Micro-Units					
Units over Time	*Linking of Units over Time*	*Period*	*Example*		
I Different				No	No
II Same	No	Short or long, not covered		Probably Not even partially	No
Same	No	Long, covered	External cohort analysis	Partially	Partially
III Same	Yes	Short	(Short) panel, laboratory experiment	Yes	No
Same	Yes	Long, not covered	Follow-up	Yes	Perhaps
Same	Yes	Long, covered	Cohort	Yes	Yes

period only, will be called an *external* longitudinal analysis if it does not connect the values (characteristics) of the cohort members at different moments. Evidently it is possible to give the mean of a variable at different ages, as one or several cohorts are observed over time without linking the various individual values for any given cohort member. Any analysis presupposing such linking is called *internal*. Analyses that use the individual cohort members as units and are not cross-sectional come into this category. Most macro-analyses of age, period, and cohort effects are external, but some are not. For instance, a study of the variation over age of the individual stability of a variable is not external.

Separating age and period effects by introducing new cohorts also gives the opportunity to study possible differences between cohorts. Some conditions may be specific to a given cohort. Obviously, however, all three dimensions of age, period, and cohort cannot be varied independently of each other. In fact, we have only two independent dimensions, as age, period, and cohort, expressed in appropriate measures, are mathematically connected. Among A (age), P (period), and C (cohort) there is the relation

$$A = P - C. \tag{2.1}$$

For instance, in 1978 (period) the cohort born in 1953 has the age of

$$25 = 1978 - 1953. \tag{2.1a}$$

Evidently the formula holds equally well when age, time of observation, and time of birth are specified in more detail, say, by day. For instance, those born on June 9, 1953, were 25 years and 74 days when they were observed on August 22, 1978 — that is, according to the formula

$$25 \frac{74}{365} = 1978 \frac{234}{365} - 1953 \frac{160}{365}. \tag{2.1b}$$

Here we are concerned with points in time rather than with intervals, which makes at least "period" a somewhat unfortunate label. However, the traditional names of the involved dimensions have been retained. The main point is that, given measures with the same precision on the three dimensions, any of them can be expressed in terms of the two others without a residual. This means that the three dimensions cannot be identified (cf. Nelson and Starr, 1972; Riley, Johnson, and Foner, 1972). In a design that varies two of the dimensions and keeps the third one constant, there is only one free variation, and as just pointed out, both dimensions in the design cannot be identified. Hence a cross-sectional design keeps the period constant and allows the variation of age and cohort, the effects of which cannot be separated. When in a survey one finds that religious interest, measured in a certain way, tends to increase with age, one cannot say whether this variation is due to an increase of religiousness by age during the lifetime of the individuals within each (or most) generations — that is, to an *age* or *longitudinal* effect — or to increased secularization from one generation (cohort) to the other in a protracted process of change over a long period of time — that is, to *cohort* or *period* effects. Of course, one may prefer one or the other explanation for theoretical reasons, but for empirical support one has to rely on sources of information other than the original cross-sectional analysis. Most probably one's theoretical preferences also stem from such sources.

Correspondingly, as already has been said, a longitudinal study of only one cohort cannot separate age and period effects without relying on some evidence from outside the project of such effects on other cohorts. The situation is made somewhat less serious by two circumstances. First, some such extra evidence is often available, although perhaps unsystematic and indirect. Usually it is strong enough to ground a theoretical conviction that age or period effects, or both kinds of effects, are reasonable and to be expected, but usually it is not strong enough to permit even a rough estimation of components of variance without rather bold assumptions. Second, many longitudinal studies are primarily concerned not with the estimation of age, period, or cohort effects in certain variables but with the exploration of causal systems or processes, where different variables enter at various ages or times and where the time-order of entering is important. These systems or processes are on the microlevel and thus deal with differences and differential effects within the cohort (or cohorts). Here, however, the problem remains to what extent the reached specification of the system or process can be generalized to other cohorts, and if so, to which cohorts. There often are some reasons to suspect that the results are somewhat specific to the studied cohort (or cohorts) or have been confounded by conditions specific to the period of observation. This assumption makes a discussion of the relations among age, cohort, and period effects relevant also to "regular" longitudinal internal analyses.

It should be mentioned that the impossibility of strictly identifying the three "external" dimensions also applies to theoretical analyses, as the proper combination of two concepts always can substitute for the third one. For instance, a cohort effect is the effect of some process occurring in a certain period, hitting or influencing age categories differentially. A period effect that is about the same in several age categories can be seen as an effect on a series of cohorts at correspondingly different ages, and if the period effect is differential over age, this means that it differs between combinations of cohort and age.

Examples of period effects on cohorts from events can be effects of the Great Depression of the 1930s and of the two world wars. French cohorts of the age of approximately twenty to thirty-five in 1914–1918, as well as corresponding English and German cohorts, got reduced size and an unusual sex ratio. The impact of the Second World War can be seen in the German, Polish, and Yugoslavian populations in, say, 1960 (cf. Keyfitz and Flieger, 1968). Less sinister effects, but still rather

profound influences on career conditions of some cohorts, can be ascribed to the changes in the educational systems, as during the 1960s.

Evidently the categories and their sizes are not fixed on any of the
three dimensions of age, period, and cohort but can be chosen to fit the
intended analysis. Often a year is a suitable unit because it covers a
cyclical period and is used as an administrative unit in many respects. If
one wants larger units, three-, five-, or ten-year intervals, and the like,
may be suggested. Smaller intervals may be preferable, as in studies of
early childhood. There, monthly or even shorter cohorts or periods may
be adequate.

Within a cohort of a time units and a period of b time units, age varies
according to formula (2.1) over a maximum range of $a + b$ time units. If
observations are evenly distributed over the cohort and period, age has
the standard deviation of

$$\sqrt{\frac{a^2 + b^2}{12}} . \qquad (2.2)$$

With observations belonging to a point in time instead of a period, age
at this point will vary a time units within the cohort and, with a rectan-
gular distribution, have a standard deviation of $a/\sqrt{12}$.

Hence, although formula (2.1) still is valid, age will vary within a
single cohort, even when the period is fixed. However, this variation will
occur only when one has assumed that age differences among cohort
members can be ignored in defining the cohort and that the difference in
age for a cohort member between beginning and end of the period can be
disregarded in delimiting the period. To the extent these assumptions are
valid, the within-cohort age variation at given period is too small to
substitute for between-cohorts variation.

Schaie (1965) has suggested a design of two-factor analyses of variance
with replication for external analyses. Two of the three external dimensions come in as factors, and the effects of the remaining one will show
as a certain pattern of interaction. A factorial design can be applied for
each pair of dimensions, and the analyses can then be compared and
evaluated. Schaie's approach is discussed extensively by Nelson and
Starr (1972, pp. 27–90) and Riley, Johnson, and Foner (1972, pp. 608–
12).

Becker's Diagram

The relations among age, cohort, and period and among the categories
of the analyses of variance in Schaie's design can be illuminated by a

well-known demographic diagram, which sometimes is named after the
German demographer Becker (cf. Wicksell, 1920, pp. 108–26) but prob-
ably is better known in a slightly different form as Lexis's diagram (cf.
Keyfitz and Flieger, 1968, pp. 589–91; Rogers, 1975, pp. 57–59; Henry,
1976, pp. 45f), after the German statistician and economist Lexis.
Becker's and Lexis's versions of the diagram are equally useful here.
Becker's form of the diagram was chosen.

   The diagram, shown in Figure 2.1, has year of birth as the horizontal
dimension and observed year as the vertical dimension. A person's birth
is denoted by a point in the position where observed year equals the year

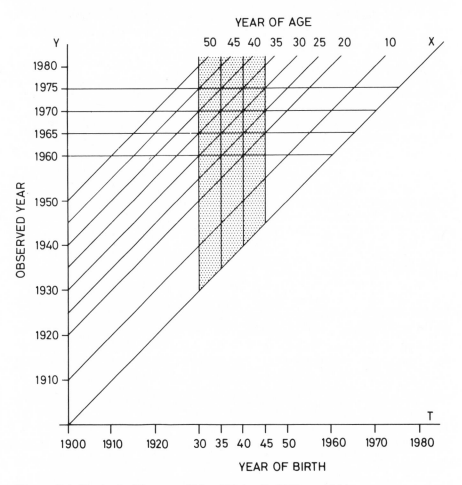

Figure 2.1. Becker's Diagram. (After Wicksell, 1920, p. 109.)

of the birth — that is, by a point on the diagonal of the axes. The person's
death is marked as a point in the position where observed year equals
the year of the death. Evidently the two points are on the same vertical
line, and the section from birth point to death point on that line signifies
the person's life. Events and observations can be located on this line at
the appropriate points of observed time. Similarly the period of a certain
condition can be marked as an interval. For instance, points of entering
and leaving the population (or sample) can be noted, when the population
is locally delimited and persons move in and out of the area. Cohorts are
delimited by vertical lines, periods by horizontal lines, and age categories
by diagonal lines (Figure 2.1).[2]

Combinations of any two of the factors age, cohort, and period as in
the analysis-of-variance design appear in the diagram as parallelograms.
Figure 2.2 shows they are of three types, each of which is built by two
half-squares, if one uses the same length of interval for all three factors,
such as a year. The orthogonal legs of the half-squares are horizontal and
vertical sections of y and t lines — that is, period and cohort lines. The

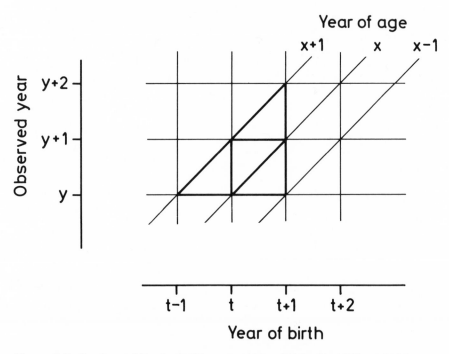

Figure 2.2. Section of Becker's Diagram. (After Wicksell, 1920, p. 113.)

opposite sides of the triangles are diagonal x lines — that is, age lines. The triangles are of two types, those with the right-angle legs above the third side and those with the legs below the third side. The first type denotes a yearly cohort observed a given year, after the cohort members have had their birthdays that year, whereas the second type denotes a cohort observed until the birthdays in the year of observation. An area bound by y and t lines signifies a cohort under a period. Thus the square bound by lines y and $y+1$, t and $t+1$ in Figure 2.2 refers to the cohort t in the year y. The diagonal x divides the square into areas referring to observations before and after the birthdays.

Correspondingly, parallelograms delimited by two y lines and two x lines refer to an age category in a period; for example, the parallelogram between y and $y+1$ and between x and $x+1$ belongs to age x as recorded in the year y. This area too is cut in two half-squares, the one to the right referring to persons born in the year t and the one to the left referring to persons born the year before — that is, to persons of the cohort t after their xth birthday and to persons of the cohort $t-1$ before their $(x+1)$st birthday.

Finally, parallelograms between two t lines and two x lines delimit cohorts at a given age, as recorded in adjacent periods. Thus lines t, $t+1$, x, and $x+1$ delimit cohort t at age x observed in periods y and $y+1$. The two periods are separated by the line $y+1$ into two half-squares.

For each area there are a number of lifelines entering and a total length of lines within the area, showing the population (or sample) under risk for the particular combination of cohort, period, and age. Furthermore, a set of events, measures taken, and the like, can be located at their possible points of occurrence in the area for the persons under risk. Note that events and observations located in vertically related areas belong to the same cohort — that is, to the same individuals — whereas elements in other areas do not.

To make choices as to the three external dimensions, their effects and interactions, one must introduce some principle or assumption. Parsimony may be considered. As already suggested, strong theoretical convictions — as to the process of aging or the impact of certain events, for example — can lead to definite preferences of models to be applied and of concepts to express such models. For instance, certain interactions may be removed from the model or the conditions of some cohorts may be assumed to be equal (cf. Mason, Winsborough, and Poole, 1973).

In an anlysis-of-variance design of the Schaie type, one should also decide what intervals to have between categories. Of course, this problem is not restricted to that particular design but is present whenever one considers having more than one cohort. The same holds even if one is not interested in external analyses but has in mind the extent to which results can be generalized to other cohorts.

If one wants to make the assumption, such as that suggested by Mason, Winsborough, and Poole, that conditions are essentially the same in different cohorts, obviously one should generally have adjacent cohorts or at least cohorts rather close to each other. This design would make the chances higher that the cohorts are subject to rather much the same events and conditions at not very different ages.

However, to the extent the same events hit the cohorts and have similar effects this can be seen as making the observations on the cohorts dependent in a way that may not be intended and not assumed in the analyses. In fact, the possibility of generalizing to other cohorts can be said to depend on the extent to which results are not contingent on such events and conditions that are specific to the cohort or cohorts of the study. To find out whether and to what degree there is such an invariance of the results, one should include cohorts subject to events and conditions as different as those one aims to generalize about. As a rule this means that cohorts should be well separated. Usually separation is made in terms of time. However, it is also possible to separate cohorts in space — for example, to have cohorts in different regions or countries.[3]

In both cases the dependence on events and conditions usually is not completely eliminated. Rather it is decreased to a certain extent — how much varies with the kind of events and especially with the kinds of conditions that are discussed. The distinction between specific and general circumstances or conditions for the cohorts is somewhat unclear both conceptually and theoretically. For instance, the career patterns of the members of a cohort can safely be assumed to depend on the specific form of the educational system, at least in certain respects and to some extent. The strength of dependence is an empirical question. The cohort may be compared as to career patterns with a cohort from the same place but, say, ten years earlier or later, when the educational system is somewhat different. An analysis of the differential impact of the system on cohorts then refers to the aspects that have changed between cohorts, whereas the many common features of the system for the cohorts are part of the general conditions of the results on, say, the differential impact of the educational system in terms of social class within the cohorts. If the second cohort was one from a neighboring country, there would probably be other differences between the educational systems, but the analytical situation would be principally the same. In both the temporal and the spatial comparisons conditions other than the educational are also likely to be different in some respects. Of course, these problems are not special to longitudinal studies but are common to all empirical studies when one wants to find out the range of relevance of the results.

RETROSPECTIVE AND PROSPECTIVE DATA

Long Period of Observation

Most ambitious longitudinal projects have long periods of observation for their cohorts (or populations). If they study more than one cohort and their cohorts are well spread out in time, this design will further lengthen the time span from the beginning of the period of observation of the oldest cohort to the end of the period of observation of the youngest cohort. To the extent this span must be contained within the span of the project, this long observation period causes problems. The protracted project will be difficult to manage economically and practically. The longitudinal questions toward which the project is oriented cannot be answered in full until the project has reached its potential — that is, before the period of observation is completed. Grant-giving bodies then either have to be content with a long time perspective, which presupposes an unusual amount of patience, or have to be fed with preliminary answers, with reports on longitudinal questions referring to shorter time spans or cross-sectional analyses of project data. Furthermore, the project leader and staff members must also be unusually sensitive to deferred gratification. Probably there will be changes of personnel and of fields of interests and theoretical orientations both within the project and within the discipline as well.

Hence, there are strong incentives to try to shorten the time span of the project without unduly shortening the period of observation. By *period of observation* I mean the period to which the empirical data refer — that is, the period in which conditions, incidents, behavior, and so on, are described. Evidently this period need not be the same as the period of actual data collecting in the project, which may be called the *period of observing*. Rather the question is to what extent one can separate the periods and shorten the period of observing (or data collecting) without side effects, which set off the gains of the reduction. Such effects may be to lower the quality of data, to extend other phases of the project (such as coding or data processing), to annoy the public, or to break ethical rules of the profession, and so on.

To separate the period of observing from the period of observation and shorten it is to postpone it, partly or as a whole. Sometimes there also are strong incentives for postponing the data collecting, shortened or not. First, to the extent alternatives and options have been kept open, one has a chance of incorporating new insights and following professional and lay discussions right up to the time of the analysis and reporting (cf. next section). Hence there is a point in collecting and processing data rather late. Second, postponing the data collecting would make it possible to study past events and conditions — to get around the obstacle often encountered in attempts to apply a longitudinal perspective, that one is out too late, because observations should have been made long ago.

The long period of observation often also leads to considerable *attrition* of cases and makes attrition a major problem of the longitudinal approach. A substantial proportion of a cohort may be affected. Cases are lost for various reasons. First, on questioning people the usual amount of refusals will be met and may increase over time, as respondents get tired of repeated questioning. Second, in areas lacking efficient population bookkeeping some cases are lost track of. Third, other cases simply leave the area or country or die. After cases move out, they usually are difficult or at least expensive to reach for questioning. They are no longer found in current local registers, and new items are no longer filed on them locally. Hence they are often dropped.

Because of various selective forces, the set of cohort cases remaining in the cohort's area of definition usually is not a random sample of the original cohort. To what extent this fact deteriorates the possibilities of generalizing results naturally depends on the size of the selective attrition and also on what generalizations are attempted. Generally losses of deceased cases can be handled appropriately without undue restrictions in intended generalizations. Usually attrition from out-migrations can be similarly taken into consideration, although at the cost of restricted generality. Finally, refusals and cases lost track of within the area of definition can hamper analyses seriously.[4]

In addition to its likely disturbing impact on analyses, attrition means increased costs and efforts. For the set to contain a sufficient number of cases even in later parts of the period of observation, it must be inflated initially. Information is then secured in the early parts of the period, as through fairly expensive interviewing, even on cases that later are lost so that the information cannot be fully utilized. Now, if data collecting could be postponed until one knew, at least for some part of the period of observation, what cases would die, move out, or disappear, perhaps one could do with a reduced set of data for them. Furthermore, possibly a shortened period of observing would bring down the number of refusals and disappearances somewhat.

Thus, there are various reasons to delay the period of observing compared to the period of observation. On the other hand, postponement also involves risks of distortion of perspective and of loss of information with time. These risks apply more to the evidence on which to base data than to data themselves and their processing.

Retrospective Data

Here one may find useful the distinction between *retrospective* and other data. To avoid the awkward term *nonretrospective,* I shall call other data *prospective,* at least in a longitudinal context. Usually the term *retrospective* is used to describe data or analyses. Here it will be applied to *data*. Generally, when data are said to be "retrospective," one compares two points or periods of time: the time data pertain to and the time at which they are *collected*. If data are collected after the time they bear upon, they are "retrospective." Here, however, a somewhat different definition will be used. The comparison is made between the time data refer to and the time at which the material they build on — that is, are coded, recorded, excerpted from, and the like — is *produced*. If data are based on evidence produced after the time they pertain to, they are here said to be "retrospective." Some data may be more retrospective than others.[5]

The definition applied here implies that data may be collected later than at the time they refer to and still be prospective. To separate the period of data collecting from the period of observation and to shorten it, one can either use retrospective data or collect prospective data at a later time. Both procedures make possible the study of past situations. The risks of distortion and loss of information refer especially to retrospective data. By definition direct observations cannot be made retrospectively. They are carried out at the observed moment or are later recorded from secondary sources such as minutes, photos, and movies, which stem from the time of the observation. Interviews and questionnaires may contain retrospective items. If used to tap the respondent's present opinions and conception of past times and conditions, such questions are not invalidated by certain sources of error that impede their application to get information on actual past conditions, opinions, and conceptions. Here only the "fact-finding" function of retrospective questions is discussed.

Recently retrospective questioning has been proposed and used to produce a kind of instant longitudinal data set by the *life-history* approach. This approach has long been used in the behavioral sciences (cf. Dollard, 1949). As advocated by Dollard, Gordon Allport, and others, it built on diaries and other personal documents and thus was not especially retrospective (Angell and Freedman, 1953, pp. 303f.), although many personal documents were ultimately based on retrospective data.

As the life-history approach is applied in a longitudinal project, the interviewee is asked for information on his or her childhood, education, family life, occupational career, and the like, more or less up to the time of the interview. Through various supports from the interviewer, the interviewee is aided in the recall of past events and circumstances. Such devices have been sophistically developed, as in studies of readership (cf. Schyberger, 1965, chaps. 5–8). The interval over which recall can be extended clearly varies with area of content, from a few days of everyday activities, such as items concerning food, reading, and fields of activity (cf. Janson and Jonsson, 1965; Walldén, 1974), to most of a lifetime for some outstanding events. However, missing recall is but one problem of retrospective questioning (Phillips, 1971, chap. 2; Cannell and Kahn, 1968). To recall an item one must have known or experienced it. To communicate it one needs both vocabulary and motivation. Even if recalled, events and conditions are seen and told in the hindsight of later circumstances and the present situation, from which they take much of their cognitive meaning and ideological significance. Especially when the answer asks for a summarizing statement of the way varying things used to be, there is room for adjustment of the past. Much information sought in longitudinal studies seems to be of this kind, such as on the father's occupation during the cohort member's childhood. Here one may suspect differential adjustments, mostly but not exclusively in the direction of promotion to higher ranks. A specification to a given age, fifteen, say, of the interviewee probably reduces this risk, but it may still be unacceptably high. It seems even more difficult to assess the validity of such retrospective items, so even when they are valid a proper degree of confidence cannot be given to them.

Problems of retrospective questioning can be illustrated from a report on a reinterview in 1974 of a national sample of persons interviewed in Sweden in 1968 on components of welfare. The number of interviewed persons was about 5,900 in 1968, when the nonresponse rate was 9 percent. Of these persons around 4,700 were reinterviewed. The field work was carried out by the Swedish Statistical Central Bureau for the official Low-Income Study in 1968 (cf. Johansson, 1970) and for the Institute of Social Studies at the University of Stockholm in 1974 (Levnadsnivåundersökningen 1974, 1977). There are no reasons to suspect the field work to be substandard.

Of the reinterviewed persons, 464 had reported in 1968 that they had at least once written an article or a letter to the editor of a newspaper or periodical. Six years later, 160, or one-third of them, denied having ever written to a newspaper or periodical (Norlén, 1977). The questionnaire contained about thirty retrospective questions of this kind. Norlén estimated the probability of a "no" answer when a truthful answer should have been "yes" and the probability of the erroneous answer in the opposite direction for thirty-two questions. His estimates of false positive answers were low. All except one were in the range between −0.01 to 0.04. Interestingly enough the one exception was the question whether the respondent could make a written complaint to a public body. Here the estimate of a false positive answer was 0.14. Some respondents may have claimed an ability they did not have, whereas others might have known in 1968 how to write a complaint but had lost this knowledge in 1974.

Still, the probability of a false positive answer on that question was estimated to be low compared to the estimates of the probability of a false negative answer on almost all questions. The false negatives got estimates from 0.05 to 0.89, with twenty-three estimates out of thirty-two on 0.20 or above, and the median estimate on 0.39. Thus, the question about writing to a newspaper had the estimated probability of a false negative of 0.15. A question about having ever taken part in a demonstration had the estimate 0.29, a question about having ever contacted an official person in order to influence him or her got the estimate of 0.42, and a question about having ever won in a pool or lottery got the estimate 0.36. The very high estimates generally belonged to questions about ever being incorrectly treated by various authorities: labor union 0.85, school 0.78, employer 0.64, and so on.

There are also retrospective documents, such as memoirs and statements made well after the incidents and situations they relate. They exhibit the same pitfalls as retrospective questioning, perhaps at least partly in even more uncontrolled forms, except usually as to costs and missing cases. There may be good arguments for asking fact-finding retrospective questions or using retrospective documents. The accuracy necessary for the intended analysis may be obtainable. There may be no better alternative available, which probably applies to the Low-Income Study just referred to.

Naturally the probable losses in validity through the use of retrospective data should be weighed against the gains made in shortening or postponing the period of data collecting. Lower validity usually means that additional analytical restrictions should be inserted and less confidence should be given to results. Although reliance on analytical assumptions and confidence in results are a matter of degree, possible sources of error and reasonable alternative interpretations become so prevalent when validity is, or can be expected to be, low that results carry little weight. Thus there is little point in shortening or postponing data collecting at the cost of validity losses beyond a certain level, which varies with the intended analysis and admittedly is somewhat indeterminate. The evaluation should be made for each study by considering the specific circumstances and with a clear view on the dangers of retrospective data as well as on alternatives.

Hill wanted to analyze family development in planning and consumership. A strict longitudinal study would follow families for a generation. To avoid "the excessive cost and awkwardness" of such a study "without sacrificing more than a few of the benefits," Hill (1970, p. 16) looked for three generations of the same family living in the same area. Of 3,000 opinion poll respondents in probability samples drawn by a Minneapolis newspaper, 125 reported identifiable three-generation linkages of nuclear families within 50 miles of the Twin Cities. These families, linked by threes as grandparent, parent, and young-married-children families, were then interviewed four times in a year with 15 families used as replacements for nonparticipants among the others. The interview dealt with current family conditions and attributes, changes in the last few months, and family and environmental history. In the first wave the loss of one family meant that the other two of the family set were also dropped. Inserting the replacements, 336 successful interviews were obtained. In later waves interviewed families were retained even if other generations of the family were not reached. In the second wave 315 families were interviewed, only three of which were lost in the two later waves. Thus 312 families took part through the whole procedure, which produced 1,239 interviews. In 300 interviews wife and husband were jointly interviewed, whereas in all other interviews the wife served as the informant (Hill, 1970, pp. 18–25). Hence the response rate was around 83 percent. In the first wave an inventory of durable possessions was obtained, and in later waves changes were noted and asked about. Through retrospective questions a history of each possession was outlined. The young families were in the first stage of family development, whereas parent families and grandparent families represented later stages. Hence "the depth of life cycle analysis" was possible for two of the generations.

It seems that Hill's well-planned and carefully executed study is not done full justice when it is presented as a substitute for a longitudinal study but without the "trials and tribulations" of such studies (Hill, 1970, p. 16). Handling the problem of attrition and telescoping the family cycle by using a cross section of three-generation families also intentionally produced a sample of families in which the generations probably were more than usually alike. This inference especially holds, since each complete family has two parental families in whose region they could live, and some parental families have more than one married child, who can live in the same region. Thus rather strong selective factors were introduced in the sample. Furthermore, the design demanded some rather strongly retrospective questions. Family histories start with conditions just after marriage and contain purchases from that time on. The husband is asked about yearly family income in thousands from the first year of marriage (Hill, 1970, Appendix B).

Similarly the Norwegian Occupational Life History Study in 1971–72 interviewed some 3,400 men divided into three cohorts of those born in 1921, 1931, and 1941, respectively, on their residential, educational, occupational, familial, household, and health conditions from the age of fourteen till the time of the interview. Questions on income were asked for every fifth year. The cohorts were nationally defined and the samples thus drawn from the whole country. The field work was carried out by the Norwegian National Statistical Central Bureau. The cohorts got non-response rates of 17 percent, 12 percent, and 17 percent, respectively (Ramsøy, 1977).

The design makes possible the instantaneous longitudinal study of three birth cohorts from the age of fourteen for periods of observation of 36, 26, and 16 years, respectively. There is no attrition of interviewed persons. However, the sample misses men who died or left the country during the period of observation.[6] Since this loss reasonably increases with age and length of period, it introduces some, presumably slight, differences between cohorts as of 1971–72. Lost cases could be drawn from population registers and background data on them taken from various registers and files. The main, or perhaps only, weakness of the design is the deliberately heavy retrospective character of data, as interviews go back as much as 36, 26, and 16 years, respectively.

To the extent such fact-finding retrospective questions really give sufficiently valid data, they are an important shortcut indeed. In view of what is known on their limitations and errors, responses to them should not be taken at face value before critical inquiry. The burden of proof here rests with those who claim their usefulness, not with those who doubt.

Governmental Microdata

As a means to check retrospective data and to let data from different sources support each other and as an independent alternative, the use of governmental (and private) microdata should be explored. For many American sociological studies this approach may not be feasible, but it probably is for some of them (cf. Angell and Freedman, 1953). In Sweden, for example, with its extensive and acceptably reliable system of population registers and files in the wide sense, governmental microdata have been employed to good results in longitudinal projects. In fact, one of the first and most influential longitudinal projects, Gunnar Boalt's (1947) study of the educational careers of a Stockholm cohort, built entirely on such data. However, with our usual independence of mind Scandinavian sociologists tend to follow American sociologists in considering secondary data as something of second-rate data. Available population registers have not been employed to their full capacity, but interest and awareness of their possibilities seem to be increasing. Ironically, this development in Sweden comes when access to secondary sources has been restricted according to the interpretation of the 1974 Data Law by the Data Inspection Board.

Governmental microdata can be classified in two categories and are employed in longitudinal projects for two main purposes. (Microdata from nongovernmental agencies play a minor role and are not discussed here.)[7] Some governmental microdata are collected for statistical or other research purposes. The prime example would be data for the Censuses of Population and Housing, but the Statistical Central Bureau, some other national boards, statistical offices, and agencies of cities have other *statistical records* of corresponding kind. In addition, many governmental agencies have files of data that they use or have used in their decision making. To the same category of *decision* or *administrative registers* and files of *process* data we allow registers for population bookkeeping. Note that files no longer used administratively because they are too old but still in the archives also are included in the category of decision registers. The statistical records, on the other hand, are never used in making decisions on individual cases of registered persons, families, companies, and the like, and generally are not available to other agencies except as tables, from which single units supposedly cannot be identified.

Data from registers and files can be used first as sampling frames and to keep track of or trace cohort members. Obviously this is a most important use. Second, information from registers and files can be used to describe cohort members and their conditions; variables for the analyses can be based on such data. The ample opportunities long provided in both respects probably are the greatest asset of Swedish social sciences in an international perspective.

As frames for defining populations and sampling of cohort members, mostly administrative registers, especially registers for population bookkeeping, are employed. These registers rather than statistical ones are used for three reasons. First, they often are closer to being comprehensive; they contain most of the population instead of a sample. Second, they are more often brought up to date than the statistical records, which usually refer to a given point in time and are renewed with rather long intervals. Third, statistical records are seldom made available with individual units identified. To protect privacy they are usually accessible to researchers only as public-use samples or in otherwise anonymous form.

For this third reason governmental statistical records tend to be less important than administrative registers to longitudinal projects also for getting variables. Even when the national statistical bureaus overcome the reluctance to public-use samples, such samples are of no direct usefulness to longitudinal projects, which require the transference of data on the individual level. This transference has been made in some cases. In the final phase of the period of observation, when no further individual linkings are demanded, the statistical agency may itself transfer its data to the project's collection of data and then anonymize them. Similarly if the agency is put in charge of the data-gathering process or of the whole project, it may link the data and hand them over in deidentified form. However, to be successful many such arrangements should include the transferring of statistical data that have been excerpted for statistical purposes from administrative registers of other agencies.

If they do so, the restriction to data already excerpted may decrease the validity of data. The main objection to the use of administrative registers and files as sources of research data seems to be the presumably low validity of the ensuing data. However, questions of validity cannot be answered in general terms but should be settled on the merits on each particular case. Obviously dossiers in decision files are not produced with an eye to making them contain good measures of the particular research project, nor are summary descriptions of cases for administra-

tive statistical reports on the activities of the agency. Such simple nota-
tions may be clearly off the target, although even the simple recording of
whether a family is known to the welfare agency as a dependency case
during a given period, for example, has proved its sociological relevance
(cf. Boalt, 1947; Janson, 1968). By going through the dossiers one may
be able to excerpt information rather to the point. Even if tedious, such
procedures may then pay off and produce data that well hold their own
against retrospective answers and perhaps also against contemporary
answers to interview questions or questionnaires.

Registers and files may contain records of interrogations. The questioning was made not for research purposes but for classificatory, eval-
uative, investigative, or therapeutic purposes, among others. This may
or may not make the informant more motivated to tell the truth than in
the research inquiry. At least the information may have been given at
the time the retrospective questioning is aiming at. One may also find in
the dossier minutes from meetings or records of decisions, about which
the interviewee is questioned in the research interview, perhaps in retrospect. If they concern matters sensitive or embarrassing to the informant, one may think the documents more reliable. There may also be
reports on investigations and direct observations made by officials as to
a cohort member and his or her situation at the time as well as letters
and statements written by the member, who expressed personal opinions
on matters at that time.

Compared to a good survey by interviews, a good register study tends
to be much less expensive per case, although not always per item of
information. It also has much fewer missing cases, since it is not plagued
by the nonresponse problem. (However, it is not as free of technical
problems as one may believe.) A series of factual information may be
found, and values of variables may be checked or documented from more
or less thorough excerpting of administrative registers and files. When
good-quality registers and files are available, excerpting probably often
provides the best way of shortening the data-collecting period without
shortening the period of observation and generally of exploring past
conditions. In any case, as to the researcher of modern history the
documents are useful to check retrospective statements by informants.

The arguments presented here may also support the use of documentary sources in sociological longitudinal studies in general, not only as a
device to shorten or postpone the data-collecting period. Furthermore,
some of the weaknesses of interviews and questionnaires also apply to
nonretrospective questions — for example, ones that concern socially or
psychologically sensitive behavior or circumstances. Even here docu-

mentary sources may be preferred. For instance, one may doubt that answers to the question whether the family is on welfare at present are more reliable than answers to the question whether the family was on welfare any time during a specified period. In both cases I am inclined to trust more completely the records of the municipal register of dependency cases.

Self-reports of crime and delinquency have been greeted as a major research-technical innovation. They have deficiencies as to reliability, but they demonstrate the high frequency of undetected delinquent and criminal acts among all investigated categories (cf. Wallerstein and Wyle, 1947, as quoted by Swedner, 1968, p. 191; Elmhorn, 1965). Furthermore, they enable criminologists to get around the socioeconomic and ethnic-racial bias of official crime and delinquency records (e.g., Nye, 1958; Dentler and Monroe, 1961; Hirschi, 1969).

However, there are also some more reserved views. In self-report studies socioeconomic and ethnical-racial factors may be rather easily blurred by differential errors in reporting and by flaws in sampling and nonresponse. Some self-report studies find difference in background between delinquency categories (cf. Reiss and Rhodes, 1961). Furthermore, as pointed out by Tittle, Villemez, and Smith (1978), at least in more recent studies, mostly on juveniles, background factors present themselves less clearly even in documentary data (cf. Janson, 1977, pp. 47–50). The results of self-report research and research based on official records may then be considered fairly consistent in terms of correlates and causes (Hirschi, 1975, p. 189). Hindelang (1978) finds records, if anything, somewhat more in accord than self-reports with data from a second type of retrospective questioning — namely, victimization data — as to racial differences in four crimes of violence. Hindelang, Hirschi, and Weis (1979) argue that self-reports are basically reliable and valid for trivial offenses, but that more serious offenses are more effectively (and with fairly little bias) revealed by some official data.

In my opinion there has been a tendency to underestimate both the weaknesses of the self-reports of crime and delinquency and the possibilities of documentary sources on these phenomena. At least this is the case when arguments mainly taken from the American scene are applied to the Scandinavian situation. There, one may assume acceptable governmental data to be more often available even as to crime and delinquency. Again, the relative merits should be evaluated in the particular situation of the research project. Project Metropolitan has not used self-reports of delinquency other than truancy and being sent out of class (Project Metropolitan, 1975, pp. 11f.). We have used both interviews and questionnaires and would have liked to do that more often than we have had opportunities to. We even asked a few retrospective questions (cf. Project Metropolitan, 1975b, pp. 27–34).

I am not at all suggesting that we abandon the interview and the questionnaire. Of course they are our most efficient instruments in many respects, such as in obtaining verbal measures of attitudes and abilities. There has, however, been a tendency to overextend the uses of these important instruments.

FADING RELEVANCE

The Problem

However much a longitudinal project can be shortened by the use of documentary evidence, most such projects with prospective data are bound to extend over a fairly long period of time. It may well take a protracted research process of some twenty years to get to the point where one can start to write up the research and to suggest answers to questions the answering of which presumably was the purpose of the project. However, not all — perhaps not even many — research questions posed some twenty years ago, if then in the mainstream of interest, are as interesting now. Perhaps, then, there is not much use for a longitudinal project (cf. Bühler, Keith-Spiegel, and Thomas, 1973, p. 865).

According to social science methods books the first step in any study is to define the question that is to be answered (e.g., Selltiz, Wrightsman, and Cook, 1976, pp. 103, 542). In doing so, one starts with a conceptual model, however vague and implicit, on the nature of the phenomena to be investigated (e.g., Riley, 1963, pp. 5f.). The empirical research project then concentrates on a number of hypotheses (e.g., Karlsson, 1961a, p. 3), which still may be vague and implicit. However, if possible, hypotheses should be explicit and precise. They may be isolated statements, but these are unsatisfactory. They should be connected in a theory (Karlsson, 1961b, p. 48). "The clear statement of a theoretically significant hypothesis related to previous research is crucial to a well-designed scientific study" (Theodorson and Theodorson, 1969, p. 191). One should have or construct a substantive theory and derive hypotheses as propositions of the theory. This is the way to arrive at explanation (Zetterberg, 1963, pp. 1–10).

When the field is little developed and it is considered premature to settle for specified hypotheses, one may work with a more open conceptual model and let one's hypotheses remain vague and mostly implicit. To gain familiarity with the phenomenon in question and perhaps to formulate a more precise research problem or to develop hypotheses, one may then attempt an *explanatory* or *formulative* study (Riley, 1963, pp. 27, 68f.; Selltiz, Wrightsman, and Cook, 1976, pp. 90f.). There are also *descriptive* studies with or without specified initial hypotheses and with varying theoretical relevance (Selltiz, Wrightsman, and Cook, 1976, pp. 101–03).

However, there is no doubt the testing of explicit, specified, and theoretically derived hypotheses is considered a more valuable form of empirical study. One should be as specific as possible and have operational definitions worked out on each concept. The perfect researcher seems to act as in the more advanced, experimental sciences with the design and analyses planned in detail, sometimes to the point of preparing dummy tables (e.g., Selltiz, Wrightsman, and Cook, 1976, p. 543). The empirical data should be carefully adapted to the specific questions one intends to answer from them. "When time has come for the actual gathering of data, one is so restricted by decisions already taken that there is not much choice left," writes Karlsson (1961a, p. 11). No data must be included just because they seem interesting on general grounds.

Naturally the longitudinal researcher prefers to contribute to the progress of the behavioral sciences by making such a verificational study with theoretically derived hypotheses rather than a mere explanatory or descriptive study. Thus he or she should proceed as just outlined. However, this seems a fairly safe recipe for how to make a longitudinal study unsuccessful by being overly rigid. First, one has to be either something of a genius or very lucky to find one's hypotheses still of general interest after, say, twenty-five years. For example, a study that started in 1964 would have been planned according to hypotheses made in 1963 at the latest. At that time the researcher probably would not have thought much on linear causal analysis of the kind just introduced to sociologists by Blalock (1961). Nor would the researcher then have known about other developments of multivariate analysis, such as Jöreskog's new approaches to factor analysis (cf. Werts, Linn, and Jöreskog, 1971) or Goodman's (1970) multiplicative models, nor would he or she have known about most packages of standard computer programs, such as SPSS and OSIRIS.

In the field of social stratification, the contributions of Lenski (1966), Blau and Duncan (1967), and Boudon (1974) would not yet have appeared, nor could the results reached by the Wisconsin group (Sewell, Haller, and Portes, 1969, etc.) have been considered, to mention only a few important works since the mid-sixties. Probably the researcher would have been more functionalistic and less Marxist in orientation then than now. As to deviance, the researcher's hypotheses would probably have been formulated when the labeling approach began to come to the fore (Becker, 1963).

Suppose the hypotheses were not in the labeling vein. Reports on them in the mid-seventies would probably have been criticized as out of touch with modern thought on delinquency and other deviant behavior and perhaps for not paying attention to certain macrosociological aspects of deviance. However, in the mid-eighties, if the hypotheses were finally evaluated then, the interest in labeling theory may have faded and been succeeded by a renewed orientation toward genetic factors. Labeling hypotheses, on the other hand, may be found to follow an early version of the theory, which had been modified already by the mid-seventies.

To the extent hypotheses put forward at the start of the project interest other researchers, these colleagues may suggest answers to the questions before the hypotheses are finally put to the test in the longitudinal project. Presumably answers based on nonlongitudinal data are inferior or at least inconclusive, but reports may even come in from other longitudinal projects that are incomplete or unknown to the researcher when he or she fixes the hypotheses.

Suggested Procedure

Hence, it seems advisable to try to arrange a procedure that makes it possible for us to take into consideration technical, theoretical, and empirical changes, progress, and opportunities that may occur during the project. In fact, it appears to be the rule for good planning generally to try to keep alternatives open as long as feasible. By postponing decisions new information can be considered until a relative satiation is reached or until a decision must be taken as the activities threaten to come to a standstill. If so, sociological methods books exaggerate the rigidity necessary in planning. After all, the designs of good buildings are often not definite until the buildings are completed.

Thus a more adequate procedure probably is first to outline the general direction of the project and its fields of interest and to plan only the first years in detail and even these with a decreasing degree of detail. For each year the planning process should then roll on, having a few years laid out in detail. To some degree one may even reverse decisions already implemented by supplementing new data from documentary sources for years gone, thus exploring originally unexpected possibilities as long as one keeps within the general outline.

Second, even with this kind of roll-on planning it is advisable, at least in the beginning, not to tie data too closely and exclusively to very specific hypotheses. Instead, and contrary to the canon of methods books, one should be sure to include data that are judged to be relevant to the project on general and unspecific grounds. This design will increase the chances to deal with other, related aspects of the field. The price to pay is the less than optimal fit to any hypothesis in particular that is likely to characterize such an all-purpose series of data. For many problems the loss of efficiency may not be important. It should also be mentioned that some problems refer to a shorter period of observation. For instance, juvenile delinquency can be profitably analyzed before the cohort has reached middle age. Again, such early outcomes of the project itself can provide reasons for making changes in the original plans as hypotheses are falsified or unexpected results appear.

Third, the rigid deductive model largely excludes the possibility of unexpected findings. This restriction, of course, holds generally and not only for longitudinal projects. Obviously the unexpected is the more important the less well founded the theory from which the hypotheses are derived.[8] Often the usage of the term *theory* is too generous in the behavioral sciences. Possibly many behavioral "theories" correspond rather more to sets of general hypotheses in more established disciplines. When we have fairly low confidence in our "theory," the deductive approach may be less rewarding than otherwise. Here Merton's term *theoretical orientation* probably describes our starting point in planning the project (Merton, 1945, p. 465; Merton, 1957, pp. 87f.). While working on the project and generally exploring a problem area, we gradually develop and perhaps change the orientation. Especially, however, we move toward a specification that may be termed a *theory of the middle range,* again in Merton's terms.

Finally, we may be optimistic enough to hope for a less passive role as to the theoretical interest of the field. Perhaps we can influence, if only modestly, the direction of the interest by bringing up a theme somewhat outside the mainstream. Here again a reference is appropriate to Merton. Already in 1948 he had pointed out that empirical research does not have the testing or verification of hypotheses as its only theoretical function. Instead "research plays an active role: it performs at least four major functions which help shape the development of theory. It initiates, it reformulates, it deflects and clarifies theory" (Merton, 1948, p. 506; also Merton, 1957, p. 103). It exerts pressure on theory in

four ways: to initiate theory, by the unanticipated, anomalous, and stra-
tegic datum ("the serendipity pattern"); to elaborate a conceptual
scheme, by new data; to refocus interest, by new methods of empirical
research; and to clear concepts, by searching for applicable concepts.

POSSIBILITIES OF LONGITUDINAL STUDIES

Comparative Assumptions

With all the troubles involved in a longitudinal study, one may ask what
it has to offer for compensation. What can be achieved by a longitudinal
study that cannot be accomplished as easily or better by other approaches? Conversely, perhaps the longitudinal approach cannot handle
certain kinds of questions and thus should be avoided when one wants
to deal with certain problems.

Comparing different approaches as to possibilities, one should probably assume them at their best. In a way, this will not be fair if some
approaches are more demanding than others. If so, one has to weigh
differences in demands made by the approaches against differences in
possibilities to decide, for instance, whether some additional opportunities offered by one approach are worth the incurred cost of increased
difficulties as compared with the cost of alternative approaches. However, actual research-technical problems probably vary more between
specific situations than between approaches and thus are not generally
inherent in the approaches.

Having completed these preliminaries, successful longitudinal studies
will now be summarily compared with successful case studies, cross-
cultural studies, experimental studies, panel studies, follow-up studies,
and cross-sectional surveys as to general analytical possibilities. Clearly,
the approaches selected for comparisons can be combined with each
other in various ways. For instance, analyses of experiments or of cross-
sectional data may also utilize data describing characteristics and conditions of earlier time periods, when such data are at hand from previous
studies, from documents or from retrospective questioning. However,
for comparisons, pure forms shall be assumed. Furthermore, in the first
place conventional applications of the approaches are considered, although some more unusual or sophisticated forms are also taken into
account — still with the limitation that they should be within the practical
and principal range of unmixed versions of the approach in question. It
should be clear from the context what combination, if any, of compared

approaches would be equivalent to a longitudinal approach as to a given aspect.

Of longitudinal studies a conventional version — that is, a study without such features as are possible as options or are specific of an actual study — is first discussed. Then options are considered. Generally, "longitudinal study" is conceived according to the narrow, research-technical definition suggested earlier (cf. Table 2.1).

Case Studies

Obviously a conventional longitudinal study is statistical and is oriented toward the analysis of cohorts. Thus the usual methodological differences between case studies and statistical studies apply. They will not be discussed here (cf. Inghe, 1960, pp. 42–55; Riley, 1963, pp. 32–77; for criminological studies, see Sutherland and Cressey, 1960, pp. 66–69). *Case study* is used here in the sense of a study of "social phenomena through the thorough analysis of an individual case" (Theodorson and Theodorson, 1969, p. 38).

On the other hand, a longitudinal project densely covering the period of observation with data provides opportunities for case studies (cf. Dollard's already quoted use of the term *long-sectional* on life histories). Potentially it thus contains a series of case studies from which findings of individual cases may be validated. Admittedly this way of analyzing longitudinal data is seldom utilized. Significantly, when it is, one may hesitate as to whether the approach is longitudinal or one of multiple-case studies. Of course, it is a combination of both, a longitudinal case-study approach. An interesting sample is Gunnar Inghe's analysis of sequential patterns of dependency (Inghe, 1960, pp. 342–98).

One may assume that an extensive longitudinal project would provide excellent opportunities for case studies. First, it would have data describing individual development and changing life-situations over a long period. Second, several cases could be so compared. However, one has to admit that the individual cases would most likely be described in less detail than in ordinary single-case studies.

Cross-Cultural Studies

A *cross-cultural study* is here defined as a study that utilizes "comparable data from different cultures in order to test hypotheses concerning individual and group behavior" (Theodorson and Theodorson, 1969, p. 89). It is not meaningful to contrast such studies with longitudinal studies, since they do not belong to the same classificatory dimension and thus are not strictly comparable. Rather one may inquire whether longitudinal projects can be cross-cultural or can be utilized for cross-cultural comparisons.

Often comparative studies use socioanthropological data nonstatistically or are otherwise nonstatistical. However, cross-cultural comparisons are also made statistically. Thus anthropological data were analyzed statistically by Murdock in his classic study (1949) and by Gouldner and Peterson (1964). In political science, social psychology, and sociology nations are compared more or less formally (cf. Merritt and Rokkan, 1966). Recent examples are Allardt's (1975) study of levels of living and welfare in the Nordic countries and Treiman's (1977) study of occupational prestige in sixty nations.

Clearly, longitudinal data can have cross-cultural relevance. As already pointed out, cross-cultural comparisons can be built in to advantage in the design by substituting cohorts from different nations or regions for different cohorts from the same area. Again, one must admit that this device is seldom used and that most longitudinal studies are large enough without being extended cross-culturally. Project Metropolitan is a case in which a cross-cultural approach was attempted but could be realized only partially (Janson, 1975, pp. 27–33). Yet parameters on individual cognitive development, educational careers, social mobility, dependency patterns, and the like, must be pertinent to sociological theory in some cross-cultural comparisons and can best be provided by longitudinal studies.

Experiments

Evidently the essence of an experiment is the testing of one or several causal hypotheses. The testing is made by manipulating crucial factors and observing differences between conditions or before and after a factor is introduced. Such tests of causal hypotheses are usually not made in longitudinal studies. Obviously, experimental manipulation is not a necessary element in longitudinal design. However, neither by definition nor in practice is it impossible to include experiments in a longitudinal project. In fact, to record long-term effects of an experiment one needs either a follow-up study or a longitudinal study. Thus an ordinary laboratory experiment directly tests a causal hypothesis but only in a short time perspective. Another well-known limitation is its sometimes relatively low "socioecological" validity — that is, its more or less artificial setting. This may be less a problem with a field experiment and even less with a natural experiment, but their likely restriction to short-term effects remains.

Occasionally natural experiments in the shape of educational or other reforms can be worked into a longitudinal design. For instance, Härnquist and Svensson in 1961 and 1966 obtained mental-test scores, marks, attitudes, educational plans, socioeconomic background, and so on, of 10 percent national samples of thirteen-year-olds in Sweden in order to follow their educational and occupational careers. At the time of the testing the new comprehensive school had been implemented in some but not all school districts. In 1961 about one-third of the pupils were in the new school, and in 1966 this had been extended to about four-fifths of the pupils. Thus it has been possible to compare results in the comprehensive school system with the results in the older elite type of school system, such as the relations between marks and educational plans in different social strata (Härnquist and Svensson, 1967) and the differences between cohorts in mean test scores in different social strata and for each sex (Svensson, 1971). Again, however, one must admit that experimental options are but seldom utilized in longitudinal projects.

Panels and Follow-up Studies

Both panels and follow-up studies employ a longitudinal perspective, and the distinction between these studies and longitudinal ones is not always clear, when it is made at all. The conventional *panel study* is an interview or questionnaire study in which the same persons are questioned in several cross-sectional waves, the questions dealing with the actual situation and changes since last time, and the waves coming fairly close during a rather short period of time. In well-designed panel studies often new respondents are brought in on each wave for comparison. Possibly most researchers accept the panel-study label also when direct observations or governmental microdata are used instead of interviews or questionnaires or when the cross-sectional data-gathering waves are spread over a rather "long" period. Whether or not the expansion of terms as to sources of data is accepted, a panel study collects longitudinal data for a certain period by the use of a special design — a series of successive cross-sectional data gatherings. Hence its analytical possibilities are included among the possibilities of the longitudinal study but are more restricted. A further restriction is imposed if the panel study is limited to a relatively short period in accordance with the practice of actual research. In actual research, however, longitudinal projects seldom cover periods as densely as panels do.

In a follow-up study one returns to the units of a previous study and records their conditions and characteristics at a much later point in time. Thus in pure form it does not cover the period between the old study and the time investigated in the return study. However, in practice this difference between the follow-up study and the general longitudinal study is often blurred, as some data for the in-between period are also supplemented. Probably many social scientists prefer to see follow-up studies as longitudinal studies. Possibly this holds for panels, too.

Cross-Sectional Surveys

A cross-sectional survey cuts through Becker's diagram horizontally; its data refer to the same time (period) but to different ages and cohorts. Thus it analyzes simultaneous interindividual variations and covariations. Age can be analytically controlled just as other variables.

The interindividual within-period variations over a broad range of ages are obtained in a longitudinal project only if several cohorts are represented as, say, in the Low-Income Study (Johansson, 1970) or the Lundby study (Hagnell, 1966; Hagnell and Kreitman, 1974; Hagnell and Rorsman, 1978). With only one cohort, age is constant and the interindividual variation accordingly restricted.

Cross-sectional variations and covariations are entirely interindividual or refer to individual variation between aspects of multidimensional profiles, whereas longitudinal variations and covariations can refer to intraindividual changes, usually compared over individuals, although sequential changes within individuals are also possible. Furthermore, in a longitudinal study variables referring to different points or periods in time can be compared and correlated, and one can decide whether one or the other change comes first. Thus a process may be described and an analysis can be brought closer to causal concepts.

Concluding Comments

It has been emphasized that the longitudinal approach can be combined with or utilized for other approaches, which are, however, usually miss-

Table 2.2. Comparison between Longitudinal Studies and Some Other Kinds of Studies.

Approach Compared with Longitudinal Approach	Characteristic of Compared Approach Missing in Conventional Longitudinal Approach	Characteristic of Compared Approach Missing in Longitudinal Approach by Definition	Characteristic of Longitudinal Approach Missing in Compared Pure Approach
Case studies	Individual case		Statistical analysis
Cross-cultural studies	Cross-cultural comparisons		
Experimental studies	Experimental manipulation		In practice: long-term effects
Panel studies	Period densely covered		Long-term effects
Follow-up studies			Period covered
Cross-sectional surveys	Simultaneous variation over age		Change of variables, time sequence of variables

ing in the ordinary longitudinal project. This absence, of course, may occur because there were no opportunities for them in the situation of the particular project or because they were not relevant to the investigations and thus not sought. Instead, even the conventional longitudinal study offers some analytical possibilities that presumably are relevant but not found with other approaches. The comparisons are summarized in Table 2.2.

The most important characteristics of longitudinal studies are that they permit the analyses of changes of variables and of the time sequence of variables and that the analyses of change and of time sequence can be extended over a long period of time. Change and time sequence obviously are essential to causal analysis even if nonexperimental. The most important principal disadvantage of the ordinary longitudinal study is its nonexperimental character, although experimental manipulation is optional. The long-term perspective is a partial compensatory advantage over the ordinary experimental study. Whether the prospects of rewards from a longitudinal project are great enough in a particular situation to justify the efforts of carrying through such a project is up to the individual researcher — and the grant-giving research council or foundation — to decide.

NOTES

1. In this section *cohort* means *birth* (or *age*) cohort. In the discussion other cohorts correspond to a series of age cohorts, if they can be subdivided into homogeneous age classes.

2. Lexis's diagram has observed time and *age* as the dimensions, which means that life lines go diagonally upward and rightward.

3. Project Metropolitan has two birth cohorts of 1953, one in metropolitan Copenhagen and one in metropolitan Stockholm.

4. In studies of mortality or geographical mobility deaths and out-migrations, respectively, evidently do not represent attrition of cases. Note also that in a strictly longitudinal study appropriate generalizations presume the set of observed cases to represent the original cohort but do not require the set to represent the cohort of the area as of a later period.

5. If an analysis deals with diachronous data on micro-units that make out a population, cohort, or sample at a given time, the characteristic "retrospective" of the analysis usually means that the analysis concerns a period or time before the given time in reference to which the set of units was delineated. Correspondingly if the analysis refers to data later than this given time, it is usually called "prospective." Thus somewhat figuratively, one may say that the retrospective analysis is concerned with the *inflow* with the analyzed set of units as destination, whereas the prospective analysis follows the *outflow* from the set.

6. One way to reduce a component of attrition is to select theoretically meaningful and interesting cohort or population areas with low rates of out-migrations. The Norwegian

retrospective study chose the whole country, which clearly is theoretically acceptable and brings strong environmental differences into the sample. In a project with a protracted period of data gathering, the geographical dispersion of cases in a national sample is expensive and heavy to handle. Project Metropolitan selected the largest metropolitan areas in the countries studied, metropolitan Copenhagen and metropolitan Stockholm. At the time of the decision these areas were assumed to have relatively low out-migration rates among those growing up there. It was also assumed to be theoretically relevant to study cohorts in these big urban areas (cf. Janson, 1975, pp. 27f.). In Stockholm a further attempt to reduce attrition was made by making the analysis retrospective up to the age of ten by defining the cohort as those who were born in 1953 and were registered as living in Stockholm metropolitan area on November 1, 1963 (Janson, 1975, p. 32). This definition closely resembles the definition applied by Boalt in his study of a Stockholm cohort, defined as all pupils who left fourth form of schools in Stockholm in spring 1936 (Janson, 1975, p. 17).

7. They are important, however, in certain fields, such as business administration and the study of popular movements.

8. By "the unexpected," I have in mind something more than the mere nonappearance of the theoretically expected results, however much nonsupport for a seemingly well-founded hypothesis may surprise the researcher. The unexpected outcome in an area with a well-established theory is most probably due to technical clumsiness or a mishap. If it is not, then it is an important finding, perhaps in the Nobel prize class, and hence extremely rare. In the less-established area the unexpected result is correspondingly less rare and remarkable but often on a par in general interest with conclusions as to the hypothesis.

3 EPIDEMIOLOGICAL CONSIDERATIONS

Johannes Ipsen

The purpose of this chapter is to recall some basic concepts and methods that pertain to the appearance, persistence, and waning of disease in groups of persons. These are the elements of epidemiology. It is assumed that the reader is more than familiar with epidemiological principles, but I hope that those who are deeply involved in intricate research problems will enjoy the relaxation of reverting to fundamentals.

Epidemiological investigations have three phases: observations, records, and reflections. The *observations* are concerned with disease, its signs and symptoms in people. The *records* are in terms of time of observation, kinds of people observed, and places where they live and work. The records may solely be those of the investigator, but more typically some or all data are furnished by others — public agencies, hospitals, primary health services, or social services. Sometimes the data can be had by stripmining; sometimes one must burrow deeply after careful surveying. The *reflections* — analysis of the data — have to do with the purpose of the investigation, which can range from mere satisfaction of medical curiosity, causation of disease, or effectiveness of prevention or cure to census of the impact of disease on society, including hazardous elements of workplaces or lifestyle.

Whatever the purpose, there is a need to conceptualize the pragmatic observations into a system of idealized parameters, whose interrelations and interactions can be numerically evaluated. The epidemiologist must therefore know statistics or at least be on speaking terms with the statistician. The latter has two missions: (1) to prevent the investigator from making false conclusions — avoiding Error I of stating that "the data show this and that" when they indeed show nothing but random variation; and (2) to turn over every stone that might support or reject a hypothesis — in other words, to specify biometric models that increase the information that is hidden somewhere in the data. Error II — "missing the boat" — is too often committed out of fear of committing Error I.

Many nonparametric tests are easy to perform and secure against false distribution models. However, when these tests are significant — and the null hypothesis can be rejected — the investigator is often deprived of an alternative hypothesis with biological meaning. Parametric tests, such as testing a linear relationship, have the advantage that they offer a quantitative statement of the relationship. If a variable increases significantly with age, for example, the regression test yields an estimate of the increase per year of age and the limits of this assessment.

There are occasions when the statistician and the epidemiologist must disagree. No statistician with self-respect can accept the evidence of one or very few cases. Yet the epidemiologist may claim that what the statistician politely terms an "outlier" is the one observation that may give a clue to a causative determinant or the source of an epidemic outbreak. This leaves the statistician cold and the burden of proof rests with the epidemiologist. He or she may either come up with supporting evidence by further observations or suggest to the statistician another model that better fits the situation.

EPIDEMIOLOGICAL PARAMETERS

Let us consider epidemiological principles and the parameters to which observations are reduced, which serve as dependent variables in the interrelation matrix. Occurrence of disease can be described as *status* and as *events*. Disease is here used generically as a changeable attribute of a person, whether perceived objectively by medical observation or subjectively by the diseased person. *Prevalence* is a status term that refers to the number of persons with a disease at a given point in time or over a given period: P_t denotes the point prevalence at time t; $P(t)$ denotes the period prevalence during the time unit that starts at time t.

The events are basically those of *entry* into and of *departure* from the diseased population group. The number of persons who enter the disease state during a given time period is called the *incidence*. It is given an adjective — annual, monthly, daily — according to the period used. (*Incidence* is often broadly used, or misused, to mean frequency, particularly in clinical jargon.) The number of "new cases" or incidence is denoted by $I(t)$. This number divided by the population considered is an estimate of the abstract probability that healthy persons, specified by kind and place, will enter the disease state during a given period. The number of persons *leaving* the disease state for various reasons — recovery, emigration, or death — is called the withdrawal or removal, denoted by $W(t)$.

The epidemiological *recurrence equation* describes the point prevalence P_{t+1}, one period after the point prevalence P_t:

$$P_{t+1} = P_t + I(t) - W(t). \tag{3.1}$$

This equation is purely pragmatic. It does not say any more than does a bank statement showing that your balance by the first of April equals your balance on the first of March plus your deposits minus your withdrawals during the month of March.

In theory, one would like to estimate probability parameters that describe the average growth and decline of the diseased population. The incidence rate $i = I(t)/N$, where N is the population at risk, is an estimate of the probability that members of the risk population will enter the disease state during the time period. The ratio of incidence rates for two population groups is called the *relative risk*. If this ratio is, say, 2.0, it can be stated that one population has twice the risk of disease of the other population group.

The removal rate

$$r = W(t)/[P_t + I(t)] \tag{3.2}$$

offers an estimate of the proportion that during a time period is removed from the diseased population (through recovery, death, or disability). A particular interest is attached to the removal rate because it has a direct relationship to the duration of disease. From equations (3.1) and (3.2) we have

$$P_{t+1} = W(t)(1 - r)/r = W(t) \cdot d, \tag{3.3}$$

which states that the prevalence at the end of a period equals the number of persons withdrawn from the diseased population times a factor d that depends solely on the withdrawal rate. Now if the rate r signifies the fraction of diseased persons who are withdrawn during a given time — for example, a year — then $d = (1 - r)/r$ is the average duration of the disease in years. Let the number of patients in a hospital at the end of a year be 400 and the number of discharges during that year be 4,000; the average length of stay at the hospital is estimated at $200/4,000 = 0.05$ year or 18 days. Similarly, in a stable endemic situation where incidence and withdrawal are almost equal, it follows that the ratio (prevalence)/(annual incidence) approximately estimates the duration of disease.

If we introduce the concept of risk population or susceptibles at a given time, denoted by S_t, the recurrence equation (3.1) can be rewritten as

$$P_{t+1} = (P_t + S_t \cdot i)(1 - r), \tag{3.4}$$

which essentially expresses that prevalence is governed by two determinants: (1) the risk of entering the disease state and (2) the forces of severity of disease that result in death, recovery, or permanent disability.

The part of the removal rate that is due to death consists of deaths during the period $M(t)$ divided by the period prevalence and is called *lethality rate* or *case fatality rate*:

$$\text{Case fatality rate} = f = M(t)/P(t). \tag{3.5}$$

The more commonly used death rate is the *mortality rate,* which is deaths over the total risk population:

$$\text{Mortality rate} = m = M(t)/N. \tag{3.6}$$

It follows that mortality rate, like prevalence, is determined both by factors that influence the occurrence of disease and by those that influence the course of the disease. A decreasing mortality rate can be interpreted ambiguously as due to prevention or to therapy and cure, unless case fatality rate is specified.

EPIDEMIOLOGICAL TRANSITION MODELS

There is a need to enlarge the classic parameter system outlined above. In order to elucidate this matter graphically, let us first consider incidence, prevalence, and removal in a sort of Markov scheme. The simplest model will take form somewhat as in Figure 3.1. The three squares indicate the three fundamental states, of which death takes a particular form, having no transition probability. The circles indicate the three

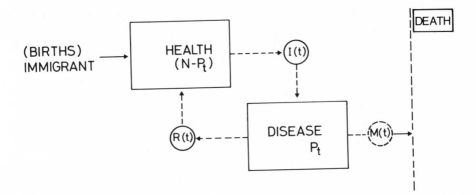

Figure 3.1. Markov Scheme.

kinds of event: onset, recovery, and death. The numbers can be trans-formed to probability estimates by dividing each event with the number in the state from which it originates. Thus:

Incidence risk $= i = [I(t)/N - P_t]$.
Removal rate $= r = [M(t) + R(t)]/[P_t + I(t)]$.
Case fatality $= f = M(t)/[P_t + I(t)]$.
Mortality rate $= m = M(t)/N$.

The duration of stay in the prevalence state is (in years or months):

$$d = [P + I(t)]/R(t).$$

Obviously there is need for more descriptive states of a disease. First, each state is a heterogeneous group, which can be characterized by the distributions of a number of variables — age, laboratory measurements, signs and symptoms, and the like. It may be suggested that there is no need for discrete stages of disease, since a given condition could be followed and described by the values of the specific variables. However, the medical care system finds it expedient bodily or administratively to transfer persons or patients from one segment of the care system to another, as presence or absence of symptoms may indicate.

In Figure 3.2 are presented several states of disease identified with level of institutional care. This enlarged diagram starts with subgrouping the "healthy" population into risk groups that are coarsely described as "low," "average," and "high." Contemporary epidemiology devotes much attention to these risk states — almost to the point of denying the

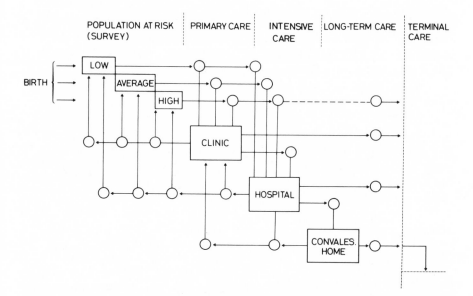

Figure 3.2. Segments of the Care System Identified with Level of Institutional Care.

existence of healthy people. The healthy population is the target for search of disease, for persons that either have conditions that are termed "nonperceived disease" or are predictive of risk. The risk attributes may change with age, be inborn, or be acquired. Low risks, for example, are persons who have acquired immunity through natural or artificial means or have habits of life that are considered preventive of disease.

The primary care, or ambulatory, state (clinic, general practice) receives new disease as well as disease in the posttherapy state. The intensive care state, identified by hospitals, is the one in which rapid changes occur through natural processes and/or therapeutic intervention. Long-term convalescent and terminal care states are those of slow progress or remitting disease.

In the extradiagonal part of Figure 3.2 are arrows that indicate incidence movements in vertical direction, either up or down. Removals are shown by arrows in horizontal directions to the left (improvements) or to the right (deteriorations). The circles indicate the number of persons who move from one state to another during a given time.

The prevalence thus consists of several compartments, each with a number of persons that depends both on the rate of influx from other states and on the rate of removal to other states. In epidemiological practice, investigators will usually find themselves placed in one of the compartments of medical care. Their access to study of the prevalent diseased population will be somewhat limited to those who arrive at and those who are discharged from that station. They can choose between three forms of epidemiological investigation:

1. *Descriptive survey of the prevalent group.* For this survey investigators can give details of clinical signs and symptoms, tests, and so on, and enumerate the subjects by a number of demographic and social characteristics. Furthermore, they can describe the course of disease during the average stay in the state in question.

2. *Retrospective analysis of the attributes of the incidence.* This analysis is the most commonly used form of search for causation. The crucial matter is to establish suitable control populations so that the relative risks of entering the disease state can be established. Usual demographic data of the population of origin are often to be had from official statistical tables, but if the causation is sought in special features of lifestyle or in exposure to specific agents, the task is far more complicated, because these attributes are not available for the base population.

Another drawback of the retrospective study lies in the fact that the selected diseased population in a given state represents prevalence of that state and not incidence, new cases. The farther the state is from the "healthy" population, the more interventions and natural changes have taken place. A typical retrospective study is that of mortality data. The dying process can be long and involve several stages in the health care system, all of which have incidence and removal rates that slur the origin of the lethal cause.

3. *Prospective study plan.* This plan offers certain advantages over the difficulty in retrospectively demonstrating a true time, place, and person relationship between onset of disease and suggested causative determinants. Prospective investigators are also placed in one of the compartments. Their concern is with the removal, whether to a more advanced state of disease or to one of improvement. They define their observational group of persons as a *cohort* — that is, a group of subjects characterized by the same attribute, such as admittance to clinic with diagnosis X, at a defined time, such as onset of event or birth year. The control cohort is then supposed to consist of subjects selected on the same time criterion, but without the attribute of the observational cohort. The dependent variable is the onset of events — changes in disease state — that occur over the observation period in both groups.

PROSPECTIVE STUDIES:
ADVANTAGES AND DRAWBACKS

In the *true prospective study* the two cohorts that are to be compared are selected at the same time and contemporaneously with the start of the observation of future events. Both cohorts must be free of the disease in question and must differ only in the attribute to be tested as a risk determinant or by some intervention that is randomly assigned to the two groups. Although the attributes of the groups under these circumstances are well defined and unbiased, the difficulty rests in attaining the events in question.

The guidelines consist first in the accuracy with which the event can be ascertained. Must it be done by a specific instrument in the hands of the investigator or can he or she rely on reports from others that are placed outside the compartmental setup? Second, the annual incidence rates of the events and the expected relative risk of the two groups will determine the length of time and the size of subject groups required to obtain data that can support or reject the working hypothesis. Time introduces "dropouts" from the study, changes the observation instrument, and — worst of all — may render the problem that seemed important at the start of the study more or less uninteresting after years of observation. New information may appear in the meantime or the setting of the investigation may gradually change. A subject may transfer from one cohort to the other over time. Statistical corrections can be performed to take care of this problem, but they are tedious and add to the uncertainty of results.

Since the length of observation period greatly adds to the costs of the study, another type of prospective study can be considered: the *historically prospective or retroprospective study*. Whereas the true prospective study implies selection of the cohorts at the beginning of observation, the historical study chooses cohorts defined by some attributes existing before the start of the observation period. For example, a study of the determinants of diseases of the circulatory system among alumni of the University of Pennsylvania was performed from 1961 to 1966. Medical records of these 45- to 55-year-old men were available from the time they entered the university in 1930 to 1935. By dividing the population of alumni according to attributes as young men (smoking habits, anxiety expressions, blood pressure, and the like), the relative risk of acquired disease could be estimated, and in several instances some astonishingly strong relationships could be established.

The most disturbing factor was the intervening world war, in which most of the study population participated actively. Yet it seemed as if this conjuncture had a randomized effect on later events of the disease entities in question.

The validity of such a study design depends essentially on the accuracy and uniformity of the information that is retrospectively gathered. In the example just cited, the health records on admission were gathered in a strictly uniform fashion, but the study deteriorated considerably after 1935, when the entrants to the university were required only to bring a statement from their family physician, which was not nearly as informative and uniform as the examination offered at the student health center.

There is undoubtedly a great advantage in the historical cohort study, which primarily rests in the time saved for observations of events between the time the cohort is selected and the termination of the study.

A third form of prospective study that embraces both the contemporary and the historical selection of the cohorts is called the *intervention study* or experimental epidemiology. Ideally intervention is an action that is instigated by the investigator with the purpose of altering the severity of disease or the development of overt disease. Hence the cohort selection should be done at the start of the intervention. However, some intervention studies are justified not if the selection of the comparative cohort is due to the action of the investigators, but when they can demonstrate that the separation into "intervention" and "nonintervention" was a random circumstance.

Demonstration of the effect of intervention is difficult unless the experimental and control groups are selected by strict randomization. For expediency, one often wishes to serve the experimental group in a defined geographic or administrative area and to keep the control in other areas — for example, to introduce a treatment in one hospital and not in another. It is extremely difficult to prove without doubt that circumstances other than the intervention are uniform in both areas. The type of patients admitted to either hospital, their social background, and so on, may differ unknown to the investigator at the start of the study.

Another procedure is to offer the intervention procedure to a total population section and then use previous experience of morbidity or mortality as an *antecedent* control. Two kinds of fallacies can occur. One is that conjunctures crop up that change the whole setting from before the study in a manner that throws doubt on the effect of the intervention. The other is that of *nonacceptance* or rejection by part of the population to which the service or treatment is offered. The rejectors must always be evaluated in some way that permits comparison with those who were exposed to the intervention. If the outcomes in both groups do not differ, the interpretation can be either that the intervention was ineffective or that the rejectors for some reason consisted of persons at less risk. If the rejectors fare worse than the treatment group, the same type of ambiguity presents itself: either the treatment was markedly effective or the rejectors were inherently at higher risk than the treatment group. At all events, it is advisable to compare morbidity and mortality for more than the disease in question. The uncertainty of deduction increases if illnesses other than the disease for which the study was designed also occur differently in the two groups.

There are many variations of the fallacies involved in both the prospective and the retrospective study. The most typical have been mentioned above, but in the following chapters examples of other varieties will be cited. Nevertheless, epidemiological studies are the most important means of assessing risk of disease and efficacy of treatment and prevention, and they add to the natural history of diseases. The manner of conducting the studies can be learned only through experience and ingenuity, perhaps coupled with a good deal of opportunism, with ability to utilize a fortuitous setting for informative observations.

4 ISSUES IN PSYCHOLOGICAL DEVELOPMENT

Jerome Kagan

The domain of inquiry we call human development is too full of contro-versy and too deficient in sturdy theory to permit any scholar to be confident of the many popular propositions that parade as conclusions. But the last two decades of research have clarified certain themes that can be grouped into four questions that dominate the books and papers written by developmental psychologists:

1. What structures are preserved in ontogeny, either in the same form, which is rare, or in altered form, which leads us to call them derivatives? For example, if it turns out that an infant's attach-ment to the mother is necessary for later adult intimacy, one would say that some psychological structure created in the first year was preserved, albeit in altered form.
2. What are the mechanisms of change in development that lead to transformation, loss, or replacement of older structures? I pose the question this way even though I appreciate that many author-ities believe that no psychological structures are ever lost or re-placed; they are only difficult to elicit.

3. What are the psychological growth functions for emergent competences or dispositions?
4. What determines differences in rate of growth of specific qualities and the content and profile of structures? This is the individual difference question so popular among investigators of personality.

All four questions involve the issue of continuity-discontinuity in development and all require longitudinal study for clarification.

FORMS OF CONTINUITY

There are three quite different ways to infer continuity in living systems. One is to hypothesize changeless elements that persist beneath the surface phenomena. The discovery of different classes of neurons in the visual cortex, each responding to different directions of movement of contours of different orientation, provides a particularly nice example of this first class.

A second strategy is to discover unchanging mechanisms that operate in varied contexts across epochs of time. In psychological development, it is believed that a nurturant role model who is perceived as commanding power acts as an incentive to provoke adoption of the model's qualities by individuals of any age.

The third basis for positing continuity rests on the assumption that two or more events in a temporal sequence are related either because some structural elements that participated in the earlier event are contained in the later one or because the earlier event established conditions that made the later event necessary. This last argument requires detecting within a sequence of many events those few that cohere in a ''causal'' chain. The stage theories of Freud and Piaget imply that selected competences or dispositions in the adolescent depend upon and are necessary consequences of historically earlier structures. But these two theories, like all essays on development, whether theoretical or empirical, are, in essence, histories. They are sets of sentences that attempt to tell a coherent story. In this sense theories of psychological development resemble both *The Origin of Species* as well as *The Rise and Fall of the Roman Empire*.

Developmental psychology, like history, consists first of descriptions of sequences of events over a given time period and, depending on the author's premises, a set of propositions that attempt to impose necessary relations among the events — the presumed explanation. But the biases of the narrator pose a major problem in both disciplines. Between any two points in time lie many more events than can be seen or recorded. The scholar must select a very small number and ignore a great many others. Between 1900 and 1978 the automobile, television, nuclear weapons, the laser, and the contraceptive pill were invented; the Germans lost World War I; there was an economic depression; Germany was divided following the end of World War II; the People's Republic of China was created; there was a long, bitter struggle in Vietnam; an American president resigned; and the prices of oil and postage increased dramatically. Which of these events are part of a coherent sequence and which are not? Only theory can produce an answer to that question.

The same problem confronts child psychologists. Between 1 and 15 months of age most infants around the world will smile to a face, show stranger anxiety, sit, stand, walk and run, solve the object permanence problem, show symbolic play, and begin to speak single words. Which of these phenomena are connected and which are not?

The developmental psychologist tries to detect which of these phenomena are structurally related and to invent reasons why. The validity of the explanation rests, in part, on the accuracy with which the theorist selects from the stream of development the events considered to be connected. And that selection is guided by presuppositions that are not always articulated, presuppositions that also influence the historian's account of a sequence of events.

Hayden White (1973) has offered an intriguing analysis of classes of historical scholarship. He suggests that every historian chooses one of four modes of employment — romantic, comic, tragic, or satirical — in describing a historical sequence. These stylistic moods refer to the author's evaluation of human nature as it attempts to reach some desired goal. The scholar also uses one of four modes of explanation — a detailing of facts, an organismic, mechanistic, or contextual interpretation. Finally, the scholar adheres to an ideology that reflects his or her attitude to change — from conservative through liberal to radical and anarchic.

If one applies this model to psychology, it would appear that most developmental psychologists are romantic, mechanistic, and liberal. They see development as inevitably progressing toward a desired terminal state; the child is seen as becoming more competent, stable, logical, or moral. The adult chooses actions, monitors affects, polishes competences, and holds beliefs that subdue the impulsiveness, liability, ineptitude, and rigidity of childhood. The explanatory mode typically chosen by developmental theorists is mechanistic; each event is related to a succeeding event through a long, gradual chain that necessarily links events and processes that can be detailed. Finally, the developmental theorist tends to be friendly to gradual change and resistant to abrupt discontinuities. One can see how the conceptions of the investigator can color, in a serious way, his or her theory of human development when put in this frame.

Human development can also be influenced by the introduction of new forces or inducers. One such inducer is the result of maturation. When the child's retrieval memory is enhanced at about 8 months of age, new psychological competences become possible, including the object concept, imitation, and separation distress. When language is inserted into the developmental process, the child is able to classify events on symbolic grounds (that is, by their membership in a class rather than by physical appearance). When reproductive fertility occurs, the adolescent is forced to recognize his or her new role, and correspondingly childishness becomes suppressed.

A less universal source of inducing events is produced within each culture. In our own society, school entrance places children in a unique social situation. They find themselves with twelve to fifteen other children of their same sex and age in a context in which intellectual talent is being evaluated daily. This situation forces all children to evaluate themselves relative to their same-sex peers and to come to the conclusion that the self is either hopelessly incompetent, of average ability, or superior to one's peers. Once that belief is articulated, important psychological changes occur, including increased or decreased motivation for academic mastery and movement toward or away from antisocial action. The large number of applicants to our professional schools leads to enhanced competitiveness and anxiety. Those who gain admission are tempted to believe they are progressing toward adulthood; those who fail are provoked to defend themselves.

DEFINITIONS OF STABILITY AND CONTINUITY

Before trying to understand why the assumption of a necessary relation between an origin and subsequent states is so attractive to Western scholars, we require a definition of terms like *stability* and *continuity*, especially with respect to psychological development. As an arbitrary terminological device we will use *stability* to refer to persistence of psychological structures and behaviors and *continuity* to refer to maintenance of psychological processes, functions, or competences, retaining the useful distinction between structure and process.

There are at least four different legitimate meanings of stability or continuity, each associated with a different empirical strategy of evaluation (see Wohlwill, 1973, for a slightly different discussion):

1. The persistence of a psychological quality as reflected in minimal rate of change in that quality over time,
2. The persistence of a hierarchical relation between complementary dispositions within an individual (ipsative stability),
3. The preservation of a set of individual ranks on a quality within a constant cohort (normative stability),
4. The necessary and contingent relation between phenotypically different structures or functions at two points in time due to the operation of specifiable processes.

RATE OF CHANGE IN QUALITIES OVER TIME: RELATIVE STABILITY OF QUALITIES

A person can be described as possessing a certain set of attributes at two points in time, each of which varies in the amount of change displayed across that interval. The four major classes of attributes modern psychologists attempt to quantify include:

1. Overt actions in a context,
2. Cognitive structures (beliefs, rules, and concepts),
3. Feeling and motivational states,
4. Cognitive processes (detection, recognition, interpretation, evaluation, recall, and reasoning).

As with the physical concepts of kinetic and potential energy, each of these constructs is assumed to exist in two states, either actualized or capable of being actualized under proper incentive conditions.

The four classes of constructs identified above are analogous to the colors, crystal shapes, and molecular structures in the chemist's working vocabulary. Although chemists trust that a few grains of salt will retain indefinitely their color, chemical structure, and capacity for dissolving into solution as long as no one disturbs them, biological phenomena are less cooperative. The amoeba changes shape continually — especially when it fissions into two daughter cells — and its internal chemical composition varies as a function of diet and immediate ecological context. Thus the description of stability in living systems is often more relative than the descriptions used for inorganic entities.

Consider two intervals in human development, each two years long, from birth to age 2 and from 8 to 10 years of age, and seven psychological characteristics:

1. Number of adjectives in the child's active vocabulary,
2. Frequency of occurrence of the Babinski reflex,
3. Amplitude of the second positive peak (P_2) in the visual evoked potential,
4. Occurrence of guilt following violation of standard,
5. Crying following the departure of the mother from the home,
6. Length of the string of numbers recalled immediately after having heard them,
7. Frequency of looking at or approaching the mother when in distress.

Some of these characteristics are relevant to only one of the age periods, and therefore it is meaningless to inquire into the stability of those qualities across the first ten years of life. The Babinski reflex and crying to maternal departure are phenomena of the first two years. Guilt and recall of digits apply to the older interval.

The other attributes occur during both periods of growth. The amplitude of the P_2 in the visual evoked potential changes a great deal over the first two years and much less during later childhood. By contrast the number of adjectives in the child's active vocabulary changes less during the first two years than it does during the preadolescent interval. Since it is unclear how much change we should expect, evaluation of the stability of a quality is often dependent on the stability of another attribute. One can say, for example, that during the first four months the amplitude of the P_2 displays greater change (or is less stable) than the occurrence of the Babinski reflex, but from 1 to 2 years of age the reverse is true. That is, if one observed one child or a thousand children each week from birth to 4 months, quantified the P_2 (in millivolts) and the Babinski response (in percent of occurrence to the proper incentive), and plotted the scores across successive months, the month-to-month differences would be greater for the P_2 than for the Babinski.

An investigator can, for any time period, quantify the occurrence of particular sets of variables, calculate the rate of change in these qualities, and draw conclusions about the differential stability of psychological qualities for a child or a group. The magnitude of the changes in raw score for each variable will display a growth function. Since the amount of change across successive time epochs will asymptote at age 2 at a lower value for P_2 than for number of adjectives, one can say that toward the end of the second year the amplitude of P_2 is more stable than the number of adjectives. That statement has empirical meaning.

When biologists declare that the first trimester is a critical period in embryogenesis, they mean the rate of change in the growth of organs is greatest during the first trimester. Change in the morphology of the central nervous system, for example, is less dramatic from 5 to 8 months than it is during the first 3 months of fetal growth.

When a particular quality stabilizes (that is, its rate of change slows), we are prone to call that attribute stable. As we shall note later, there are intervals during development when certain behavioral dispositions display such slowing. Rate of change in a measurable quality is perhaps the most meaningful definition of stability in living systems, and when rate of change in one quality is compared with that of others there is a sense of enhanced understanding.

The reader will notice that these statements refer to objectively quantified, observable phenomena. Many pschologists are more interested in the stability of hypothetical constructs. They prefer to discuss the stability of intelligence, attachment, or emotional lability, not the amplitude of the visual evoked potential or the number of adjectives in a child's vocabulary. These scientists have been frustrated because of absence of consensus on the observable phenomena that index the constructs. Consider a psychologist interested in the differential stability of the constructs of intelligence and dependency across the first five years of life. The investigator will be forced to use qualitatively different measures at 1 month and at 5 years, each of which bears an uncertain and highly controversial relation to the constructs. As a result, some contend that the statement, "Intelligence is more stable than dependency during the first five years," is at the moment without empirical meaning.

IPSATIVE STABILITY OF A RESPONSE HIERARCHY WITHIN A CHILD

A closely related definition of stability refers to the relative dominance (or frequency of occurrence) of one response relative to a complementary response within a child over a period of time. This idea has been called *ipsative stability*. Suppose a child has two reactions in his or her repertoire that are displayed with differential frequency in a specific context. Under these conditions it is meaningful to ask, Is a child's tendency to display response *A* in preference to response *B* stable over time? The reader will note that this statement differs from the one that asks whether the rate of change in variable *A* is more or less than the rate of change in variable *B* over the same interval.

Consider two responses a child can make to a maternal request: obedience or disobedience. Suppose a particular child is always more likely to obey than to disobey across successive sets of 100 parental requests. For each set of 100 requests, the child obeys 75 percent of the time and disobeys 25 percent of the time. We would be entitled to conclude that the dispositional preference to obey rather than to disobey showed stability. But the rate of change for acts of obedience and disobedience across successive six-month periods might be very similar or very different. Thus the persistence, within a child, of a tendency for one response to dominate a complementary reaction does not have the same meaning as the rates of change of these two responses in the same situation. Both are meaningful but different forms of continuity.

When parents remark that their child has always been shy, they may not mean the child now withdraws and has always withdrawn from other people. I suspect they mean that, relative to the tendency to initiate contact with strangers, their child is more likely to be timid. This is the meaning of ipsative stability we have just considered. Although ipsative stability is meaningful, it is not the definition typically used by psychologists.

NORMATIVE STABILITY

Most psychological data are not amenable either to statements describing rate of change in a quality or qualities or to ipsative stability. Rather, most investigators are interested in the stability of individual differences in one variable across various time periods. The evidence used to make this judgment is based on a comparison of the differential magnitudes of a certain variable assigned to a group of subjects across time.

Consider an obvious example. The statures of 100 children are assessed every six months from 1 to 5 years of age and correlation coefficients computed. The correlation from age 1 to 5 is likely to be between .4 and .5, and it is concluded that height is a stable attribute of children. However, this is not equivalent to stating that height does not change or that height is more or less stable than another physical attribute. The normative statement that stature is stable means that the *differences* in height of the 100 children have remained somewhat constant, despite sizable changes in stature over the four-year interval.

In a recently completed longitudinal study infants were administered the same visual episode at 5, 7, 9, 11, 13, 20, and 29 months while the duration of their attentiveness to the episode was quantified. In one procedure a child watched a hand move an orange rod across a traverse of 180 degrees until it contacted a bank of three light bulbs that lit upon contact. The lights remained on for several seconds and then the rod was returned to its original position. This procedure was repeated for ten trials. The child then saw a transformation of that event for five trials and then three re-presentations of the original event. In one analysis we computed the ratio (for pairs of successive ages) of the difference in fixation time between two successive ages divided by the mean fixation time for that pair of ages for trials 2 through 5 of the original standard. A low ratio indicated minimal change relative to the absolute amount of attentiveness; a ratio of 0 indicated no change. Figure 4.1 shows the ratio for trials 2 through 5 of the original presentation of the standard. The ratio was lowest from 9 to 11 months, meaning that absolute attentiveness

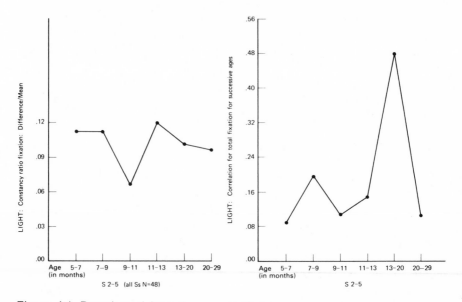

Figure 4.1. Duration of Attentiveness in Children.

changed least across that two-month period (Kagan, Lapidus, and Moore, 1978).

Now compare that developmental function with the magnitude of the Pearson product moment correlation coefficient for fixation time across the same successive two-month periods. Note that the correlations are typically low (less than .20) for all pairs of ages except for the period 13 to 20 months, when the coefficient was .48. This analysis suggests that the subjects tended to retain their relative rank for fixation time for the period 13 to 20 months, even though fixation times changed more, in an absolute sense, from 13 to 20 than from 9 to 11 months. Similar results were found for attentiveness to other visual and auditory episodes.

The special character of normatively based propositions about stability of individual difference is seen more clearly when standardized scores are used, as they are for IQ. Absolute scores on the subtests of the Wechsler Intelligence Scale for Children change over age, but because they are standardized within an age cohort, all the real change due to development in psychological competence is removed. All that is left is the relative standings of the children. When textbooks say that children's intelligence is stable from 5 to 10 years of age, they do not mean that cognitive ability is stable; it is not. They mean that the differences in test scores within a cohort of children remain stable, despite dramatic changes in the abilities that accompany growth.

Suppose biologists postulated a concept called *health* and operationalized it for a particular period by counting the number of colds and fevers; measuring absolute gains in height, weight, and strength of pull; and quantifying time to recover from infections. These six variables display characteristic changes over the first ten years of life. Suppose a biologist standardized, within age, each of the six distributions for a thousand children, correlated the transformed scores by successive ages, found an average correlation of .5, and concluded that health was a moderately stable attribute across the first ten years of life. That statement may strike the reader as misleading; it is what psychologists have done in studying the stability of IQ (see McCall, 1977).

In the influential book *Stability and Change in Human Characteristics,* Bloom (1964) equates high correlation coefficients across successive age periods with stability of the psychological characteristic. After noting that the correlation between IQ scores at ages 5 and 17 is about +.80, he suggests that intelligence is stable. In the final chapter after summarizing data revealing that correlations during the early years of development gradually increase in magnitude, he treats growth in the size of the correlation coefficient as if it represented growth of the characteristics and concludes that the early environment is of crucial importance.

CONTINGENT RELATION AMONG STRUCTURES
OVER TIME

Each species displays invariant sequences of sets of behaviors. Young macaques mouth other monkeys, but this response eventually vanishes, giving way to rough-and-tumble play. Initially human infants play with one toy at a time, then with two toys simultaneously, and finally they play with toys in a symbolic manner. The existence of replicable, invariant sequences in the ontogeny of all species poses the theoretical problem many have tried to solve. Which of the responses in these sequences — if any — are part of a necessarily continuous process? Further, for these sequences, what is the relation among the structures characteristic of each phase of the sequence? A tangled ball of strings is composed of many separate segments of different length. We pick up the end of one and want to know if it is short or winds its way back to a distant origin in the center of the ball.

How does one know which responses are members of a necessarily continuous sequence and, more important, how do we determine the nature of the structural connection between successive phases of an ontogenetic sequence, when there is such a connection? (We assume that at least in some sequences the structural overlap may be minimal.) Let us consider a concrete example from infancy.

Among the many responses that emerge between 5 and 12 months of age, three new behaviors include comparative scanning of a new and an old toy (about 6 months of age), crying and inhibition of play to adult strangers (about 7 months), and reaching for a toy hidden under a cloth (about 8 months). These behaviors are quite different in their surface form. Yet it has been conjectured that they are part of an emerging competence involving the ability to retrieve the past and to hold the retrieved schemata and current perceptions on a stage of active memory (Kagan, 1976). One might speculate further that the ability to remember the location of a hidden object — Piaget's notion of the object concept — builds on the prior competence to recall that an event occurred in the past.

Stated succinctly, this meaning of continuity is concerned with the necessary relations between the hidden structures and competences of one stage and those of another, as each is embodied in sets of different public actions. The connection is concretized as a process in which the structures or functions of one era are incorporated, completely or partially, into the present:

> The ontogenetic formation of the intelligence includes a series of stages . . . each one of which has its origin in a reconstruction, on a new level, of structures built up during the preceding one. And this reconstruction is necessary to the later constructions which will advance beyond the former level. In biological terms, each generation repeats the development of the preceding one, and the new phylogenetic variations as they appear during ontogenesis extend this reconstruction of the past. [Piaget, 1971, p. 147]

Something like this must occur a great deal of the time. The child must know the meaning of number before he or she can add or subtract. Similar examples abound. But that is not sufficient reason for assuming that all invariant sequences imply connectivity, even though we can always invent an explanation that is reasonable. The ability to speak a language is always preceded by a period, prior to about 10 months, when the infant points at a toy he or she wants. But is the pointing reaction a necessary antecedent to the later speech? Could the prior stage have been omitted? The reader will recall Leonard Carmichael's (1926, 1927) anesthetized ambystoma larvae that swam without prior practice, even though under normal conditions of growth the swimming movements are always preceded by a stage when much smaller motor movements are observable. But those small movements are not necessary for the mature swimming response. Since not all invariant sequences are epigenetic, we must be skeptical toward fast and easy claims of such forms of continuity unless logic, data, and theory provide coherent support for the claim.

Theorists, like detectives, enjoy speculating on the relation among disparate events separated by years and linking pieces of apparently unrelated evidence into a coherent story. Freud believed that excessive resistance to toileting in a 2-year-old and compulsivity in a 12-year-old were part of a continuous sequence. Piaget has contended that the infant's kicking of a mobile and the concrete operational groupings of a 7-year-old belong to a common sequence.

Some believe the attachment of the infant to the caretaker is necessary for a deep love relationship to be possible in adulthood or that stimulation of cognitive development during the first three years is necessary for intellectual competence during later childhood. There is, of course, insufficient evidence for any of these speculations. Development represents a grand puzzle, with each scholar guessing at the past's contribution to the present or, on occasion, the present's contribution to the future.

We have now considered four popular meanings of stability of structure and continuity of process: (1) the rate of change in a quality over time, (2) the persistence of a particular hierarchy of related responses within an individual, (3) the persistence of a set of ranked differences among children on a psychological quality, and (4) connectivity of processes and hypothetical structures across phases of development. Emmerich (1968) addressed this issue in an earlier essay where he differentiated among a developmental view (epigenesis), a differential view (normative analysis), and an ipsative view of continuity and change.

Additionally some regard regularity as a form of continuity; it was the core meaning of growth for the ancient Greeks and Chinese. Development contains cycles that repeat themselves — the menstrual cycle is an obvious example. Each part of that cycle contains an orderly set of changes, each part of which is connected to the next. Since the end of one cycle often acts as an incentive to the next, one assumes a connectivity. But regularity seems a more accurate descriptor for this phenomenon than continuity.

CLASSES OF CHANGE

All four types of continuity considered above permit some change to occur. In some cases structures are preserved or enhanced; in others the new quality is dependent on the existence of earlier ones. But even though many surface changes have a close link to the past, it is not necessarily true that every new quality contains remnants of what came before. Some qualities in the present are replaced; others may vanish. In both cases it is not clear that structural heirs survive.

Let us consider in a little more detail the four classes of change — two of which are accompanied by stability of structure or continuity of process; the other two are not. We might call these four enhancement, derivation, replacement, and disappearance.

Enhancement

In enhancement a particular psychological structure or process becomes better articulated or a process more efficient, but the essential nature of the psychological quality remains unchanged. This idea has its clearest analogy in morphology. Once neurons or muscle spindles form, they grow in size but do not change their fundamental structure. Similarly many assume that understanding of the concept *mammal* becomes elaborated and better articulated with growth but always retains some key structures over the period of change. Additionally some psychologists contend that the psychological process of recognition memory becomes more efficient and accurate with age but does not undergo qualitative alterations after the first three to five years of life.

Derivation

Although there is a relation between enhancement and derivation, there is also a subtle distinction. In derivation, which is closely related to the connectivity meaning of continuity, the structure or process that emerges from an earlier one is a transformation of the original and requires its prior presence. In embryogenesis the mature genital is a derivative of the genital bud. It is not an enhancement of the original tissue but a transformation built from it. Although the haploid gametes produced by meiosis are qualitatively different from the parent cells that gave rise to them, they are a material derivative of them.

In psychology many theorists believe that the experience of guilt following a violation of a standard must be preceded by a period when the person fears loss of parental love. Even though the two emotions are different in phenomenology and incentive, the later quality is presumed to be a derivative of the earlier one. Or consider a child who, upon seeing a zebra for the first time, infers that it possesses the characteristics of eating and sleeping. That insight is a derivative of existing knowledge; namely, that all animals eat and sleep. Piaget has argued for more profound derivatives; for example, the conservation groupings are assumed to be derivatives of the structures of the earlier sensorimotor and intuitive stages. Most psychologists regard much of development as constituted of long chains of derivatives — a process or competence grows out of a prior one, and aspects of the former are incorporated into the later entity.

Replacement

We now come to a form of change that is often ignored because, on the surface, it resembles derivation. In derivation part of the ontogenetically older form continues to exist in the new entity, be it a structure or a process. Fear of loss of love is presumed to remain as an incentive even after guilt emerges as a derivative. In replacement the earlier form vanishes. More important, however, is the fact that although the prior existence of the parent form constrained the nature of the potential replacement, it is often the case that more than one replacement could have occurred. The early form did not determine the new one; the new entity was not contingent on the earlier structure or process, even though it followed it.

Consider the growth function for apprehension to an unfamiliar peer that emerges between 11 and 20 months of age. Before 11 months there is little or no apprehension to an unfamiliar child of the same age. Apprehension to a peer, which appears soon after the first birthday, is followed by a loss of the inhibition by 30 or 36 months. Was the inhibition a derivative of earlier fears, such as adult strangers, or the result of new cognitive capacities that permit the child to generate questions he or she cannot answer? Pairs of children who saw each other monthly from 13 to 27 months showed more apprehension at 20 months of age, after each pair had seen each other seven times, than they did initially when they were 13 months old. These data suggest that a new cognitive ability, rather than some structural product of past experience, was responsible for the inhibition and its demise. Although rough-and-tumble play follows mouthing in infant macaque monkeys, it is not obvious that the former required the presence of the latter.

Replacement is a common form of change in history. The child-centered attitudes of the late eighteenth century replaced the authoritarian patriarchy of the 1600s, but the latter did not determine the former. Similarly the use of wet nurses, which ceased in England after the mid-eighteenth century, was replaced by more continuous maternal care. The emergence of new attitudes between 1650 and 1800, which included celebration of sensuality, child centeredness, and personal choice of marital partners, was due to changes in economic and social factors. It is not obvious that the new family was a derivative of the older one; if different economic and social events had occurred, the replacements might have had a different quality.

It is important to distinguish among invariant sequences in which one structure or competence replaces another and those which are derivatives of preceding ones. The generations of antibodies to rubella virus, which are produced for years following the introduction of the antigen, are true derivatives, as is the persistence of genetic material through generations. But the appearance of Huntington's chorea or menopause is a less obvious derivative and seems to be a replacement of ongoing functioning.

Psychological development may contain many replacements that are classified as derivatives. The fear of strangers shown by 8-month-olds replaces the friendly, smiling posture 5-month-olds display to strangers. The avoidance at 8 months is not a derivative of the earlier amiability but a replacement due to the introduction of new cognitive competences. Reciprocal play between two 30-month-old children replaces a period of timidity that peaked between 15 and 20 months. It is not necessary that the timidity occur before the reciprocity of play. New knowledge and the emergence of executive processes permit children to conquer their fears and to initiate reciprocal interactions with unfamiliar children. There are many examples in psychological development in which maturation of a new competence or an external demand leads to the establishment of a structure that replaces an old one. Replacements imply discontinuity; derivatives imply continuity.

Disappearance of Structures or Processes

Finally there are changes in which a structure, state, or process vanishes and is not followed or replaced by a functionally related one. The trellis cells of the central nervous system vanish after they have accomplished their mission of guiding neurons to their destination, and "in vertebrate animals the main role of the notochord is apparently to participate in the formation of the embryonic nervous system. Once the backbone has appeared, the notochord has no further function and largely disintegrates" (Gordon and Jacobson, 1978, p. 112). Indeed, neurobiologists suggest that during development many synapses decay and many neurons die — synapses and cells that participated in prior experience (Edelman, 1978).

In a similar sense, the Moro reflex and the 6-month-old's babbling also vanish without apparent replacements. As fear of the dark is conquered by the growing child, it is not necessarily replaced by another fear.

Classes of Change in Ontogeny

Biological evolution, which may provide a fruitful metaphor for psychological development, contains illustrations of all four classes of change. There is an enhancement in the size of the cerebral cortex within mammalian evolution. The mammalian eye is a derivative of the eye of earlier vertebrate forms. The amphibian feet replace the tail fin of fish, and reproduction through fission vanishes.

Consider some illustrations of the four classes of change for psychological qualities, where by psychological quality we mean a competence-performance unit. Motor skills typically become enhanced with development; they become more efficient, faster, smoother, and, where appropriate, more forceful. But the basic form of the act often remains unaltered. Language provides a good source of derivatives. When a child first utters the passive sentence, "He got hit by his father," instead of the active form, "His father hit him," we assume that the passive sentence required prior mastery of the competences necessary for the older form. When negatives appear as a new entity in the child's speech, the child will first say, "No go," and later, "I no want to go" and "I do not want to go," as apparent derivatives of the earlier, simpler phrase. Beliefs, by contrast, are often replaced. The attitude that education is good because it permits pursuit of a skilled vocation replaces a former belief in its irrelevance, but the new belief is not a necessary consequent, only one of several. The older child might have developed the belief that education is good because it permits understanding or facilitates economic gain. Finally, a belief in ghosts, the babbling of infancy, the 2-year-old's uttering of strings of unrelated numbers, and probably many thousands of representations of forest scenes and facial expressions that have never been removed vanish from the psychological repertoire.

It is likely that these four classes of change are not evenly distributed across the life span. Since the newborn is developmentally incomplete, it is likely that maturational processes permit the introduction of new competences. As a result, we are likely to see replacement and disappearance more often than derivation and enhancement during the early years. With growth, structures and processes come to have a longer life and derivatives are apt to become more common.

Flavell (1972), who has written an elegant essay on types of developmental sequences, posits five classes of change. He calls them addition, substitution, modification, inclusion, and mediation. We shall try to summarize the essence of the distinctions among these classes; the reader is urged to consult the original monograph for details.

In *addition* (which is similar to our notion of enhancement), two related dispositions develop at different times, but the earlier one remains active or operative even after the later one emerges. In one sense, the later one is added to the former. Flavell offers as an example the fact that when the 2-year-old becomes capable of a symbolic mode of apprehending objects he does not lose his capacity for an enactive mode.

In *substitution* (which is similar to our notion of replacement) the earlier disposition is replaced. "Thus development here consists in the complete substitution of a later acquired form for a functionally similar but formerly different, earlier acquired one, rather than in the mere addition of the former to a cognitive inventory already comprising the latter" (Flavell, 1972, p. 291).

In *modification* (which is similar to our concept of derivative) the new form is "some sort of improved, perfected, and matured version of X_1; some sort of transformed, derivative, or variant of X_1; in brief, some sort of modification of X_1 in the direction of cognitive maturity" (Flavell, 1972, p. 298). Flavell suggests that differentiation, generalization, and stabilization are three forms of modification.

His fourth class of change is called *inclusion* and is closely related to the old notion of hierarchic integration. A disposition begins to develop and at some point becomes coordinated with a larger cognitive whole. We have suggested that inclusion is one form of a derivative class of change.

In the final form of change, *mediation,* a disposition facilitates or mediates a new response but does not become a part of the new structure.

Although Flavell (1972, p. 292) is reluctant to acknowledge the possibility of structures vanishing completely ("it is a fair guess that X_1 is, in fact, seldom if ever irrevocably banished from the repertoire"), he does urge investigators to be more receptive to the possibility that developmental sequences that appear to be invariant and cumulative over time might well be cyclical and sequence violating. He writes, "We developmentalists would also do well to enrich our vision of cognitive growth by taking seriously the possibility that it has significant asequential aspects" (Flavell, 1972, p. 344).

WHAT IS PRESERVED?

A quarter century ago a great deal of the empirical research on early development was under the influence of two ideologies, psychoanalytic theory and intelligence testing. Both ideologies ascribed general qualities to the young child and assumed that the child possessed an internal disposition that was preserved but took different disguises during different periods in ontogeny. The child's intelligence was reflected in babbling to an examiner at 4 months, knowing the meaning of *orange* at 3 years, and remembering five numbers at 6 years of age. Oral anxiety was present in feeding problems at 12 months and severe depression in early adulthood. These were bold hypotheses, Platonic in conception, which captured the imagination of many scientists and graduate students. They did so for me. Many of us went off like Don Quixote trying to affirm their obvious validity. I spent twenty years trying to generate quantitative proof that the differences in behavior seen during the first two years of life were preserved in some way for the next decade. These ideas do not dominate the essays in this book, and that is progress.

The tendency to posit general attributes has been replaced by the study of much more specific variables. Investigators study coherent patterns of facial movements, not *emotion*; sleep patterns, not *regularity*. Even the Brazelton procedures contain many different scales. No one suggests that we compute a mean score across all the scales. Studies of temperament also focus on specific behavioral dimensions. I suspect that our descriptive terms and theoretical constructs will continue to become even more specific. Activity level, for example, will have to be parsed, as will sensitivity and fear. For example, in our own laboratory we have found no relation between signs of anxiety to an unfamiliar person (we code inhibition of play, clinging to the mother, and crying) and similar behavioral signs of anxiety to separation from the mother in children 13 to 29 months of age. This conclusion is verified by the work of others who also report little or no relation among behavioral signs of fear to different incentives. The variable *fearfulness* is not likely to be theoretically useful. A descriptive classification term applied to the child without a statement of the incentive context is incomplete.

This principle of context specificity is also valid for cognitive processes, like memory, investigated in older children. For example, many investigators find correlation of less than .2 among recall memory performances for pictures, words, sentences, and numbers. This lack of generality is not restricted to American or European children. Sellers (1979) found low correlations across a variety of memory tasks in rural Costa Rican children. Similarly Rogoff (1977) found low correlations between recall scores for orally presented sentences and for visual scenes in preadolescent children living in northwest Guatemala. Further, Rogoff found that the child-rearing antecedents of the two recall performances were different. That is, the best predictors of verbal memory were different from the best predictors of pictorial memory. Michael Moore and I have been working with preadolescent reading-disabled boys; this group also provides data indicating no correlation between memory for sentences and memory for pictures and no correlation between recognition memory and recall memory.

These results and conclusions are a far cry from suppositions that led to constructs like intelligence and oral anxiety. Thus, if there is preservation of structures and processes in ontogeny, it is likely to involve very specific attributes. Investigators keen on finding these derivatives should frame their questions in extraordinarily specific terms.

This conclusion is also applicable to temperamental qualities that, in my opinion, have the best chance of preservation. If I had to predict what temperamental quality had the greatest chance of being preserved over the first five or six years of life, I would describe it in the following way: the tendency to inhibition of spontaneous activity upon encountering uncertain situations in which the child has no appropriate response. Let me present some evidence for this claim. Some of the initial evidence for this hypothesis is summarized in our recent book (Kagan, Kearsley, and Zelazo, 1978). We studied 32 Chinese children and 32 Caucasian children. Half of the children were being raised in a day care center and half at home. The children were studied from 3½ through 29 months of age. The most provocative finding was that the Chinese children were more likely than the Caucasians to be inhibited when placed with an unfamiliar woman or child. Additionally the Chinese children were likely to inhibit babbling when they were shown a discrepant visual event, and they displayed more stable heart rates when looking at visual information. The Chinese children had an average heart rate range of 3 to 4 beats while looking at interesting chromatic slides; the Caucasian children had cardiac ranges of 8 to 10 beats. In addition, although the cross-age continuities for behavioral variables like attentiveness, vocalization, and irritability were low and only significant across 2- to 4-month periods, the cross-age correlations for heart rate range were high for periods of 9 to 13 months.

We recently replicated this finding with two longitudinal cohorts of Caucasian children. One cohort was seen from 13 through 22 months, the other cohort from 20 to 29 months. Although these independent samples were shown a different set of materials, heart rate range was again stable over an 8- to 9-month period. Additionally the children who were the most likely to cry and become motorically inhibited when an adult modeled some difficult tasks or when each was placed with an unfamiliar child tended to have more stable heart rates than those who were less inhibited. A physiological basis for this prediction is reasonable. Under normal conditions the variability of the cardiac cycle is under vagal control and the cardiac cycle is being monitored by respiration. When the child is aroused, sympathetic tone begins to dominate parasympathetic tone, and the relation between respiration and heart rate is broken. As a result the heart rate tends to rise and to stabilize. That is, when the child is aroused (due to vigilance or fear) one expects higher and more stable heart rates.

Some of us who work with temperamental variables believe that these dispositions may be acquired during pregnancy. Patterson, Potter, and Furshpan (1978) have found that there is a period in the embryogenesis of the autonomic nervous system of the rat when the local chemical environment of the neuron will determine whether it becomes permanently cholinergic or adrenergic. It is not beyond reason to suggest that if the mother is under extreme stress when this decision occurs in human development, physiological changes accompanying the stress might influence the chemical environment of the embryo. One might expect the ratio of adrenergic to cholinergic neurons in these fetuses to be different from those growing in a nonstressed mother. The ratio of adrenergic to cholinergic neurons might very well affect postnatal temperament.

But preservation of any disposition requires a preserving environment. A disposition — either a temperamental attribute or a learned habit or attitude — is not a fixed structure. It is not a "gem," and the child remains malleable to some degree. It is extremely difficult to find a disposition that cannot be changed under certain environmental conditions. Recognition of this fact represents an important change in our view of development. In the past many scientists studying human development held a tape-recorder view of ontogeny, which implied that every experience that was registered was preserved. One of the hardiest relations in psychology is the association between social class and various cognitive performances. This relation seems due to the fact that each social class environment contains a preserving set of experiences that shapes the psychological profile. Moreover, clinical studies show that some children who had stressful environments during the first two or three years of life were able to show remarkable recovery of normal functioning when their environments became much more benevolent. More recently Genie, a girl who was deprived of normal experience for almost 11½ years, made remarkable recovery after she was taken out of her home setting and placed in a more normal environment for a few years (Curtiss, 1977).

I once saw a 2½-year-old girl who had been locked in her room since birth with a sister who was one year older. When both children were taken from the home they had no language, were fearful, and of course were untestable. Both girls were adopted by a middle-class family and have made remarkable progress over the last fifteen years. I visited them when they were both adolescents and could find no evidence of pathology in the younger girl. The older girl seemed more anxious, but was functioning adequately. She had no obvious psychopathology.

The difficult question we cannot answer concerns the age when we can detect the psychological strands that are likely to be preserved. That problem remains unresolved. I am prepared to celebrate any empirical demonstration of long-term preservation of individual qualities seen in 2-year-olds. If such preservation exists, however, I suggest it will be subtle, fragile, and likely to be related to the child's temperament. I have one positive instance. My colleagues and I studied sixty-eight 10-year-old children whom we had seen earlier at 4, 8, 13, and 27 months of age (Kagan, Lapidus, and Moore, 1978). We gave a large battery of tests to the 10-year-olds and related their performances to individual differences in attentiveness, play, irritability, and activity during infancy. The only hint of stability was a slight association between a disposition to show the smile of assimilation to representations of faces at 4 and 8 months of age and the tendency to be reflective on the matching familiar figures test at 10 years of age. Because the smile of assimilation during infancy is heritable, there may be at least one temperamental quality that has a life beyond infancy. Although the association between smiling and reflectivity was statistically significant, it accounted for only 8 percent of the variance. But it is a precious 8 percent and we regard it as a prize.

However, from 6 to 10 years of age forward there is obvious preservation of a great many attributes, especially those related to school achievement and social behavior with peers. No one argues with that statement. But these behaviors enjoy supportive environments. For example, schools segregate on academic ability during the opening years, and children learn their qualities and are treated as competent or incompetent; as a result, ranks will be preserved. This preservation also occurs for behaviors involved in peer interaction. Once a child decides she is popular or unpopular her behavior with peers tends to be preserved. The critical change that has occurred during the last quarter century is that the burden of proof has shifted from those who argue that there is little permanence from infancy forward to those who say there is. That change in empirical obligation is healthy. Nothing is proven; the case for stability of variation in attributes from infancy forward has been reopened for investigation. This new attitude of openness can only be good for the field.

MECHANISMS OF CHANGE IN ONTOGENY

The next question concerns change. What has been transformed, replaced, or lost and how shall we conceptualize the forces that lead to changes in psychological profile? When behavioral and psychoanalytic theory were dominant, habit, motivation, and conflict were major constructs to explain change. Today cognitive theory is ascendant, and one prevailing view is that the maturation of the central nervous system permits new cognitive competences to emerge, as long as the supporting environment supplies some tamable variety. In Piagetian language, tamable variety means events that require accommodation. But variety may be actualized in many different ways. This view is quite different from one that says that habit, anxiety, and motivation change as a function of particular material experiences in the environment (the amount of affection or playful interaction between adults and children).

Let me summarize two relevant sets of findings that support this view; they come from our own laboratory. The first has to do with an enhancement of retrieval memory, usually seen at about 8 months of age. The results of a decade of empirical inquiry into the functioning of the infant has shown a remarkable concordance of events that seems to emerge during the last three to four months of the first year of life. The infant will now display greater attention to a variety of discrepant events than he or she did at 6 months of age. For example, if masks or drawings of human faces are shown to children, attention is prolonged at 4 months, lower at 7 months, and then increases through the second year. Additionally the child will now show motor inhibition to an unexpected event. Before 7 months the infant typically reaches at once for a novel object that is presented after repeated presentation of a familiarized standard. However, an 11-month-old shows a short but obvious delay before reaching for the novel object. It also appears that the infant who can crawl does not always show avoidance of the deep side of what looks to him like a cliff until after 7 months of age, even though he or she is capable of perceiving the difference between the deep and shallow sides. Inhibition of play is also the dominant reaction of a 1-year-old to the introduction of an unfamiliar child.

There is also a dramatic increase in the probability of signs of distress or fear to an event whose major characteristic is that it is a discrepant transformation of a schema for an earlier experience. The child will show anxiety to strangers beginning at 7 to 8 months of age, and that tendency grows dramatically between 7 months and the end of the first year, after which it declines. The growth function for separation distress is also similar among children being raised in the United States, barrios in urban Guatemala, subsistence farming Indian villages in the Guatemalan highlands, Israeli Kibbutzim, or !Kung San bands in the Kalahari Desert and among infants diagnosed as suffering from failure to thrive. Signs of distress following the mother's departure tend to emerge at 8 months of age, rise to a peak at 13 to 15 months of age, and then decline.

One of the most reliable phenomena of this period of life is what Piaget has called *object permanence*. Prior to 8 months most children will not retrieve a prized toy that they watched being hidden under a cover, whereas after 8 months of age the retrieval is reliable.

I believe that the temporal concordance among these phenomena — increased attentiveness, inhibition, object permanence, and distress to strangers and to separation — is due to the maturational emergence of several related cognitive abilities. These include the enhanced ability to retrieve a schema related to present experience, despite minimal incentive stimuli in the immediate field, and the ability to retain the old schema and the new experience in active memory while comparing them in an attempt to resolve their potential inconsistency. Several studies support the claim that retrieval memory improves during this period; they are summarized in our recent book (Kagan, Kearsley, and Zelazo, 1978). The enhancement in these competences can be used to explain the universal growth function for separation distress. After departure of the mother the 10-month-old child generates from memory the schema of her former presence in the room and holds that schema in active memory while comparing it with the present. If the child cannot resolve the inconsistency inherent in that comparison, he becomes uncertain and may cry. Since the 6-month-old is unable to implement these cognitive functions, he does not become afraid.

We also have been studying longitudinally groups of children between 13 and 30 months of age, both in the home and in the laboratory. In one group of six children (followed every three weeks from 17 to 27 months) we noted that between 17 and 21 months a coherent set of behaviors emerged. During the last half of the second year there is a major enhancement in the child's preoccupation with adult standards, affect displays appropriate to successful or unsuccessful mastery, improved quality of performance on problems set by adults, the appearance of commands and requests to adults, and language that describes the child's own actions. The similarity in time of appearance and rate of growth of these behaviors among and within various samples implies that these diverse psychological phenomena are likely to be inevitable consequences of maturational changes in the central nervous system. We hazard the guess that the two major psychological victories of this period include the establishment of the first standards, followed by the emergence of awareness of one's actions, intentions, states, and competences.

We have called this latter function *self-awareness*. The apparent sudden-
ness in the appearance of these behaviors is likely to be dependent upon
more continuous changes in the underlying physiological substrate.

What is the contribution of past functions and structures to these new
behavioral qualities? Consider the appearance of signs of anxiety (crying,
clinging to the mother) after watching a woman demonstrate a play
sequence with some toys (for example, the woman has a doll cook food
and feed it to the family). The signs of anxiety typically appear between
18 and 22 months, and we interpret this reaction as indicating that the
child is now aware of her inability to imitate the model. The enhancement
of memory at 8 months is a necessary prerequisite for the display of
anxiety to the woman's behavior, for the child must be able to retrieve
the model's action in order to recognize she cannot perform it. But the
new competence also seems to require a new endogenous function. If
the child merely continued to do what she had been doing — an implicit
supposition in nineteenth-century developmental theory — the new competence would not have occurred. New behaviors do not always emerge
as habits get stronger or better articulated. Often a new endogenous
process must be inserted into the stream of development. I am pleased
to see that many reports now involve the careful study of changes in
specific dispositions with growth. This strategy was essential to progress
in the laboratories of nineteenth-century embryologists. As the embryol-
ogist remains mystified by the appearance of new structures, like the
neural crest, we remain mystified by the appearance of object permanence at 8 months and self-awareness at 20 months.

GROWTH FUNCTIONS

We now appreciate that the development of many dispositions is not
linear. Many psychological qualities behave like trellis cells; they have
a period of growth and significant function and then disappear. Consider
a psychological example. In one study in our laboratory infants 13 to 29
months viewed pairs of identical slides. We noticed that between 17 and
21 months many children would look first to the right side of the screen.
This behavior occurred during the time the children were speaking one-
morpheme utterances. After they began to utter two-morpheme sentences
they began to look with equal probability to the right and left sides of the
screen. This bias to look to the right occurred only when the child's
speech was emerging. Perhaps a special state of neural organization,
which is occurring as speech first matures, forces the child to look to the

right. But once that early phase is over, the disposition vanishes. There are probably thousands of such individual inverted U functions. Such functions seem to hold for crying to maternal departure, offering a toy to a peer, and distress to a model. Each act appears at a certain time and then vanishes. Some of these dispositions, like the Moro or the smile of assimilation to a face, may have no future consequences. Others may lie dormant for long periods of time and affect future states. I recall a girl in the Fels sample who had an unexpected preschizophrenic break soon after leaving home for college when she was 18 years old. When I read her early record, I noticed that during the first two years of life she rarely showed signs of anxiety or fear. Everyone in her family thought she was a very well adjusted child, much less irritable than her older sister. Perhaps this lack of fear was an anomalous sign of a temperamental disposition that made a contribution to the pathology she showed rather suddenly in late adolescence. I believe some structures may be preserved, but I also believe that a great many structures simply vanish from the repertoire; they are erased from the tape.

INDIVIDUAL DIFFERENCES

There are two major classes of variation in psychological profile among children. The first pertains to differences in rate of development, the other to differences in structure. American psychologists are generally more interested in differences among children than in uniformities because American child psychology has traditionally been pragmatic in tone. The differences among American children in academic success and adoption of approved cultural values have been striking and remain so. Our society wants to be egalitarian, and differences in academic talent and motivation, which are so hard to change, bother citizens. Hence we want to understand them so we can minimize them. The guesses as to the reasons for individual differences reflect a strong empiricist bias in psychology. Most investigators codify specific social experiences, believing that a specific class of objective external events will have a fixed and inevitable effect on children. But as Victor Denenberg has said many times, one must always expect interactions.

As to the cause of differences in specific dispositions, skills, motives, and beliefs, I remain puzzled. Most psychologists favor reliance on four mechanisms that monitor growth and produce differences among children. The mysterious law of effect is certainly one. Although we do not know how it works, it seems to be useful, especially with respect to overt behavior. Observational learning and the reaction to the press of problems that force accommodation are two other mechanisms. Identification with role models is another. I noted above that there is a strong empiricist bias in psychology. There is the belief that if one could document all the relevant events a child experienced, one would be able to predict behavioral outcomes, without taking into account the temperament and private interpretations of the child. I suggest, with considerable humility, that this is not a reasonable supposition. We must try to discover ways to quantify the child's typical reaction to uncertainty and his belief systems. The effect of a sibling depends on the sex of the child and how he or she had been treated beore the arrival of the infant. There is no uniform effect of a sibling, just as there is no uniform effect of attending a day care center or experiencing parental divorce. The child is not impelled to react to every change in stimulation or every "stressful" event. It is time we accepted the principle of interaction and tried to obtain measures of the organism. I appreciate the enormous difficulty involved in meeting that demand, for we have not yet developed appropriate methods. But we should begin that task.

III METHODOLOGICAL BASES OF LONGITUDINAL RESEARCH: *Tools*

5 DISEASE REGISTERS

Annalise Dupont

CASE REGISTERS IN EPIDEMIOLOGICAL STUDIES

Wing (1975) has identified three characteristics of case registers that make them especially important as research instruments in epidemiology:

1. The registers contain unduplicated counts of the contacts of each patient and thus avoid selection biases inherent in data available from any single facility.
2. The registers contain information on the population of a particular area or nation; this census data can be utilized to calculate rates.
3. The registers contain data on each patient for every episode of care; thus the history of the patients can be ascertained.

I would like to add a fourth characteristic: The units of registers may be the affected persons, hospital stays, or episodes of out-patient treatment, and the like; it is possible to use such units as starting points for many different investigations concerning, for instance, treatment, death rates, and social conditions of the patients.

Case registers may be established *primarily* for clinical purposes, as systems for linking all the case records for each patient. Other case registers are designed for research. Some are designed and used for both kinds of purposes. However, in the following discussion, I am especially concerned with the registers that can be used for planning and monitoring services and for research.

Among the tools of epidemiology, the case register has been used increasingly for many purposes, especially during the last twenty-five years. However, the history of registration goes back much further in the history of epidemiology. At the beginning of this century, interest in chronic disease had already developed, and case registers had been started in Europe. In Denmark the registration of chronic illness began in the mid-nineteenth century. Mental illness, mental retardation, speech defects, and other chronic handicapping diseases have been cumulatively registered on a nationwide scale since the beginning of this century.

The topics of registration vary according to time and geographical area. Some Western European countries, where registration of chronic handicapping diseases started about 1910 (Westergaard, 1928), continuously register the same conditions and diseases. In Denmark, mental illness has been constantly registered since 1910, and the old files have been important for research in this field. But interest in the registration of some diseases, such as tuberculosis, is decreasing. However, the register still receives notification of all cases. New registers of great interest have been started; for example, the heart register in 1972 and registration of abortions in 1973 (*Prioritering i Sundhedsvæsenet*, 1977).

Sometimes it can be difficult to distinguish between an epidemiological case register and a case register that is of no use in epidemiological studies. For a register to be epidemiological, the data of each patient must be traced to his or her first attack of illness. Epidemiological case registers are used in many countries, especially the United States, Japan, the United Kingdom, Denmark, Norway, Iceland, and some Eastern countries like the USSR (Mombour, 1975). It is not possible in this short survey to give a description of all the registers in the different countries; only some examples will be mentioned.

THE TECHNIQUE OF THE REGISTERS

After the Second World War, when there was growing interest in war veterans and other chronically ill persons, a tool of great interest became available: the computer. With the possibility of computerizing the data of the registers, a new era began. The pioneers were psychiatrists behind some area-bound registers in the United States, such as the Monroe County psychiatric register (Gardner et al., 1963). Later some European countries also started computer-based registers, especially in the field of psychiatry.

The technique of the register is dependent upon the possibility of identifying individuals. Some years ago I was asked to give advice to some psychiatrists who wanted to set up a psychiatric register in Iran. The idea was not possible to carry out, as a person in Iran often takes a new name when he grows up and finds out that he wants to be another person with another name; only a small proportion of the population is aware of their birthday and year.

The difficulty of some of the British registers has been the identification of persons. Many of the linkage problems described by Acheson (1967) are the results of lack of identification numbers for the population. In this regard we are very lucky in Denmark to have the CPR number: all persons get a ten-digit CPR number when born, which makes all kinds of registration very easy. The CPR number is used in the cumulative Danish Psychiatric Register; see Figure 5.1 (Dupont, 1974, 1979).

Conditions Registered

The first topics of registration were the illnesses and chronic diseases of importance for the person's health and invalidism. Later it was found more important to register the well-defined diseases of interest; for instance, the different types of cancer. Today we have reached the next step and want to register the unit of diseases, such as those described by abnormalities of the chromosomes or of the enzyme system.

Some General Outlines of the Difficulties, Biases, and Pitfalls

The more it is possible to refine the technical instruments and the designs of both software and hardware of computer-based systems, the more important it is to be aware of biases.

A nationwide register of all cytogenetic cases of a population is based upon the individual observation of all the laboratories of the whole country. It is obvious that this registration gives very important information. However, if a laboratory is especially interested in one of the anomalies and takes care to count a higher number of cells in order to find as many

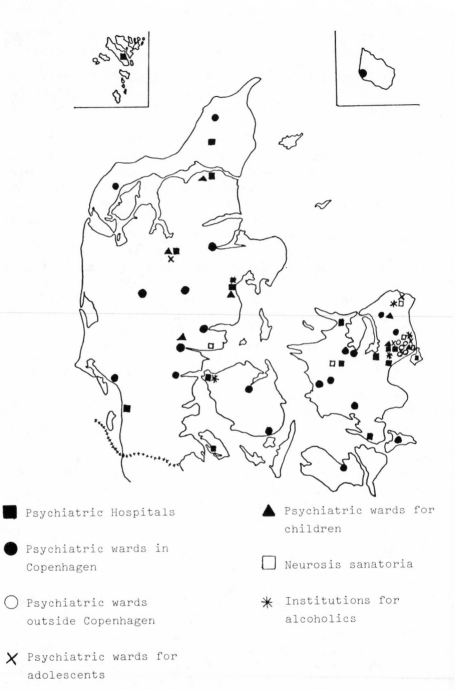

■ Psychiatric Hospitals	▲ Psychiatric wards for children
● Psychiatric wards in Copenhagen	☐ Neurosis sanatoria
○ Psychiatric wards outside Copenhagen	✳ Institutions for alcoholics
✕ Psychiatric wards for adolescents	

Figure 5.1. The Cumulative Danish National Psychiatric Register.

persons as possible with the specific anomaly, an especially high prevalence of this disease is found. Other laboratories are not interested in this special disease and are only counting the necessary and normal number of the cells and therefore find few cases. The entries of a register must be based on the same methods used by all the agencies referring to the register. Otherwise, the results must be balanced according to the biases.

The registration of psychiatric illness, for example, is based upon the following data: name, identification number (CPR number), whether this is the first time the patient has been admitted to a psychiatric bed, diagnoses according to the ICD code, and the manner of admission and discharge. But no information is given of the social status or the degree of education of the patient. The reason for this modesty in design is quite simple: there is no tradition of training medical professionals to make a general coding system of the patient's social status and education uniform and useful for the eighty agencies of the register. Some criticisms have been directed toward the diagnostic system (Babigian et al., 1965). However, it is astonishing how constant the diagnoses of, for instance, psychiatry can be: the well-known cross-sectional studies by Strömgren and co-workers have shown that psychiatric diagnoses of chronic patients have seldom been changed, and now they have been controlled with the use of five-year intervals since 1957 (Weeke and Strömgren, 1978).

A recent survey revealed that it is much more difficult to define a person's first entry in a system. If a researcher wants to study the first admissions of a special diagnosis — for instance, schizophrenia — (Gam, 1980), it is obvious that he gets a group from the register that is in two ways biased: (1) too many are wrongly called first admissions because their very first admission in a psychiatric hospital took place earlier than stated but was forgotten by the informer, and (2) a patient is said to be admitted for the first time because he is referred from a bed of an acute receiving unit to a more chronic bed of the same system, and both entries are labeled first admissions. Very clear definitions, criteria, and instructions to all the coding professionals may reduce such errors.

USE OF CASE REGISTERS FOR LONGITUDINAL STUDIES

The case register can be used to conduct *longitudinal research,* such as follow-up studies. The groups may be chosen by demographic criteria (according to age, sex, birthplace, and the like) or by other criteria, such as the type of agency or the period of time in which the patients were treated.

A longitudinal study could be conducted by using registered data in which one-day prevalence rates are analyzed at a specific date with, for instance, five-year intervals. Such cross-sectional studies are longitudinal and based upon an epidemiological case register. By comparing prevalence rates for cross sections, information can be obtained on trends in the distribution of various demographic data, such as age, race, and sex categories, in terms of the care received; for instance, day patient care or hospital bed care or diagnoses and length of treatment over a period. There are two advantages in utilizing a register to carry out a longitudinal study: (1) As the register contains data that have been continuously gathered over a period of years, it can give the researcher greater flexibility in specifying the particular period he or she wishes to examine. (2) As the data have already been collected and are immediately available, the time and expense involved in conducting research are significantly reduced.

Longitudinal studies of a group of the population limited to a geographical area are possible (Kastrup et al., 1976) if the register contains a coding system for the residence of the patients. Many registers today contain no less than three codes for each individual: the municipal region of residence, the municipal region from which he was first admitted, and finally the municipal code for his birthplace.

Also *cohort studies* are possible based upon the registration systems. As an example I would like to mention a newly performed study of what is called new long-stay patients with psychiatric illness (Weeke et al., 1979). Studies of this kind have been performed in the Camberwell register; in the Danish psychiatric register it has also been possible to perform such studies based on cohorts of patients who entered the system and stayed for more than one year. The computer program for such studies is rather sophisticated, and it must be taken into consideration that some patients could leave their hospital beds for a short time but not conclude the actual hospital stay. In our study as in the British studies, we made the choice of nine days for the stay outside hospital without disturbing the total period.

The general registration of mental illness has been combined with other registers — for instance, twin registers — and with certain groups of adopted offspring whose parents were examined for mental illness, as in the well-known studies by Schulsinger and others where the register of adoption has been combined with the psychiatric register (Mednick et al., 1974). Longitudinal studies of special groups at risk could be based on the information from the register; for instance, in a study of the offspring of schizophrenic parents. The well-known Danish prospective newborn baby study by Zachau-Christiansen (1972) and others is now approaching the age groups in whom it is very important to study the prevalence of psychiatric illnesses, especially schizophrenia.

The design of the study could be modified in many ways; for instance, the group at risk could be treated or divided into treated and nontreated groups. The well-known Milwaukee study (Garber and Heber, 1976) in mental retardation could be mentioned as an example of longitudinal prospective studies where the background was the study by Heber and other psychologists of the population at risk of mild mental retardation.

Combining two registers may give information about groups at risk; for instance, combining the register of cancer with the register of death, or the register of traffic accidents with the psychiatric central register (Kastrup et al., 1977), and so on. In Denmark a nationwide register of somatic illness (*Fællesindhold*, 1976) based upon annual tapes from all hospitals may be of enormous importance for research and planning. It may be possible, for instance, to trace throughout a lifetime the sequences of a traffic accident of a child, an inborn error of metabolism, or a congenital malformation. It will also be possible to combine the somatic and the psychiatric nationwide registers.

FUTURE OUTLINE OF RESEARCH IN LONGITUDINAL PROSPECTIVE STUDIES BASED ON REGISTERS

According to the still-growing knowledge of computer-based registers, it is obvious that methods could be refined, design of the registers improved, and other data and variables included. Here especially the need of a linkage of the medical data with sociological data is an obvious new possibility and may improve the use of many registers. However, I am not too optimistic about an expansion of the registers. I am especially afraid that the rather hysteric or uncontrolled aversion against registers in the population is working against us. Almost every week I confront this problem in the telephone calls or letters I receive as responsible medical head of the psychiatric register. From the daily newspaper cuttings I have collected some cases, and almost every day attacks have been directed against registers (the CPR register, the psychiatric register, and so on). The problems of confidentiality of registers has been described by Baldwin et al. (1976).

CONCLUSION

The case register is a valuable instrument in the field of research. Its advantages to investigators include an unbiased study population on duplicated counts of contacts with services and hospitals, longitudinal information on each patient, access to the past, immediately usable data, and a reduction in the cost of amount of time involved in conducting research. However, before interest can be generated in the register as a data source potential, researchers must have some idea of how it can be manipulated and of its biases. Here we have discussed several types of national studies that can be applied to register data. These include cross-sectional, longitudinal, and other approaches, and hopefully the application of such methods to the register will stimulate research areas that were not amenable to investigation prior to the establishment of the cumulative case register.

6 GENETICS AND CLASSIFICATION

Fini Schulsinger and Hanne Schulsinger

Longitudinal studies are always aimed at studying the interaction between genetic predispositions and various experiential factors. If this aim is not conscious to the researchers, they are apt to fail in their research or they need more than usual luck to find anything of real interest.

THE ROLE OF GENETICS

In behavioral research, and also in most research on physical illnesses, the genetic predisposition is a construct that is not well defined. The characteristics of the biological bases of the genetic predispositions are known only to a small extent with regard to their modus operandi as well as their exact location. Therefore we frequently have to work with constructs based on statistical risk figures for various types of relatives of the ill probands.

This fact means that evidence for genetic factors is based more frequently on correlative data than on strictly causative data. In spite of

103

this relative weakness, it is profitable to take into consideration Johanssen's old formula:

$$\text{Genotype} + \text{environment} \rightarrow \text{phenotype}.$$

The following negative examples will be informative:

The Danish National Institute for Social Research (Socialforskningsinstituttet, 1968) published a large study on problem children in 1968. From primary school classes in the city of Copenhagen, the city of Randers, and the rural parts of the county of Randers, 641 children were selected by their teachers as problem children in accordance with some preset criteria. The problems were truancy, unreliability, aggressivity, and other transgressive behavior, but problems of other types such as inhibited, anxious, or withdrawn attitudes were also included. From the remaining pool of school children (more than 7,000) 641 were randomly selected as nonproblem control children. Behind the study were assumptions that certain social factors were responsible for the problem behavior. No attention was paid to the fact that the children might have had different genotypes. Johanssen's old formula thus was modified into

$$\text{Environment} \rightarrow \text{phenotype}.$$

The main results were as follows:

Of the total pool of school children from the grades in question, 8.3 percent were problem children, but they were not evenly distributed in the three geographical areas. In Copenhagen the distribution was over 10 percent, in the rural areas below 5 percent, and in the city of Randers a percentage in between.

When compared with the control group, a few more of the problem children lived under bad social and housing conditions. But the vast majority of problem children did not live under such bad conditions, and thus they could not have been responsible for the development of the problems.

A few but not many more of the problem children came from broken homes. A few more problem children had mothers who worked full time outside their homes. Likewise, neither of these two conditions could be responsible for the manifestation of problems.

The problem children were more frequently punished by their parents than were the nonproblem controls. The punishments were related to the transgressions as well as to the inhibited behavior.

The report concluded that any parent carried a risk of having problem children. It was suggested that family counseling be offered to families independent of their social problems.

On the whole, the large and neatly performed study did not find striking evidence for social factors as causes of behavioral problems. But this does not mean that social factors play no role in this context. If the design had been different, such that the "genotype" were under control, the results might well have differed and the primary assumptions been confirmed. If the problem children had been matched with nonproblem control children whose parents showed the same composition as those of the problem children with regard to a history of psychiatric hospitalization, then it might well have resulted in evidence for social factors as *precipitating* factors. The old formula

$$\text{Genotype} + \text{environment} \rightarrow \text{phenotype}$$

should be used such that one of three elements is defined, another is under control, and the third then is the dependent variable — in this case, the environment. In zoology and botany the formula has been used this way since the beginning of this century, whereas social, behavioral, and medical researchers concerned with human subjects have been more reluctant to use it.

To emphasize the point above, a second Danish study (Ekstrøm, 1972) will be briefly reviewed. A psychiatrist studied approximately 300 teenagers who all suffered from gonorrhea. He found that their social background was comparable to the social background of the general child and youth welfare clientele. They came to a larger extent from broken homes, and so on. This result was of course interesting, but not really surprising. It did not tell us why the majority of teenagers with a poor social background do not get gonorrhea. The direct reason for this was — understandably enough — that those with gonorrhea had earlier and more frequent sexual contacts than the others. But why do some teenagers with a poor social background have more frequent sexual contacts than other teenagers with the same social background? The psychiatric interview did not disclose this reason. One possible explanation could be a genetic predisposition toward psychopathic behavior (Schulsinger, 1972). To test this hypothesis we would have to use the formula

$$\text{Genotype} + \text{environment} \rightarrow \text{phenotype}$$

as follows: the phenotype, gonorrhea, is defined; the environment is under control (child and youth welfare characteristics); and the genotype would be the dependent variable.

These two examples demonstrate clearly the shortcomings of the concept that all children are born alike into this world but are exposed to different environments and therefore have different outcomes. Many people are aware of the Laingian viewpoints on the family as the cause of schizophrenia. In addition there are several other theories on the family role, such as those by Lidz and by Bateson. But, as pointed out by Gottesman and Shields (1976), it has never been demonstrated that schizophrenia manifests itself in a person who does not have a schizophrenic relative. The family researchers simply did not go to the trouble of reporting whether there were ill family members, because they *believed* that the illness was due to psychodynamic factors alone. They excluded the possibility that certain children with a genetic liability or vulnerability might be less resistant to unlucky emotional constellations in the family. At the same time they never really took the trouble to try to explain why only one or two children and not all children in the suffering families got schizophrenia. Thus, neglect of the role of a genotype not only invalidates the research but also provides the fuel for futile scholastic conflicts.

To conclude this discussion with a positive example, a type of study will be described that has not yet been realized, but probably will be so in the near future. It has been shown that certain relatively frequent diseases — seronegative arthritis, diabetes, and psoriasis — occur in persons who, ten to thirty times as frequently as the general population, are carriers of certain defined human leucocyte antigenes (HLA) (McDevitt and Bodmer, 1974). But most likely, experiential factors are important for the manifestation as well as for the severity of such illnesses.

If we were interested in further information on the effect of such experiential factors, the greatest payoff would come from a study of specially selected groups of young, not yet ill, subjects who were carriers of these HLA antigenes. It could be a waste of time and effort to study a sample of which only a minority were carriers. It may well turn out then that, for example, carriers of the "arthritis" antigene run a very high risk if they work outdoors during winter, whereas noncarriers may rarely get this particular type of arthritis under any condition. A study like this might be worthwhile to carry out. It would throw light on the importance of a possible genetic vulnerability, and it might be possible to estimate whether specific or general prevention of the arthritis would be most feasible.

Thus, the role of genetics in longitudinal research is to make meaningful the study of environmental factors. It is meaningful to study why the experiential factors in many instances have a different effect on different individuals.

METHODS IN HUMAN GENETIC RESEARCH

Family Studies

The traditional method in human genetics research has been that of family studies. In this method the scientist sets out with a sample of persons who suffer from the condition in question. The prevalence of this condition among various types of relatives is examined. The distribution of the condition may then make it probable that genetic factors are effective or not. The differences in the distribution between the first-degree relatives (parents, siblings, offspring) and more distant relatives may speak for or against a special mode of inheritance, such as a Mendelian mode.

This family method has yielded enormous amounts of important information. But it has one particular weakness: the closer the relationship between members of a family, the more uniform the environment will have been.

In order to overcome this methodological weakness, it is preferable to study the relatives of probands who, early in life, were adopted by nonbiologically related adoptive parents and reared by them. A number of studies using adopted samples to examine hereditary factors in certain behavioral disorders have been published: in schizophrenia, by Rosenthal et al. (1968) and Rosenthal (1974); in psychopathy, by Schulsinger (1972); in criminality, by Hutchings and Mednick (1974); in alcoholism, by Goodwin et al. (1973, 1974, 1977); and in suicide, by Schulsinger et al. (1979). More are in progress.

The phenomenon of adoption can be utilized in different designs (Rosenthal, 1971):

The family study design. The biological and adoptive relatives of ill adoptees and of nonill control adoptees are studied with regard to the disorder in question — and possibly also related disorders.

The adoptees study design. Adoptees are selected as probands on the basis of their biological parents' having the disorder under study. Adoptees whose biological parents do not have the disorder serve as a control sample.

The cross-fostering design. Adoptees are selected whose biological parents are healthy, but whose adoptive parents show signs of the disorder under study. This method was used by Wender et al. (1974).

The nonadoptive study design. To elucidate the possible effects of adoption itself, the previous design can be supplemented with the nonadoptive study design, in which are studied nonadopted probands who have spent most of their childhood with their biological parents of whom one or both were ill.

There is no principal reason not to use these designs in the context of physical illnesses, about which the possible roles of environment and heredity have not yet been sufficiently clarified. In general, however, adoptive designs are usually dependent on the following facilities:

A central register of adoptions, from which the nonfamily adoptions can be ascertained;

A national, or at least regional, complete population register, from which information can be elicited on family relationships;

National, or at least regional, registers of the disorders under study.

Also necessary are responsible administrators of these registers, who conceive of research as beneficial and who are cooperative in working out safeguards to be observed as a condition for permission to use the registers in question. The constellation of facilities listed above does not exist in many countries, but more and more disease registers are under development.

Twin Studies

The twin method has now been in use for more than 100 years. A pair of monozygotic twins have the same genetic endowment, whereas dizygotic twins are like ordinary full siblings in this respect. It is therefore generally assumed that if concordance of a disease or trait is considerably higher among monozygotic than among dizygotic twins, then hereditary factors play an important role. Theoretically the concordance rate in monozygotic twins should be more than double the concordance rate among dizygotic twin pairs.

It should be noticed that concordance can be expressed pairwise as well as probandwise. Pairwise concordance expresses how many pairs are concordant out of the total number of pairs under study, which can be very illustrative. But when the results of twin studies are to be compared with other types of family studies, it is more realistic to express the concordance as a probandwise concordance — that is, how big a percentage of all the affected subjects have a cotwin also affected. This procedure is in agreement with the principle of expressing concordance between relatives in family studies other than the twin studies.

In the field of behavioral genetics doubt has been raised with respect to the interpretation, described above, of the difference in concordance rates between monozygotic and dizygotic twins. Critics of the interpretation hold the view that monozygotic twins usually experience a much more uniform environment than do dizygotic twins. This uniformity of environment, then, could be the cause of the higher concordance rates. Confronted with reality, however, such an explanation could hardly be true.

An example from twin research in schizophrenia clearly demonstrates these problems. The major contemporary studies show an approximately 40 percent concordance for monozygotic pairs and approximately 12 percent for same-sexed dizygotic pairs (see Figure 6.1).

If the difference between MZ and same-sexed DZ twins, as the figure shows, is approximately fifteen times as great as the difference between the DZ twins and ordinary siblings varying in age and sex, and this was explained by a greater environmental uniformity, this uniformity should be fifteen times as great as the uniformity for DZ twins and ordinary siblings. Such uniformities are not in agreement with common sense.

The twin method is still a powerful method to demonstrate that genetic factors play a role in the transmission of illness or deviance. A special version of twin studies, however, is very effective in the search for environmental factors of importance: the study of MZ twin pairs discordant for the condition under study. Differences between members of such pairs can be explained only on experiential grounds. In principle, it would be most effective to study twin pairs from birth and prospectively into adulthood to avoid all the shortcomings of retrospective data. But this

	Relationship		
	MZ	DZ	Siblings
Concordance rate	40	12	10
Differences	>300%		20%

Figure 6.1. Concordance Rate for Schizophrenia in Twins and Other Siblings.

would require larger samples because it is not known from birth which pairs will turn out to be discordant.

In schizophrenia research the method has been very valuable, even if the studies have been carried out retrospectively on discordant pairs. The most detailed and up-to-date studies were carried out at the National Institute of Mental Health, Bethesda, Maryland, by Pollin and co-workers (Pollin and Stabenau, 1968). They found in their series of eighteen discordant pairs that the twins who eventually became schizophrenic showed the following characteristics:

They had suffered more asphyxia during delivery.
They were shorter and lighter at birth.
They suffered more frequently from infections with possible CNS affection during childhood.
They had more soft neurological signs as adults when compared with the nonschizophrenic health cotwins.

As part of these studies, parents and other siblings were carefully examined. It then turned out that many twins who became schizophrenic had a very complicated relationship (ambivalent and hostile) with the more psychopathological of their parents. This means that the twins who were the smallest and most ailing were also reared in a less favorable psychological atmosphere. In our opinion such spiraling interactions between biological and psychosocial traumata illustrate life itself.

CLASSIFICATION

Genetic studies — be they twin or pedigree studies — face special problems with regard to the diagnostic classification of cotwins or other relatives. These problems are specially distinct in longitudinal studies of populations at a high, possibly genetic, risk for the disorder in question. The problems can be outlined this way:

1. In genetic studies one does not want to miss registration of pathology that — even if weak—could be genetically related to the disorder under study.
2. During the consequently thorough examination of the relatives of affected probands, one finds a number of relatives with clear-cut pathology, in spite of the fact that these relatives function very well socially and therefore are not patients or "cases."

Problem 1 has implications for the choice of disease concept. This is illustrated very elegantly in Gottesman and Shields' (1972) study of schizophrenic twins. They prepared case histories of the cotwins of the schizophrenic twin probands and asked six experienced clinicians independently to make a diagnostic classification of the cotwins. The six judges had different backgrounds and therefore also different concepts of schizophrenia. Some had a broad concept, some a narrow, and some an in-between. The results indicated that a concept that was neither too broad nor too narrow yielded the most valid results.

Any deviation from the broadest possible disease concept, however, implies a risk of losing interesting information on relatives — or prospectively studied subjects at high risk. The solution to this problem is to employ the "spectrum concept" of the disorder under study. With regard to schizophrenia, use of the spectrum concept has been illustrated by Kety et al. (1975); Rosenthal (1974) also provided important evidence for this approach. It turned out to be possible to create a reliable and valid spectrum: chronic schizophrenia, doubtful chronic schizophrenia, acute schizophrenia, and borderline schizophrenia. Results indicated that the acute schizophrenias were less genetically related to chronic schizophrenia than were the borderline cases. Eventually the spectrum was extended to include a softer part, comprising schizoid personalities and inadequate personalities. The softer the spectrum, the more "noise" can be expected, but in the Kety et al. study even the distribution of the soft-spectrum disorders among relatives seemed to be in part genetically determined. The spectrum concept applied to the genetics of psychopathy was illustrated by Schulsinger (1972), who developed it in a simple fashion into a quantitative instrument to characterize whole families.

So far we have been preoccupied with rather traditional concepts and spectrum components as illustrated by the reported schizophrenia studies. The traditional concepts must be used for the selection of probands — as the starting point — in the genetic studies of well-known disorders. But if we want to learn more about the nature of the disorders than is already known, we must operate with more flexible disease concepts than the traditional ones.

An example from Mednick and Schulsinger's 1962 Copenhagen High-Risk Study (Schulsinger, 1976) illustrates this point. The study began in 1962 with examination of 207 children of severely schizophrenic mothers, when the children were between 10 and 20 years old. Ten years later, between 1972 and 1974, this group was reexamined, and this time it was very important to carry out a clinical evaluation of the outcome; that is, to make a diagnostic classification of the sample. It was important that all psychopathology be registered. We could expect to find both a group with distinct schizophrenic psychopathology and groups with other types of psychopathology, in addition to well-functioning persons with or without discreet deviations in personality, contact, and thinking. It was anticipated that groups falling outside the traditional diagnostic practice would also be present. These expectations determined the development of the clinical procedures.

In order to obtain the highest possible reliability of the diagnoses and to make the results comparable with those of other authors, two diagnostic interview instruments were selected. Both were currently in international use: the PSE (Present State Examination, 9th ed.) and Catego program (Wing, Cooper, and Sartorius, 1974) and the CAPPS (Current and Past Psychopathology Scale) and DIAGNO II program (Endicott and Spitzer, 1972).

The advantage of using these standardized interviews lies in the absolutely uniform way in which the data are processed during the simulated diagnostic procedure, thus favoring the possibility of reliable diagnoses. These interviews are not at all as rigid as questionnaires or rating scales; they are basically clinical and are performed as a daily-life psychiatric interview. The difference from the free, unstructured interview lies in the fact that the interviewer has to rate a standardized set of symptoms and personality variables. The PSE and CAPPS were originally developed from patient samples; both (especially PSE) have, however, been used in studies on normal, nonpsychiatric populations. Nevertheless the PSE and CAPPS interviews have their shortcomings, particularly when used on a sample with an expected large variation in psychopathology, ranging from clear-cut schizophrenic patients to borderline states, personality deviations, and neuroses to those without any psychopathology.

In order to describe these conditions, each with presumably varying degrees of severity, one has to add more finely nuanced observations to these traditional and relatively wide-meshed psychiatric interviews. This is a way to avoid overlooking characteristics that might be of importance for possible later understanding of the nature of the disorders. Therefore a number of variables were selected that were of uncertain diagnostic significance but considered by many experienced clinicians as relevant in the assessment of discreet or latent psychopathology. These variables consisted of additional characteristics of the interviewees, including scales that evaluated thought structure, cognitive functioning, ego organization, ego identity, ego maturity, emotional contact qualities, and the like, all dimensions of general psychological functioning. Included also were a number of traits that potentially might illustrate what Dohrenwend, Egri, and Mendelsohn (1971) call *positive functioning* — that is, creative interests, goal directness, empathy, humor, spontaneous verbal production, and the like — which in general could be conceived as coping and strengthening personality resources.

Diagnostic Classification

The whole 3½-hour clinical interview resulted in three diagnoses — the PSE and Catego, the CAPPS and DIAGNO II, and the interviewer's — for each interview subject.

Even if all three categories of "diagnosticians" followed ICD 9th edition (WHO, 1967), there were differences in the use of the categories. For example, neither PSE and Catego nor CAPPS and DIAGNO II applied the diagnosis of pseudoneurotic schizophrenic borderline state, which was a crucial category in this study. Most of the subjects classified borderline state by the interviewer were classified schizophrenic by the CAPPS and DIAGNO II and schizoid character deviations by the PSE and Catego.

Another example of the problems of cross-national classifications was that the Catego program was the most conservative (narrow) in diagnoses of schizophrenia (diagnosed 10 schizophrenics), the DIAGNO II evidenced the broadest definition (diagnosed 30 schizophrenics), and the interviewer took up the middle ground between the two (diagnosed 13 schizophrenics). (The interviewer's diagnosis of schizophrenia was based on the Danish psychiatric tradition, which is mainly Bleulerian; that is, the presence of primary symptoms is most important. The Catego program classified schizophrenia on the basis of Schneider's first-rank symptoms. And DIAGNO II placed a relatively heavy weight on any single Bleulerian secondary symptom, such as hallucinations and delusions.)

These differences in definitions and delineations did not have serious effects. The three diagnostic instruments showed a great degree of overlapping within the total schizophrenia spectrum. Thus the greatest part of the surplus of DIAGNO II schizophrenia diagnoses was categorized pseudoneurotic schizophrenic borderline state by the interviewer.

For the preliminary analyses of the clinical outcome we decided to use one diagnosis instead of all three. This diagnosis, outlined in Table 6.1, was made on the basis of consensus. The use of consensus is a feasible and straightforward method as a starting point in research that relies far more on description than on experimentation. The consensus

Table 6.1. 1972 Follow-up Diagnostic Status of High-Risk and Low-Risk Subjects. (Low-Risk Subjects in Parentheses.)

	Interviewer	CAPPS DIAGNO II	PSE CATEGO	"Consensus" Diagnoses
Schizophrenia	13 (1)	30 (6)	10 (1)	15 (1)
Borderline states (including schizoid and paranoid personality disorders)	71 (5)	20 (1)	35 (3)	55 (4)
Psychopathy	5 (4)	2 (1)	4 (4)	5 (4)
Other personality disorders	26 (10)	3 (2)	22 (9)	22 (9)
Neuroses (symptoms and character)	34 (44)	31 (16)	43 (38)	30 (33)
Nonspecific conditions	0 (0)	43 (17)	24 (17)	13 (11)
No mental disorder	23 (27)	44 (47)	15 (17)	25 (27)
Other conditions (including affective and paranoid psychoses)	1 (0)	0 (1)	20 (2)	1 (0)
Disagreement among the three diagnoses				7 (2)
Total	173 (91)	173 (91)	173 (91)	173 (91)

Source: Schulsinger, H., 1976.

diagnosis was based on agreement between at least two of the three diagnostic sources and within eight main diagnostic categories.

The Problem of Caseness

It should be borne in mind that the sensitivity of the interviewer in the observation of possible psychopathology was deliberately very high. The sample was "overdiagnosed," except for the category "No Mental Illness." Only a minor part of the total sample, however, can be conceived of as being mentally ill in the traditional sense. As mentioned earlier, psychopathology may very well be described in individuals with a satisfactory functioning at work and at home.

On the basis of results from PSE and Catego studies of general population groups, John Wing et al. (1978) have developed an Index of Definition of Syndromes. This index is an expression of the degree to which a subject suffers from specific psychiatric syndromes. The Index of Definition of Syndromes is calculated from PSE scores on the basis of amount and quality of symptoms and has shown a high degree of reliability and validity. Table 6.2 shows how the application of Wing's Index of Definition of Syndromes makes our diagnostic results comparable with traditional morbidity rates from other genetic and epidemiological studies.

It should be mentioned, however, that not all the possible "cases" and even not all the definite "cases" were in earlier or current treatment. For example, six of the fifteen schizophrenic "cases" had not yet been admitted to psychiatric departments at the time of the interview examination. This leaves intriguing questions about our traditional disease concepts and classification, which perhaps will be clarified in the future follow-up examinations of this sample.

The longitudinal research design also shows its advantages with respect to the interpretation of psychopathological phenomena.

Aspects of Classification and Outcome

So far we have described some technical solutions to the problems of classification in studies of populations at genetic risk. These solutions are necessary tools for a meaningful selection of probands in genetic studies.

Table 6.2.   1972 Follow-up: PSE Index of Definition of Syndromes Distributed by "Consensus" Diagnoses in High- and Low-Risk Groups. (Low-Risk Subjects in Parentheses.)

	Minimal Specific Syndromes (PSE)*	Definite Specific Syndromes (PSE)**
Schizophrenia	0 (0)	14 (1)
Borderline states (including schizoid and paranoid personality disorders)	16 (1)	10 (1)
Psychopathy	3 (2)	0 (0)
Other personality disorders	2 (5)	0 (1)
Neuroses	6 (8)	1 (4)
Nonspecific conditions	0 (0)	0 (0)
Other conditions (including affective and paranoid psychoses)	0 (0)	1 (0)
Disagreement among the three diagnoses	2 (2)	1 (0)
Total	29 (18)	27 (7)

* Corresponds to PSE Index B_3. It is included to be on the safe side, so as not to miss possible cases.

** Corresponds to PSE Indices of $C_3C_2C_1$.

Source: Schulsinger, H., 1976.

But if we look back at the old formula

$$\text{Genotype} + \text{environment} \rightarrow \text{phenotype},$$

where phenotype corresponds to diagnosis, we can understand the limitations of using the traditional concepts of the diseases. We can imagine two persons of the same sex and age who receive the same diagnostic classification; for example, schizophrenic. One person might, however, be someone with a very strong genetic liability and good psychosocial experiences, whereas the other might be less liable but exposed to a rough and anxiety-provoking childhood.

In order to disentangle the genetic and experiential contributors, it is also necessary to have a flexible attitude toward classification of outcome. The prospective longitudinal method teaches us a certain flexibility of our disease concepts. Subjects diagnosed as schizophrenic at one follow-up may well turn out not to be schizophrenic at a subsequent follow-up but to suffer from a borderline condition or a personality disorder. Such results are emerging and will be published eventually. Fluctuations that may increase our understanding will show up only in longitudinal research.

Another aspect of flexibility may be illustrated by the fact that certain psychophysiological variables (fast recovery and high responsivity) according to Mednick (1978) are correlated, not to a diagnosis of schizophrenia, but to the presence of hallucinations and delusions embedded in the interview data.

A third example comes from Walker et al. (1980), who used path analysis to demonstrate, among other things, that certain environmental childhood factors contributed to schizophrenia-related variables derived from factor analysis of interview items outside the PSE and CAPPS.

Finally it should be noted that repeated diagnostic follow-up examinations, each resulting in traditional classification, may not be the best way of getting information on causal relationships. Based as they are on purely descriptive criteria and cross-sectional data, the diagnoses may be of limited value for the understanding of outcome. Detailed reports of psychological and biological characteristics, of life experiences, and of social and cultural conditions may contribute more to our understanding of outcome.

SUMMARY

Longitudinal studies invariably aim at the classification of experiential factors — their type and their role.

The present chapter illustrates the necessity of taking genetic factors into consideration during studies of experiential factors. Human beings are not born alike into this world, and they may therefore react differentially to the same environment. In other words, the chapter advocates a diathesis-stress model of disease.

Genetics has been described in the context of a tool for longitudinal research. Only methods of obtaining genetic data have been described and not the modes of genetic transmission (Mendelian, polygenetic, and so on).

A crucial problem in human genetic studies and in longitudinal population studies in general is the problem of assessing clinical outcome. Therefore we have described problems and techniques in this field as well. The examples are drawn mainly from the project described by Mednick, Schulsinger, and Griffith in Chapter 15 of this book.

7 STATISTICAL MODELS FOR LONGITUDINAL STUDIES

Karl G. Jöreskog

The characteristic feature of a longitudinal research design is that the same measurements are obtained from the same people at two or more occasions. The purpose of a longitudinal or panel study is to assess the changes that occur between occasions and to attribute these changes to certain background characteristics and events existing or occurring before the first occasion and/or to various treatments and developments that occur after the first occasion. A schematic illustration of a two-wave longitudinal design is given in Figure 7.1.

Several chapters of Nesselroade and Baltes (1978) deal with the conceptual and substantive issues and with the logic of causal model building in longitudinal research in developmental psychology and education. Other chapters of the same volume deal with specific methodological problems. Wiley and Harnischfeger (1973) have given an account of the conceptual issues in the attribution of change in educational studies. In the sociological literature there have been a number of articles concerned with the specification of models incorporating causation and measurement errors and the analysis of data from panel studies (see, e.g., Bohrnstedt, 1969; Heise, 1969, 1970; Duncan, 1969, 1972, 1975b). Other papers dealing with methodological problems are Lord (1963), Thorndike (1966),

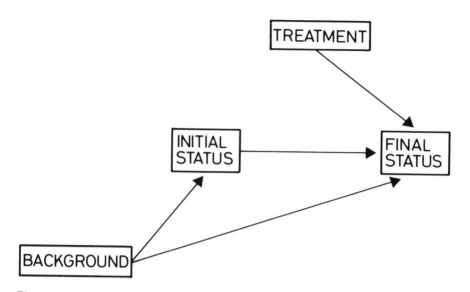

Figure 7.1. Schematic Representation of a Two-Wave Longitudinal Design.

Härnqvist (1968), Cronbach and Furby (1970), and Bergman (1971). Complex models involving multiple measurement and/or several occasions have been considered by Harris (1963), Jöreskog (1970), Corballis and Traub (1970), Nesselroade (1972), Corballis (1973), Bentler (1973), Fredriksen (1974), Jöreskog and Sörbom (1976, 1977), and Olsson and Bergman (1977).

This chapter summarizes a previous paper by the author (Jöreskog, 1979). We consider several models suitable for analyzing longitudinal data. The general setup is that of a longitudinal study where the same or similar quantitative measurements have been obtained at two or more occasions, possibly from several different groups of people. The models cover a wide range of applications and are relevant for psychological and educational measurements as well as for social and socioeconomic measurements.

A distinction is made between change in level and structural change. The models for change in level consider the measurement and assessment of change at the group level. They deal with the estimation of growth curves describing the means of the variables as functions of time. The growth curves, which are usually specified to be polynomials of a specified degree, may be different for different groups of people and for different variables, but one can test the hypotheses that the growth curves are the same or parallel for different groups and/or different variables. The growth curves can often be estimated more precisely if the autoregressive nature of the repeated measurements is taken into account in the model. Growth curves can be estimated under various autoregressive models with the computer program LISREL of Jöreskog and Sörbom (1980) (see Sörbom and Jöreskog, 1981).

Structural change occurs when the relationships between variables within or between occasions change over time. In the study of change in level, the variables can often be treated as error-free, but in the study of structural change it is necessary to consider the measurement properties of the variables in terms of their validities and reliabilities.

One of the most difficult problems for a social scientist, when it comes to the formulation of a causal model, arises because many of the concepts and constructs that he or she wants to work with are not directly measurable (see, e.g., Torgerson, 1958, Chap. 1; Goldberger, 1972; Duncan, 1975a; and Heise, 1975). Although such hypothetical concepts and constructs, or latent variables, cannot be directly measured, a number of variables can be used to measure various aspects of these latent variables more or less accurately. Thus, while the latent variables cannot be directly observed, they have operational implications for relationships among observed variables. We may regard the observed variables as indicators of the latent variables. Each indicator has a relationship with the latent variable, but if we take one indicator alone to measure the latent variable, we would obtain a biased measurement. By using several indicators of each latent variable, we get a better measurement of the latent variable.

Another reason for using latent variables in behavioral and socioeconomic studies is that most of the measurements employed contain sizable errors of measurement (observational errors), which, if not taken into account, can cause severe bias in the results. Errors of measurement arise because of imperfection in the various measurement instruments (questionnaires, tests, and so on) that are used to measure such abstractions as people's behavior, attitudes, feelings, and motivations. Even if we could construct valid measurements of these traits, it is usually impossible to obtain perfectly reliable variables. Special care must be taken to obtain measurements that really measure the latent traits or hypothetical constructs that one is interested in measuring.

A common experience in two-wave longitudinal studies is that the initial status is the best determinant or predictor of the final status (see, e.g., Lord, 1963). Therefore, if one is interested in attributing change to certain background variables, one must find some way of effectively eliminating the initial status from the final status. This statement has been taken to mean that one should study difference scores (final scores minus initial scores). However, it is not necessary to do so; the important thing is that both background variables and initial measures be included in the model as determinants of final measures. In multiwave studies one can determine the effect of the background variables on the dependent variable at various points in time.

Often it is not possible, or even desirable, to specify the model completely, since there may be other models that are equally plausible. In such a situation it is necessary to have a technique of analysis that will give information about which of a number of alternative models is (are) the most reasonable. Also, if there is sufficient evidence to reject a given model because of poor fit to the data, the technique should be such as to suggest which part of the model is causing the poor fit. The computer program LISREL of Jöreskog and Sörbom (1980) provides the flexibility and is based on a very general model. This computer program is designed to handle various models for recursive and interdependent systems of latent variables and measurement errors.

In presenting and discussing the various models, it is convenient to use a path diagram. In the path diagram observed variables are enclosed in squares, whereas latent variables are enclosed in circles. Residuals (errors in equations) and errors of measurement are included in the diagram but are not enclosed. A one-way arrow pointing from one variable x to another variable y indicates a possible direct causal influence of x on y, whereas a curved two-way arrow between x and y indicates that x and y may correlate without any causal interpretation of this correlation. It is convenient to write the coefficient associated with each arrow in the path diagram. When the coefficient is omitted, it means that it is one. For one-way arrows such coefficients will be (partial) regression coefficients (path coefficients), and for two-way arrows they will be covariances. In the special case when all observed and latent variables are standardized, these coefficients will be correlations. With these conventions it is possible to write down the model equations from the path diagram. In order to define the model completely, it is necessary only to specify the assumptions about the origin and unit of measurement of the variables involved and the distributional assumptions.

Figure 7.2 shows a two-wave, two-variable model with two variables measuring the same construct at two occasions. A common experience in this situation is that the errors (ϵ's) for the same variable tend to correlate over time because of retest effects. Figure 7.3 shows a similar model without correlated errors but with a background variable affecting

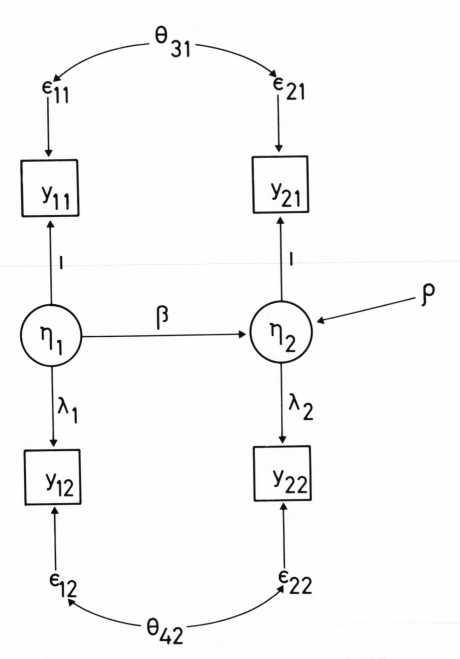

Figure 7.2. A Two-Wave, Two-Variable Model with Correlated Errors.

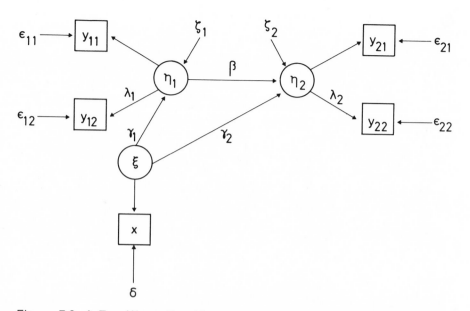

Figure 7.3. A Two-Wave, Two-Variable Model with a Fallible Background Variable.

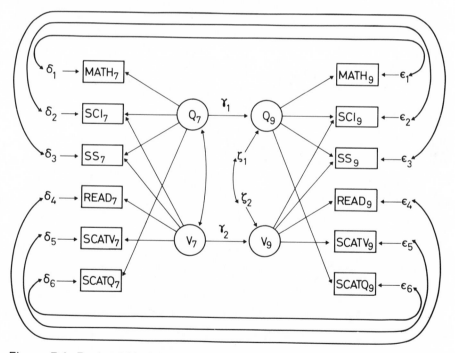

Figure 7.4. Revised Model for the Measurement of Change in Verbal and Quantitative Ability between Grades 7 and 9.

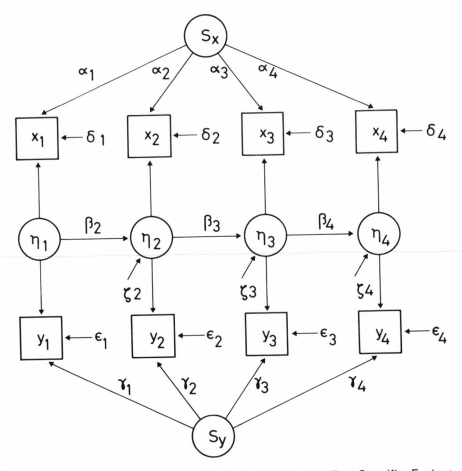

Figure 7.5. A Four-Wave, Two-Variable Model with Test-Specific Factors (Model B).

the latent variable at both occasions. A two-wave multivariate model with errors for each variable correlated over time is shown in Figure 7.4. LISREL can be used to estimate such a model and to test for misspecifications in different parts of the model. A four-wave, two-variable model is shown in Figure 7.5, in which the error correlation over time is assumed to be accounted for by a test-specific factor for each variable.

8 BIOLOGICAL MEASUREMENTS IN LONGITUDINAL RESEARCH

Peter H. Venables

The biological measurements feasible to employ in this field are those that are noninvasive, easy to use, and relatively non–time-consuming in application. The types of measures that have been used fall generally under three heads:

1. Electrodermal activity
   a. Skin conductance
   b. Skin potential
2. Cardiovascular activity
   a. Heart rate
   b. Vasomotor activity
3. Cortical activity
   a. "Ongoing" EEG
   b. Event-related potentials

Of these measures, by far the greatest amount of attention has been given to skin conductance activity, with heart rate and cortical activity receiving somewhat less attention, and little work being carried out on skin potential or vasomotor activity.

125

In addition to the considerations outlined above, the choice of measurement used is normally made with reference to some theoretical position, some heuristic stance, or some prior knowledge held by the investigator. Thus, for instance, the use of an electrodermal conditioning procedure adopted by Mednick and Schulsinger in their first study in 1962 (e.g., Mednick and Schulsinger, 1968) was made in part on the basis of a theoretical view of the development of schizophrenia enunciated by Mednick in 1958. Subsequent studies from the Copenhagen laboratory have used extensions of the same technique because they build on the data already collected and other material — for instance, on adult schizophrenics — that has come to hand in the meantime.

Types of activity measured may be considered to fall under two heads: (1) tonic, ongoing activity and (2) phasic activity in response to stimulation. In the case of tonic activity, it is necessary to collect the data in conditions that are comparable over subjects. If, for instance, measures of skin conductance level (SCL), skin conductance fluctuations (SCF), heart rate level (HRL), and a frequency analysis of the EEG were used to measure "arousal" in an initial "testing" period of data collection, very clear instructions need to be given and other reassuring steps taken to persuade the subject that he or she is not going to receive stimulation and should relax and rest for a specified length of time.

In the same way that standardization over subjects is an essential prerequisite for the collection of tonic activity data, so standardized stimulation methods are important for the collection of phasic data. The method used in the Copenhagen studies is that of a standard auditory stimulus tape. With care this method ensures that each subject receives comparable stimuli at the same specified times and that response data are collected that are comparable over subjects. The use of a stimulus tape procedure greatly facilitates the use of computer analysis techniques.

The advantages in the use of such a procedure should be seen against the disadvantage of the inability to adjust the timing of stimulus presentation to the ongoing state of the subject. Thus if the subject were one showing a large number of spontaneous fluctuations of skin conductance (SCF), then manual presentation of stimuli would be made to ensure that as far as possible the subject was relatively quiescent at the time of stimulus onset. Standardized tape presentation of stimuli sometimes results in the loss of ability to measure a response because of its superimposition on underlying and ongoing activity.

It is possible that use of on-line computer control of stimulus presentation could result in a better, more flexible stimulation system. However, practical attempts to take account of the state of more than one physiological data channel in the search for quiescence before data presentation result in impossibly long delays between successive stimuli. These delays lead not only to a different presentation rate for each subject but also, in practice, to delays in a total testing program because some subjects take longer than others to process. In general the advantages of a standard tape system outweigh those of more flexible systems.

METHODS

Standard Stimulation

Auditory Stimulation.   A well-tried method makes use of a two-track stereo tape recorder of high quality. On one track of the tape recorder the auditory stimuli to be used are recorded; the other track is used to record trigger signals that may be employed to give information to the computer on the timing of stimulus onsets and/or to produce event marking on paper records on the polygraph or EEG recorder.

Difficulties that have to be taken into account and that demand the use of the highest quality of recorder and recording tape are the "dynamic range" of the system, the amount of "cross-talk" between channels, and the extent of "print-through" between adjacent layers of tape on the reel.

By *dynamic range* is meant the extent of recordable sound between the quietest and loudest stimulus intensities. On most recorders the range is about 40 to 45 dB. Consequently, if a conditioning paradigm is being recorded on tape and it is desired to use a 100 dB stimulus as the UCS, then the quietest sound that may be used as the CS is in the region of 55 to 60 dB. If, for instance, a poor-quality recorder were used to produce the very loud UCS, then the background noise level in the absence of a signal would be very high and might exceed the value of 60 dB that might be required for the CS stimulus. Difficulties also arise in eliminating cross-talk between tracks if very loud stimuli are recorded on one track and a trigger stimulus that has to be electronically recognized with adequate sensitivity is used on the other track. This factor appears to necessitate the use of at least ¼ in. reel-to-reel recorders; the narrow tape width of cassette systems is not adequate to stop cross-talk when using stimuli of the range required for this purpose. A further additional difficulty is encountered because of "print-through" of loud signals from one tape layer to the next, resulting in "ghost" signals' being heard at times before the wanted signal. This factor imposes a top limit on the intensity of signals that may be recordable. Some alleviation of the difficulty is afforded by the use of thicker qualities of recording tape instead of the "long-play" variety.

Greatest control over perceived stimulus intensity may be achieved by the use of headphones rather than loudspeakers. The intensity of stimulation varies with the amount of free air space trapped by the earphone surround, which is in part a function of ear size and amount of subject's hair. Best results are probably obtained by headphones with a hard earpiece that fits on top of the pinna instead of surrounding it, although this earpiece is in general less comfortable for the subject and does not afford a means of attenuating external sounds.

Preparation of the stimulus tape may best be achieved by a system under computer control where oscillators and electronic switches are activated by logic pulses. It is most important to recognize the changes in stimulus quality that are brought about by the rise time of auditory stimuli; appropriate electronic techniques to ensure controlled rise time should be employed (Hatton, Berg, and Graham, 1970). Intensity of stimuli should be measured at the headphone by the use of a microphone coupled to an "artificial ear" and a sound level meter.

Visual Stimulation.   Presentation of visual stimuli may also be controlled by the use of a magnetic tape system. With the same type of electronic circuitry that is used to detect the "trigger" stimuli on the control channel of the recording, trigger stimuli may be used to activate systems for presenting visual stimuli. These may, for instance, be lights of the gas-discharge kind, with fast and controllable rise and fall times, or slides in an electronically controlled slide projector.

A potentially more convenient control of complex sequences of stimuli may now be achieved — in a possibly less expensive way than by using tape-recorded stimuli — by the use of large-scale integrated microprocessors and memories. This system is particularly convenient for visual stimulus sequences and may also be used for auditory stimuli.

Psychophysiological Measurement

Skin Conductance Activity.   It is physiologically realistic to view the conducting pathways in palmar skin as being made up of sweat glands and an epidermal conducting pathway connected at one end by the overlying electrode-electrolyte system and at the other by underlying dermal and other tissue. Sweat glands formed in this way are like resistors in parallel and consequently add as their reciprocals; it is, however, more convenient to think of conductance as the reciprocal of resistance and of conductances therefore as directly additive. On this basis, having n more sweat glands active means that n more units of conductance may be added to an existing level. It is thus physiologically reasonable to measure exosomatic electrodermal activity in terms of conductance rather than of resistance. The use of constant voltage circuitry has the immediate advantage that recording is directly in terms of conductance.

Suitable circuits for this type of measurement are shown in detail in Lykken and Venables (1971) and Venables and Christie (1973). These circuits, however, maintain constancy of voltage by a "passive" method, and more recently an appropriate and more accurate active form of constant voltage circuit has been presented by Lowry (1977) and by Venables and Christie (1980). Either the active or the passive form of circuit also necessitates the provision of a "suppression" system whereby the large value of skin conductance level (SCL) may be suppressed and measured, leaving the smaller-amplitude skin conductance response (SCR) that is superimposed on the SCL to be amplified and recorded at a higher gain. Circuits for the automatic control of suppression are now becoming available (Venables and Christie, 1980). These obviate the need for vigilance on the part of the busy operator in the manual operation of the suppression control to maintain his or her recording within pen limits.

Recommended electrodes are the silver/silver-chloride variety using either sodium or potassium chloride in physiological concentrations as the electrolyte. Suggested sites are those indicated as "bipolar placement" in Figure 8.1. Full details of all procedures are provided in Venables and Christie (1973, 1980).

A schematic version of a skin conductance response is shown in Figure 8.2. Here it may be seen that in addition to two magnitude measures, SCL and SCR amplitude (measured in micromhos), there are three temporal components of the response; namely, latency, rise time, and half recovery time. Two further derived measures may be calculated; these are "rise rate" or "recruitment" — that is, micromhos per second gained during rise time — and "recovery rate" — that is, micromhos per second lost during half recovery.

Expected values of SCL are 2 to 100 micromhos/cm² electrode area, with most values lying in the range 5 to 20 μmhos/cm². Values of SCR amplitude will most probably lie in the range 0.01 to 0.5 μmhos/cm². Latencies range from 1.0 to 3.0 secs, rise times from 1.0 to 2.5 secs, and half recovery times from 1 to 15 secs.

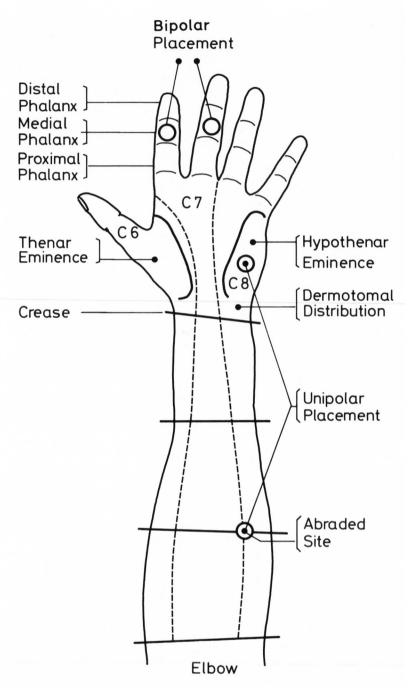

Figure 8.1. Electrode Sites.

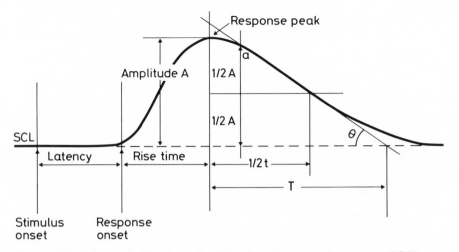

Figure 8.2. Schematic Version of a Skin Conductance Response (SCR).

Skin Potential Activity.   In contrast to skin conductance measurement, which demands the use of an external source of potential, endosomatic activity is measured as a potential difference existing between two points on the skin. The usual placement of electrodes for measuring SP is the unipolar one shown in Figure 8.1, with the active site on a palmar surface and the inactive or reference site on an area of the forearm, mildly abraded in the case of adult subjects or unabraded in the case of children.

Using silver/silver-chloride electrodes and 0.5% KCl as the electrolyte, values of skin potential level (SPL) recorded will range from -70 mV to $+20$ mV, the polarity being referred to the palmar site.

Skin potential responses (SPR) may be uniphasic negative, biphasic, and, more rarely, uniphasic positive and triphasic in form. Because it is not possible to determine the relative contribution of negative and positive components of any one response, it is not advisable to attempt to measure amplitudes. Instead responses are best classified according to their waveform. It is important to note in this instance that a biphasic SPR is usually accompanied by an SCR with a shorter recovery time than a uniphasic SPR.

Heart Rate.   Although the electrocardiogram (EKG) contains a considerable amount of information, it is not usual in this field to use measurements other than those of rate. It is perfectly feasible to use data of this kind collected by palpation of the radial pulse, as has been demonstrated by Wadsworth (1976), using subjects from the Douglas sample (Chapter 11). It is, however, more convenient to record EKG while measuring other variables, thus allowing the calculation of phasic elements of response (HRR) as well as tonic ongoing levels of activity (HRL).

For convenience it is probably easiest to record the EKG from Standard Lead I; that is, with electrodes on left and right arms. There are, however, two disadvantages to the use of this lead. First, with young children particularly, it is prone to disturbance by movement artifacts; second, there is more likelihood than with some other leads of the record's showing T waves as large as the QRS complex and consequently leading to difficulties in single-pulse identification by level-sensing circuits. Other electrode placements such as sites on the chest are preferable from these points of view, but they do, of course, create other difficulties. Later usage of the data is most convenient if a single shaped pulse is available on every heart beat. Suitable circuits for forming such pulses are available in Brener (1967).

Although this section is introduced under the heading "Heart Rate," it is worth noting that measurement of cardiac activity in terms of rate is probably the result of physicians' counting the number of beats in a set period. Interbeat interval (IBI) is a measure that probably has more physiological meaning and is more normally distributed than HR (Jennings, Stringfellow, and Graham, 1974). IBI should be used in preference to HR. The use of cardiotachometers has also led to another convention that needs modification. With these instruments, HR is presented at each beat; thus the time base of a recording is in terms of "physiological" rather than real time. As cardiac data need to be represented alongside other data having a real-time base, the recommendation is that the convention of its presentation in terms of IBIs at ½- or 1-second intervals be adopted. This, however, does necessitate the use of computer analysis to calculate IBI values in time intervals as a function of the partial values falling in those intervals. The other advantage of using a real-time base line is that time can start with stimulus onset and consequently does not require the use of artificial conventional procedures that arise when the base line is in terms of physiological time. It is, however, important to take account of the mathematical constraints involved in combining HR or IBI data against a "real-time" or "biological-time" base line (Graham, 1978).

Vasomotor Activity. Vasomotor activity is most conveniently measured by photoplethysmographic techniques. A suitable method obviating many of the disadvantages of earlier systems is given by Tamoush et al. (1976).

Two variables may be measured: pulse volume (also known as blood volume pulse) and blood volume. The former is the change in the volume of the blood vessels (for example, in the finger or ear lobe) occurring at each heart stroke; the latter, the longer-term change in blood volume occurring as a result of vasodilation or constriction occurring at the peripheral site. Pulse volume measured at the ear lobe and suitably shaped may provide a more convenient measure of heart rate (IBI) than that measured from the EKG. The use of measures of vasomotor activity indexed by changes of blood volume has received little attention in this area, although Janes and Stern (1976) have employed this technique.

Cortical Activity. EEG is normally recorded from scalp sites defined by the International Ten-Twenty system (Jasper, 1958). These sites are shown in Figure 8.3. While normal care of silver cup electrodes provides satisfactory recording in most instances, measurement of the contingent negative variation (CNV), with the necessity of recording slowly changing or DC potentials, requires the use of silver/silver-chloride electrodes. Conventionally, ongoing EEG used in the clinical type of evaluation is recorded from a large number of sites, whereas event-related potentials — averaged evoked responses (AER) and CNV — are recorded from a more limited range of sites. In this case placement is often on the vertex site C_z, from which nonspecific recordings are obtainable. Ongoing EEG material may be processed by using filters and integrators to provide measures of abundance of activity in frequency bands, or the recording may be subject to period analysis or frequency or spectral analysis by using Fast-Fourier transform techniques (see Rémond, 1977, for a full review of methods). The AER or CNV again necessitates the use of computer processing either with "hard-wired" special-purpose computers such as the CAT or now more normally general-purpose "laboratory computers." An example of the use of EEG techniques in high-risk research is given by Itil et al. (1974).

Analysis of Psychophysiological Data

General Considerations on the Nature of Psychophysiological Data. In contrast to the use of psychophysiological techniques in an experimental setting, their use in longitudinal prospective studies faces conflicting problems. In the first instance, as typically a large number of data are collected at some expense at an unrepeatable point in time, it is

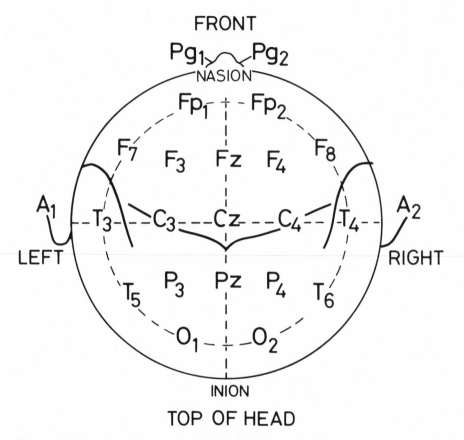

Figure 8.3. Standard International (10–20) Electrode Placement.

important to derive as much from the material collected as is feasible. On the other hand, it is only too easy to become overwhelmed by too much data that are probably only one facet of a larger study. This material has to be reduced in size without substantial loss of information to relate it to other data collected at the same time and to other material that may be collected in the future.

The problem of data reduction is one that is faced in other areas of longitudinal studies, but there are some special problems in dealing with psychophysiological material. These are particularly concerned with missing data. Nonavailability arises from two sources: first, the subject may not respond on a particular occasion because, for instance, he has habituated; second, the response that has been given may be unmeasurable because of, for example, movement artifacts. Reduction of data by, say, factor analysis has therefore to be approached with care, as N^s of correlations in a matrix from which the analysis might start may differ, thus rendering the analysis illegitimate. To some extent the nonresponsivity of subjects may be diminished by the nature of the standard stimulus material used, and care may be taken to reduce artifacts to an absolute minimum; nevertheless there is an inevitable and legitimate amount of zero data that must be taken account of in analysis procedures.

Storage of Data.   Data for psychophysiological investigations have in the past typically been in the form of paper recording scored by hand. The sheer bulk of the material presents a storage problem, and when the data have to be stored under tropical conditions, as in the Mauritius study, the problems are immense. The results of hand scoring are typically transferred to computer coding sheets from which cards are punched, but the bulk of these materials in a large study also presents storage problems. The only feasible form of storage, in this case, is in digital magnetic tape form; indeed, the labor and cost of forming a "clear" set of computer cards when the correction of errors has been carried out on the magnetic tape suggest that the final form of data storage should be magnetic tape. Nevertheless, tape is vulnerable, and adequate precautions have to be taken to have several master copies stored in different places, to have these run through at intervals of about six months to minimize print-through, and always to carry out day-to-day work on a "working" copy.

It is, however, more convenient to collect the original psychophysiological data on analog magnetic tape. This has the advantage of storing data in a relatively nonbulky form that can be easily reanalyzed when some new method becomes available sometime after the original study has been undertaken. Data in this form are of course essential if computer techniques such as time series analysis of heart rate, spectral analysis of EEG, or measurement of event-related potentials are to be carried out.

Recording at slow speed and playback and analysis at a higher speed may allow considerable savings in time. Experience has shown that, even without rewinding, data on analog magnetic tape appear to be preserved in an adequate form after five years' storage. A difficulty that does have to be faced, however, is that intercompatibility of analog instrumentation tape recorders is much lower than with digital machines; unless the original recorder is available at a subsequent playback stage, replay after an interval may be difficult. For this reason it is probably useful either to record directly onto digital tape via an A/D system or to digitize the analog-recorded material at the earliest opportunity. These procedures also allow copies of the data to be made more readily than with analog tape, but in the case of EEG material, for instance, the bulk of stored material is increased.

The extent to which an investigator may feel it necessary to record and preserve any of the media — paper record, analog tape, magnetic tape — depends somewhat on personal preference. However, experience with tape storage now indicates that it is less vulnerable than was at one time feared; consequently paper records may be destroyed after the investigator is assured that the taped data are adequate.

Other practical issues have to be considered in setting up a system for the storage and analysis of psychophysiological data. These include the recording speed of paper record — to allow adequate measurement of temporal events — if this medium is the only one available. The recording speed of the analog tape recorder has to be chosen to encompass the frequency bands required, and the numbers of channels available have to include, in addition to data channels, a track for recording stimulus events. If a voice channel is also available, it is often invaluable for annotating the record in the event of subject difficulties, breakdowns, and the like. In the case of digital recording, the main decision is that of sampling rate and whether it is more convenient to digitize all channels on the same tape or, for instance, to record the EEG material on one tape and the more slowly changing electrodermal data on another. In practice, from the same session the EEG data occupy about three times more bulk than the electrodermal data. Heart rate data probably occupy, in turn, about one-third of the bulk of the electrodermal data.

Depending on the facilities available, it is also important to examine the time economics of using laboratory minicomputers or large computers in analysis. Experience suggests that the ideal solution is to record data on analog tape and to digitize separately "high"-frequency (for example, EEG) data and "slow"-frequency (for example, EDA) data on a minicomputer. The major analysis of the "high"-frequency data such as spectral analysis is then carried out at high speed by using the power of the large computer, while the analysis of the slow data such as skin conductance material, which requires much editing with a visual display, is carried out on the laboratory computer.

Electrodermal Activity: Skin Conductance. The particular characteristic of skin conductance activity is its range of variability between subjects and the lability within subjects. Thus in a sample of subjects at risk for schizophrenia, some will show no responsivity whatsoever, and the only measure available is that of SCL. On the other hand, the major characteristic of those offspring of schizophrenic parents in the original 1962 Copenhagen study who eventually broke down with schizophrenia is their extreme responsivity. Along with responsivity to specific stimuli goes a tendency to exhibit a large number of skin conductance fluctuations (SCF), which, having the same form as SCRs, can be misinterpreted as responses. Probably the most conservative method of identifying responses is the use of latency criteria. Figure 8.4 shows the latency criteria used in the Mauritius study. In the case of the responses to specific, orienting, conditional or unconditional stimuli, responses are scored only if they have latencies in the "window" 1 to 3 seconds after stimulus onset. *B,* or pre-UCS, "conditioned" responses are identified if they occur 4 seconds before and 0.5 seconds after stimulus onset.

Aspects of the responses thus identified that are scored are those shown in Figure 8.2 and outlined in the section on skin conductance activity. SCL is identified as the level at the point of inflexion of the base line at which the response starts or, in the absence of a response, at which SCL is at a point 2.0 secs. after stimulus onset. If a response occurs, then a value of latency will be measurable; if there is an identi-

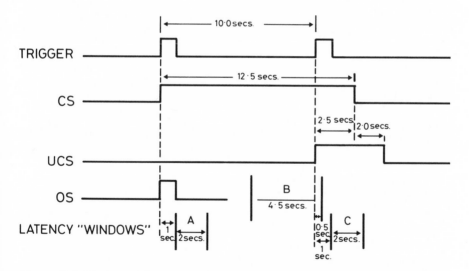

Figure 8.4. Timing of Stimuli on Auditory Tape and Definition of Responses by Latency "Window" Criteria.

fiable peak of response, a value of amplitude and a rise time are scorable. In a labile subject an SCF may appear before peak SCR is reached, and if identification of SCR peak is equivocal, then, conservatively, neither amplitude nor rise time should be scored. In this instance, of course, no measure of half recovery time will be available. In a labile record this recovery measure is the most vulnerable SCR component to interference, and the amount of missing data on this important component unfortunately tends to be large.

Table 8.1 shows the intercorrelation of components of the SCR derived from data from Copenhagen collected in 1972 on children of mean age 11 years. The magnitude of the correlations does not in fact differ substantially from the degree of those derived from data collected in Mauritius and in the United States (for example, Venables and Christie, 1980, p. 48). Several points may be noted in relation to the scoring of data. First, there is a fairly substantial correlation between rise time and half recovery time (this is 0.77 in data for the USA). Second, it should be noted that latency is relatively independent of the other temporal variables. It should also be noted here, although the point will be taken up later, that both the "derived" measures, half recovery *rate* and recruitment, are related to amplitude and to each other.

Another particularly difficult issue concerns the measurement of the "amplitude" variables where a mean figure for data over trials or subjects is required. There are two possibilities: a mean value may be derived only from those responses with nonzero values for which the term *amplitude* is standardly used; alternatively "magnitude" may be calculated where individual SCR amplitudes are averaged with zero entries from nonresponse trials included. Prokasy and Kumpfer (1973) suggest that this magnitude measure should not be used, as it confounds frequency and amplitude measures that do not necessarily covary.

The point, however, is difficult to maintain, as the definition of nonresponsivity depends on the gain of the system used, and it is in practice impossible to separate "real" nonresponses from those where the *S* responded but the response was at that time too small to measure.

It would appear appropriate to use the magnitude measure (including zero responses) where, for instance, a matrix of correlations with this variable for each response has to be calculated. Only in this way can the numbers entering each correlation be the same and thus make further application of multivariate technique legitimate.

It is, of course, inappropriate to include zero values in the calculation of mean latencies, rise times, or half recovery times, and for that reason the use of these data in multivariate analyses is apparently not possible

Table 8.1. Correlations between Components of the SCR to an Initial Orienting Stimulus. (Subjects: 11-Year-Old Children. Max. N = 260.)

	Level	Latency	Rise Time	Amplitude	1/2 Recovery Time	1/2 Recovery Rate	Recruitment
Level		−.14	−.01	.33	−.12	.34	.47
Latency			.25	−.12	.18	−.16	−.18
Rise time				.17	.54	−.18	−.13
Amplitude					.12	.67	.86
1/2 Recovery time						−.23	−.02
1/2 Recovery rate							.80
Recruitment							

without prior reduction. Part of the reason for employing factor analytic technique with magnitude data is to provide material that would allow grouping of responses, so that, for instance, the sixty response measures available from the Mauritian material might be reduced by at least a factor of ten (Venables, 1978). Therefore a mean recovery or rise time measure might be allowable for each subject or each group of responses derived by analysis of magnitude data, which would thus make possible the use of this component in multivariate analysis.

Another approach, one used successfully by Mednick et al. (1978), is to use a rationally derived index that summarizes a large amount of data. In this instance the index is the product of recovery rate and responsiveness, where *responsiveness* is taken as the percentage of measurable responses in the entire 1962 electrodermal examination. Mean recovery rates were taken from conditioning, tests for conditioning, and extinction testing. It should be noted by reference to Table 8.1 that recovery rate is related both to amplitude and to recovery time; thus in this usage, where an "overall" index is required, recovery rate is to be considered a useful way of combining data from these two relevant sources. Data from Mauritius (Venables, 1978) show that a close analog of this measure appropriate for those data and called "recovery rate index" was more reliable than other "cleaner" measures that had been used. In a similar way an appropriately calculated "recruitment index" might prove useful in practice but apparently has not so far been used.

Cardiac Data.   As described in the section on heart rate, it is recommended that cardiac rate data be analyzed on the basis of interbeat intervals (IBIs) calculated in real time. This procedure necessitates the use of a laboratory minicomputer to detect R-wave peaks from the analog recorded EKG, to time IBIs, and to calculate IBI values at time intervals and record the result on digital tape. The process is facilitated by a program that includes a blanking period after the R-wave to inactivate the system from operation by a following T-wave. The advantage of using a computer-based system rather than a hardware blanking technique is that the blanking period may be made variable by including a set of tabled values that may be used to vary the blanking period as the HR changes. It may also be useful to top-cut filter the EKG before A–D conversion to minimize muscle artifact. The amplitude spectrum of the EKG has its maximum value between 5 and 20 Hz, whereas most muscle activity lies in the frequency range above 20 Hz. The eventual analysis of the digitized data may then be carried out on a minicomputer or preferably on a large general-purpose computer, with its greater speed.

Three approaches to analysis are possible: (1) analysis of critical points in the phasic heart rate change record; (2) the application of analysis of variance of trends, taking into account more than critical points in the record; and (3) time series analysis. The first is advocated by Gatchel and Lang (1973) and is in some ways analogous to the analysis of skin conductance data insofar as it involves searching for aspects of the cardiac response within certain latency windows.

The points of interest to be identified are:

B — base-line sample (average IBI two seconds prestimulus),

D_1 — longest IBI during the first two seconds after stimulus onset,

A — shortest IBI subsequent to D_1 and within the first five seconds after stimulus onset,

D_2 — subsequent longest IBI before the eighth second after stimulus onset.

Bull and Lang (1972) describe nine possible measures derived from these indices but suggest that the most important are $A-D_2$, shown to be an index of habituation, and $B-D_1$ and $B-D_2$, reflecting deceleratory trends and as such associated with attentional behavior.

Wilson (1974) has developed a series of computer programs, under the acronym CARDIVAR, concerned with the trend analysis of cardiac data. It is possible to see a use for these programs in studies where specific groups of subjects may be identified and group differences in the shape of cardiac response curves may be anticipated. However, if, as is so often the case in longitudinal work, data reduction of material from individual subjects is required for subsequent entry into a multivariate analysis, then the points-of-interest type of analysis developed by Lang and his colleagues is probably more appropriate.

The major difficulty with analysis of heart rate data is that rate is constantly varying, and phasic responses as a result of the presentation of a stimulus are to be seen as deviations from a changing rather than steady base line. Furthermore, as each successive cardiac beat is not independent in value from the beat that preceded it, analysis of the data by the use of analysis-of-variance techniques is not strictly legitimate.

Developments in the analysis of cardiac data with the use of time series analysis are therefore important. These have been described by Jones, Crowell, and Kapuniai (1969) and Crowell et al. (1976). In the analysis proposed, the lack of independence between successive beats is removed by means of autoregression, where each observation is predicted from past observations. If these predictions are successfully carried out, the difference between predicted and actual observations represents the random or unpredictable component of the observation at any given time. Statistical tests can then be used on these random differences. The Jones, Crowell, and Kapuniai (1969) model uses a first-order autocorrelation procedure. This model has been developed by Lobstein (1978) and is reported to cope successfully with the variability in heart rate arising from sinus arrhythmia and other sources.

The output from the program CHANT that carries out the appropriate analyses is in the form of "t" values, which give the significance of the differences between predicted and observed values at a particular time. These t values can be used to form a "response" curve and consequently can be used in a points-of-interest type of analysis such as that developed by Lang and his colleagues and described earlier. In this case, however, the data adequately take account of prestimulus variations in base line, and values at points of interest are differences that may be unequivocally ascribed to stimulus effects. The amount of data generated is still large, however, and further reduction is probably necessary to achieve a limited set of indices capable of informatively describing a subject's cardiac response characteristics.

EEG Data.   The precedents for the use of electroencephalography in longitudinal studies of populations at risk are few. Itil et al. (1974), in the only major study that appears to be available, provide a basis for work in this area in their opening sentence: "Even though no pathognomonic EEG characteristics for schizophrenia have been discovered, two major types of EEG findings have been identified in the past 40 years as seen frequently in schizophrenic patients." In a series of studies, however, including the one just quoted, Itil et al. (1972, 1974, 1976), using visual evaluation of EEG records and computer analysis of the same material, showed that in adult schizophrenics and psychotic children, in addition to the children at risk for schizophrenia, there was evidence of slower, faster, and less activity in the alpha band than in the EEG frequency spectrum of normal subjects. This type of finding suggests that spectral analysis of the data is a useful procedure. In addition the data showed that the children at risk evinced less amplitude variability than normal, a finding in line with that of Goldstein et al. (1963, 1965), who used the Drohocki (1948) type of integration of EEG activity.

The choice of available techniques for analyzing EEG activity is, however, large and growing, as indicated by a recent review edited by Rémond (1977). The sensible approach at this time would appear to be to obtain the best recordings of EEG technically possible, to analyze them by a suitable but not too time-consuming range of techniques, and to be in a position to make use of suitable developments in analytic techniques as they become available.

Additionally, because experience with particular techniques is to be sought in the laboratories that are best equipped to deal with them from both a software and a hardware point of view, it would appear to be a suitable strategy to make recordings of data freely available to other workers if they have the capacity for making use of the material. Developments in classification of subjects by processes of numerical taxonomy of brain functions under the title of "neurometrics" have been generated by John and his colleagues (John et al., 1977). The possibilities offered by these techniques in the longitudinal field need to be explored. However, the analytic processes involved will clearly not be available in smaller laboratories, and the cooperation of larger laboratories may be required if more general use is made of the procedures.

Itil et al. (1974) also employed event-related potential techniques in their study. In spite of a somewhat pessimistic view of the present use of these techniques, which was the outcome of a "benchmark" conference on the area in Virginia in 1977 (Callaway, Tueting, and Koslow, 1978), Itil and his colleagues do appear to have suggested that high-risk children differ from normal ones by having shorter AER latencies. Perhaps the most important feature of this type of work for longitudinal studies is that it results in a relatively limited set of indices for each subject, thus allowing the comparison of this sort of data with epidermological material to be made more readily.

FUTURE DEVELOPMENTS

Certain promising areas of work appear not to have been used in longitudinal risk studies. Depending on facilities available, it may be worthwhile adopting some of these in future work.

Smooth-Pursuit Eye Movements

Holzman and Shagass and their colleagues (e.g., Holzman, Levy, and Proctor, 1976; Shagass, Roemer, and Amadeo, 1976) have shown that the EOG eye tracking of schizophrenics in following a pendulum target is not smooth but has a "cogwheel" appearance. Instead of smooth pursuit there are velocity arrests, which show up clearly on a differentiated EOG record.

Perhaps the most relevant of Holzman's findings in the present context is that poor eye tracking is found in a large percentage of the otherwise normal relatives of patients. Recent work (Holzman et al., 1977) has suggested on the basis of a twin study that an important part of the variance in eye-tracking performance has a genetic attribution. The technique has the advantage of being simple and takes little time in data gathering, some ten swings of a pendulum providing sufficient material for analysis.

Augmentation-Reduction

Using event-related potential techniques, Buchsbaum and his colleagues (Buchsbaum, 1975, 1976; Landau et al., 1975) have shown that the phenomenon of "reduction" is characteristic of many schizophrenic patients. By *reduction* is meant a paradoxical decrease in components (typically P100–N140) of the visual evoked potential (VEP) as stimulus intensity increases. There are some suggestions on the basis of twin studies of a heritable factor determining this feature of VEP performance.

The advantage of the technique of longitudinal studies is that the procedures involved may, on the basis of the work already reported, be highly standardized and the results expressed as a limited number of variables.

Blood Platelets

If it is feasible in the course of the total investigation to collect a small amount (20 ml) of blood, then the evidence suggests, albeit with some dissenting voices, that the analysis of platelet monoamine oxidase activity and platelet serotonin (5HT) may provide useful leads. There are by now a host of studies in this field, but recent work is represented by Murphy, Donnelly, Miller, and Wyatt (1976), Schildkraut, Herzog, Orsular, Edelman, Shein, and Frazier (1976), and Nies, Robinson, Lamborn, and Lampert (1973). The last study shows that data from twins suggest a heritability of platelet MAO level of 0.83; the Schildkraut et al. (1976) study suggests that reduced platelet MAO activity is characteristic of schizophrenic patients with auditory hallucinations and delusions, but not of other schizophrenics. (It is this subclass of schizophrenics whose breakdown is predicted by skin conductance variables in the Mednick and Schulsinger 1962 study [Mednick et al., 1978].) Platelet MAO activity has been used as a risk indicator in its own right by Buchsbaum, Coursey, and Murphy (1976). These authors screened 375 college students for platelet MAO activity levels. The upper and lower 10 percent were interviewed and family history obtained. Low MAO probands or their families were found to have more frequent psychiatric problems and problems with the law and a higher incidence of suicide or suicide attempts than did high MAO probands. The authors suggest that "reduced MAO levels . . . may predict vulnerability to psychiatric disorder." At a more speculative level, Stahl (1977) suggests that "an analysis of platelet 5HT pharmacodynamics may serve as an appropriate model for determining certain functions of CNS 5HT . . . and . . . promises to generate new insights into several neurologic and psychiatric disorders . . . ."

Laterality

Some time ago Flor-Henry (1974) suggested that there might be evidence of lateralized dysfunction in psychiatric patients. In brief, he suggested that in psychopaths and schizophrenics there may be disorders of the left temporal lobe, whereas there is right-hemisphere involvement in affective disorders. In work using bilaterally measured SCL, Gruzelier (1973) and Gruzelier and Venables (1974) have provided data suggesting left-hemispheric dysfunction in schizophrenics. In psychopaths, Hare (1978) has shown that "high ratings of psychopathy were associated with slow recovery of the skin conductance response, but only with 120 dB fast rise time tones and only in the left hand." Similar work has been conducted by Myslobodsky and Horesh (1978) with depressed patients.

This impetus suggested in 1972 that high-risk investigations then commencing in Copenhagen should employ bilateral measurement of electrodermal activity. The material has not been fully analyzed, but results suggest that there is a tendency for signs of abnormality to be evident in risk groups in left-hand leads (and hence left hemisphere, as evidence suggests ipsilateral connections) but not to the same extent in right-hand leads. It is perhaps noteworthy in this context that the original 1962 Copenhagen study used a left-hand site for recording skin resistance, and the Mauritius data also employed the left hand for skin conductance. Much more work needs to be done in this area to establish the laterality of pathways relating hands to different areas of the brain before a very definite statement can be made.

CONCLUSION

The use of biological measurement in longitudinal research has to be undertaken with a range of constraints in mind. Some of these have already been mentioned and include particularly those concerned with overall design of the project. If, as may well be the case, a large number of subjects have to be tested in a fairly short time, then two things are inevitable: first, only a limited time in the total program will be available for biological measurement; and second, as more than one subject will probably be tested per day, some will be tested in the morning, some in the afternoon, and some before or after other aspects of the study characterized by varying degrees of stressfulness.

Data from Mauritius (Venables et al., 1981) show that in electrodermal and cardiac measurement, significant amounts of variance are attributable to time of day of testing, season of testing, sex of subject, age of subject, race of subject, and interactions among these variables. Clearly one must note, and if necessary take into account, these variables in relation to the major topic of prediction of risk. Because longitudinal research nearly always starts with subjects in childhood, one must take into account states at the time of testing that are due to the age at which the subject is tested and, in line with this, the normal changes in the variable under investigation that may be expected as the child grows older. Thus, for instance, basal heart rate at age 3 may be about 100 beats per minute (in a white population) but will normally fall to about 75 beats per minute by age 15. Similarly about 40 percent of a 3-year-old group may be expected to respond electrodermally to a 75 dB 1,000 Hz tone on its first presentation, and by age 15 about 95 percent of the population will respond to a similar tone.

As is always the case in longitudinal studies, what is measured depends on the theoretical stance of the investigators. However, at this time — several years after the first major attempt to use biological measures in longitudinal research on a large scale — there is available sufficient material to suggest what may be useful variables to include in any study. Possibly the greatest need is to try to settle on a minimal standard set of techniques to be included in all studies, thus attempting to ensure a degree of comparability across studies.

The other major requirement of research in this area is to attempt to overcome some of the bottlenecks in data analysis that have occurred because of inadequate means — in hardware, software, and personnel — to mount analysis immediately after data collection. The present state is that in general such techniques are available, and any future research starts off with the bonus of having built on the hard-won experience of earlier studies.

IV EXAMPLES OF LONGITUDINAL RESEARCH:
Birth, School, and Clinical Cohorts

9 A PROSPECTIVE LONGITUDINAL STUDY OF THE RELATIONSHIP BETWEEN OBSTETRICAL FACTORS AND CNS DAMAGE

Henk J. Huisjes

Obstetricians do their best to prevent adverse effects of the complications of pregnancy and delivery on the fetus and newborn. Nevertheless the incidence of cerebral palsy is about two per thousand, and more than half the cases are of perinatal origin (Woods, 1976). If the concept of a "continuum of reproductive casualty" (Lilienfeld and Pasamanick, 1955) is true, then lowering perinatal mortality may well lead to a rise in the number of children with brain damage. Some doubts are now arising with respect to this concept, based on the observation that infants can develop normally after an extremely complicated perinatal period, such as pre-term birth with severe asphyxia, provided adequate neonatal care was given. In fact one of the greatest feats of medicine in recent decennia has been the steadily rising prospects for low birthweight babies (Davies, 1976). However, it is not at all clear why some children acquire perma-nent and severe cerebral damage after relatively minor perinatal compli-cations, whereas others emerge unharmed from a seemingly disastrous pre-, peri-, and postnatal period.

This contribution could not have been made without the unfailing cooperation of all the members of the Groningen Perinatal Project. I am grateful to Dr. John O'Brien and to Professor Heinz Prechtl for reading the manuscript.

BRAIN DAMAGE IN THE FETUS AND NEWBORN

Pre- and Perinatal Causes

To clarify the issue, we shall have to consider briefly the pre- and perinatal complications known as the most important causes of brain damage in the fetus and newborn. The human brain grows and matures from an early stage of gestation onward, until well into adult life. This process and its vulnerability were described by Dobbing in 1973. During the last trimester of gestation the glial cells are proliferating rapidly, and this continues at a slower rate until the end of the second year after birth. Slowing down of the antenatal growth spurt of the brain may occur in intrauterine growth retardation (defined poorly as a birthweight below a certain centile — for example, the fifth — for gestational age). It may be caused in several ways, one of the most important, from a clinical point of view, being pre-eclampsia. This condition, characterized by hypertension, proteinuria, and edema during the third trimester of pregnancy, is concomitant with vascular pathology leading to insufficient perfusion of the placenta and thereby to a reduction in the supply of nutrients and eventually of oxygen to the fetus. This process results in slowing down of somatic growth, which affects also the fetal brain, although to a lesser extent than most other organs. In extreme cases hypoxia may lead to fetal death.

Thus the fetal nervous system may be damaged in two ways: first, by restricted proliferative growth and a reduced number of glial cells; and second, by "chemical trauma": hypoxia and acidemia. Chemical trauma is especially liable to occur during parturition, when placental circulation is temporarily arrested during uterine contractions, resulting in hypoxia when placental transport capacity has already been limited by disease, such as pre-eclampsia. Other conditions in which hypoxia during delivery can occur are breech presentation, prolapsed cord, and postmaturity. The incidence of mechanical trauma during delivery resulting in cerebral hemorrhage is low nowadays, when an adequate standard of obstetrical care can be provided.

Notwithstanding the greatly improved prognosis of low birthweight babies, preterm birth is a third notable variable associated with brain damage. Causes of spontaneous preterm birth are rarely known, and thus the contribution of preexisting conditions can hardly be estimated. The difficulties of neonatal adaptation to extrauterine life are, however, well known. They arise as a consequence of the immaturity of a large number of enzyme systems, the most conspicuous of which is that involved in the formation of surfactant by the alveolar cells of the fetal lung. The earlier birth occurs, the more serious are the problems to be expected. Few neonates survive birth prior to the twenty-eighth week of pregnancy.

That prematurity, growth retardation, and hypoxia are important factors in the causation of brain damage is substantiated by several studies. The relationship between these factors and neonatal neurological abnormality found in the Groningen Perinatal Project will be discussed later. Not all children with brain damage, however, were born underdeveloped, preterm, and/or hypoxic. Some of them, of course, have congenital anomalies or inborn errors of metabolism. Others are victims of such more or less rare congenital infections as toxoplasmosis of cytomegaly. As mentioned before, birth trauma is now relatively rare. Diseases acquired during childhood, such as encephalitis, are responsible for other cases of brain damage.

Of special interest are those cases in which no cause can be found. This may partly be due to the fact that obstetrical and neonatal data may be inaccurate or even completely lacking; but even where well-kept patient records are available, frequently no indication of pre- or perinatal complications is found in retrospective studies. There are three possible explanations for this situation:

1. There is an unrecognized postnatal cause.
2. There is a congenital anomaly not accessible for existing diagnostic techniques.
3. There are single or multiple pre- and perinatal factors as yet unrecognized as causes of damage to the fetal nervous system.

In the present discussion it will be the third possibility, together with the three major obstetrical causes mentioned above, that will concern us principally.

Obstetrical management of both "normal" and high-risk pregnancy and delivery must aim at preventing not only (the effects of) growth restriction, preterm birth, and hypoxia but also (of) those lesser known complications liable to affect the developing fetal nervous system. A prerequisite for attaining this goal is insight into the relationship between these variables on the one hand and the condition of the nervous system in the neonatal period and in later childhood on the other hand. The neonatal period is of specific interest in this respect because the relationship with pre- and perinatal circumstances is likely to be stronger then than at a later age when intercurrent diseases and environmental influences have made their impact on development.

Pre- and Perinatal Variables

The extremely complicated processes resulting in the birth of the fetus reveal themselves to the clinician in a very indirect way. There is a great distance between brain growth and increase in size of the uterus as palpated by the obstetrician. Yet the two are related, and apart from serial ultrasound measurements of the fetal biparietal diameter, too cumbersome to carry out in each of a few thousands of gravidae, there is no way for the obstetrician to get more direct information on brain growth during pregnancy. Chemical derangements constituting a potential threat to the brain can be measured during and after delivery by blood gas analysis, not in blood samples from the cerebral blood vessels, but from such remote sources as the fetal scalp during, and the umbilical artery and vein after, delivery. Symptoms such as vomiting during pregnancy, uterine blood loss early in pregnancy, and even hypertension or intra-uterine growth retardation may be found related to later dysfunction of the brain without having any relevance for obstetrical management, since symptoms, but not the causes of the abnormality, may be influenced.

It is only natural that most investigators have sought the causative role played by such common final variables as growth retardation in the neonate (representing all processes restricting multiplication and differentiation of nervous cells), preterm birth (for disturbed maturation), or neonatal asphyxia (for acute or subacute chemical trauma), and that in most studies the effect of these entities is clear. Even now, however, the discussion goes on as to whether the deleterious effect of being born too early is more harmful than that of being born too small, or whether the reverse is true. Even more important, it is by no means clear why some growth-retarded, preterm, or asphyxiated infants survive unscathed while others die or remain crippled for the rest of their lives. Perhaps it is to this question that longitudinal studies must seek the answers. From Prechtl's (1968) work it has become clear that reduced optimality of pre- and perinatal health is more often associated with brain damage than is any single adverse event, even one serious enough in itself to cause injury. In our follow-up study of children born to mothers with severe hypertensive disease of pregnancy, we reached the same conclusion: there may be a direct influence of the hypertensive disease in pregnancy on the function of the fetal nervous system, but this relationship is by far exceeded by the effect of the whole gamut of associated complications (Huisjes et al., 1975). To be able to adjust obstetric and pediatric management, it is necessary to recognize the associated factors better than we do at present.

Parameters of the Condition of the Nervous System

It is notoriously difficult to get an insight from the literature into the late sequelae of pre- and perinatal complications. This is mainly due to the lack of consistency in the parameters chosen. Often no distinction is made between low birthweight caused by preterm birth and by intrauterine growth retardation, although the consequences of both for the organism are fundamentally different.

The function of the nervous system may be tested in a variety of ways, ranging from purely somatic neurological examination to IQ measurement. In order to reduce the disturbance caused by intercurrent disease, it is imperative that the test or tests used for a longitudinal study be equally applicable in the neonatal period and in later childhood. For obvious reasons this excludes IQ and a number of other tests. In the second place, in studies concerning the relationship between pre- and perinatal circumstances and the development of the nervous system, emphasis should be placed on those aspects of the nervous system least subject to environmental factors. Intercurrent diseases and social circumstances will always provide "noise" and must be accounted for as far as possible, but the distorting effect is more marked when the examination techniques used are directed at behavioral aspects of the function of the nervous system. In the third place, the choice of the parameter or parameters is at least partly dependent on the purpose of the study. When the relationship with pre- and perinatal circumstances is sought, it is less important that an integral qualitative picture of all the aspects of the central nervous system be obtained, even though this of course represents more the well-being of the individual than any partial aspect. On the contrary, it is essential that the parameter used be quantifiable and that subsequent measurements in the same individual be comparable. In other words, a usable test could very well be an "abstraction" of nervous function, such as biochemical or morphological measurement.

It has been the merit of Prechtl and his group to standardize neurological examination of the full-term newborn and of older children. Extensive manuals of the methods have been published (Prechtl, 1977; Touwen, 1976). In previous studies it was shown that there existed a good relationship between the obstetrical optimality score and the neurological findings in the newborn (Prechtl, 1968). Moreover, the prognostic value of the neonatal results for neurological findings at 2 to 4 years was high. Even though some aspects of the function of the central nervous system are not covered, it appears that this rigorously standardized examination technique very well serves the purpose of studying the relationship between the pre- and perinatal circumstances and the development of the nervous system.

THE GRONINGEN PERINATAL PROJECT

Purpose and Scope

The Groningen Perinatal Project started in 1975 as a collaborative enterprise of the Departments of Obstetrics, Developmental Neurology, and Pediatrics of the University Hospital, Groningen, the Netherlands. The objective of the project is prevention of damage to the developing nervous system and limitation of the sequelae of damage once it has occurred by (1) improvement of obstetrical and neonatal care and (2) early recognition and referral for treatment of children with neurological abnormalities.

The main questions asked were: What is the relationship between pre- and perinatal conditions on the one hand and neonatal and later abnormalities of the nervous system on the other hand? More specifically, are there any variables that, in association with the commonly known causes of brain damage, such as preterm birth, growth retardation, and asphyxia, make them more likely to result in neurological syndromes than when these causes occur alone? Are there other, hitherto unknown variables or combinations of variables resulting in brain damage?

All the infants born at the Department of Obstetrics, University Hospital, Groningen, the Netherlands, were subjects of the study. Unlike most large obstetrical units outside the Netherlands, this department does not serve an unselected population. About half the patients are booked as cases for the teaching unit. The other half is made up of patients referred for advanced obstetrical care and the relatively few patients referred for acute assistance during delivery. Thus the population ranges from normal pregnancies and deliveries to seriously abnormal ones. Due to the high percentage of home deliveries — about 40 percent — in the region, normal pregnancies are underrepresented, as are acute complications during labor, which are preferably referred to other hospitals. Although the local population is not truly represented, a wide range of cases, from normal to highly pathological, is present. This was considered advantageous for the purpose of the study.

The first cohort of some 1,500 newborns was examined between 1 July 1975 and 31 December 1976. Since then a second cohort has been examined, but the results have not been evaluated as yet. All term-born children were examined as soon as possible after the third day of life.

Preterm infants were examined at the time their gestational age would have been about 40 weeks. The examination was carried out according to the standardized method described by Prechtl (1977) by two research physicians.

All children found neonatally abnormal are being reexamined at the age of 18 months, together with a control group of neonatally "optimal" children. The same group will be followed up until at least 4 years of age. Apart from this main body of subjects, a smaller group of children, born both growth retarded and asphyxiated, and a selection of neurologically suspect newborns are being reexamined. Both reexaminations are carried out according to a standardized procedure, described by Touwen (1976).

In the organization of both neonatal and later examinations, the importance of completeness was emphasized. This resulted in the loss of only forty subjects at the neonatal examination, only three of them by refusal to cooperate, the rest for technical reasons, such as early discharge from the hospital. At the first follow-up examination not one child had dropped out, except for one who had died from multiple congenital anomalies. Several hundreds of obstetrical, neonatological, and neurological variables were collected and stored on magnetic tape.

Methods of Analysis and Some Preliminary Results

For a preliminary analysis of the relationship between pre- and perinatal factors and neonatal neurological findings, the 1,507 infants from single pregnancies, born in the first cohort and examined in the neonatal period, were divided into five categories: growth retarded (below the tenth centile for birthweight), acidotic ($pH_{v.umb.}$ < 7.20), both growth retarded and acidotic, not growth retarded and not acidotic, and pH unknown. This categorization was made separately for full-terms and preterms.

Acidemia was almost twice as frequent in full-term growth-retarded infants (18.0 percent) as in full-term infants with an appropriate weight for gestational age (9.6 percent). In preterms the difference was slightly larger. Sixty-eight (4.8 percent) of the 1,431 full-terms examined were considered neurologically abnormal. Infants who were both growth retarded and acidemic had the highest frequency of abnormality (17.2 percent), followed by growth retarded (9.8 percent) and acidemics-only (6.5 percent). The control group of normal-weight children without acidemia showed the lowest incidence of neurologic abnormalities (3.4 percent) (Table 9.1). In the preterm children the percentage of abnormals was

Table 9.1. Neonatal Neurological Abnormality in Relation to Acidemia and Growth Retardation. (Overall Incidence of Abnormality = 5.3%.)

	Full-Term		Preterm		
	Total No.	Abnormal (%)	Total No.	Abnormal (%)	Total
Control	1008	3.4	42	14	1050
Acidemic	107	6.5	5	(20)	112
Growth retarded	132	9.8	13	(15)	145
Acidemic and growth retarded	29	17.2	6	(33)	35
Unknown	155	5.8	10	(10)	165
Total	1431	4.8	76	16	1507

much higher: 16 percent. Although the numbers are smaller, the distribution over the groups seems to follow roughly the same pattern as in the full-terms. The results confirm the role played by growth retardation, preterm birth, and asphyxia in the causation of dysfunction of the neonatal nervous system.

In the second approach a detailed analysis is made of each case history of both the abnormal and the control group in order to detect whether different obstetrical or neonatological management might have influenced the outcome. The results of this analysis are published extensively elsewhere (Huisjes et al., 1980; Jurgens-van der Zee et al., 1979; Touwen et al., 1980).

SPECIFIC PROBLEMS IN CONNECTION WITH FOLLOW-UP STUDIES OF NEWBORNS

Analysis of Data

Neurological function in the neonate and older child can be relatively clearly defined, provided one chooses standardized and comparable parameters. The situation with regard to obstetrical and neonatological data is much more complicated. In the Groningen OBDAT-data base, which functions as the source of obstetrical variables for the Groningen Perinatal Project, 191 obstetrical variables concerning each gravida delivered are routinely stored. Many more could have been collected and are of possible relevance to the problem. Nevertheless it was the most practical way to use the extant file, supplemented with some data obtained specifically for the purpose of the study a few days after delivery and with the neonatological data.

Among the possible ways to analyze the relationships between pre- and perinatal variables on the one hand and the developmental neurological findings on the other is the one devised by Prechtl. He used an optimality score for both the obstetrical and the neurological data and studied the relationships between the two scores. An optimality score is the number of a group of predefined optimal conditions present in a given case. This approach is extremely suitable for studying the structure of an existing relationship. However, it offers little opportunity to recognize specific situations leading to neurological dysfunction, which are amenable to clinical management.

This purpose is served even less by statistical procedures, such as correlation matrices of factor analysis carried out on the whole material. In general, the sheer mass of data, accumulated in a computer file, tends to distract from reality. By finding correlations, profiles, and factors, insight in what really happened may be deepened, but the usefulness of such results is determined by numerical limitations. They will not lead to the recognition of rarely occurring variables leading to damage to the fetal or neonatal nervous system unless the investigation is carried out on a huge scale.

Even in the most favorable of circumstances, statistical analysis will not be the ideal procedure to reveal why in a certain clinical situation a particular decision was or was not made. The nature of obstetrical management is such that it is just this kind of question that has to be answered: should elective Caesarean section be performed or should a trial of labor be allowed first? Should labor be induced as early as possible in intrauterine growth retardation or not? Solutions to these problems will not often be found by analyzing the data base. Perhaps they can be extracted from the patient records, although anyone who has ever studied those documents will recall moments of exasperation. Nevertheless in addition to studying the optimality scores, analyzing specific groups of cases, and applying statistical procedures to the whole material, we undertook a detailed study of the histories of selected cases.

On the basis of the patient records, an accountability analysis was carried out (Birch et al., 1970). The extent to which the pre- and perinatal periods were disturbed was defined according to criteria known from the literature to be related to brain damage. In any case answering one or more of these criteria, it was assumed that brain damage, if present, was caused by the abnormalities found. This left us with a residual group of neurologically abnormal children in whom no such severely adverse circumstances could be found. In a way, this is the most interesting group, but on the other hand, preliminary results have shown that serious late sequelae are almost exclusively found in the first group. Possibly the second group is characterized by transient influences leading to neonatal morbidity of short duration. This possibility is currently being examined.

Completeness of Follow-up

A second problem pertaining to longitudinal studies in general is the attrition rate. In most studies of postnatal development, follow-up rates vary between 50 and 70 percent. This percentage is largely determined by the amount of energy one is willing or able to spend on keeping in contact with moving families. Another important factor is the motivation of the subjects — in this case, the parents of the subjects. Clearly the design of the study is of importance. Prospective projects such as ours, where the subject can be followed from the time of entering the study, have an advantage over those in which follow-up is based on retrospective selection. Even there, in our experience from another project, it is possible by motivation and proper techniques of tracing to achieve a high rate of follow-up. The size of the project has some importance, as will be discussed later.

The consequences of incomplete follow-up are difficult to assess completely. There is always a reason for dropout, be it through moving out of the area, unwillingness to cooperate, or failure to trace the subject. Higher social classes are more mobile, socially backward people often lack a permanent address, and locating adopted children is often difficult. As some important obstetrical variables, such as preterm birth, tend to be associated with socioeconomic circumstances, incomplete follow-up may very well introduce bias.

From the beginning of the project we therefore gave high priority to complete follow-up. Circumstances were advantageous in that Holland is a small country, so that even families who moved to the opposite side of the country could be visited. Another favorable factor is the apparently growing interest among the general public in the safety of pregnancy and birth. The reduction of family size is accompanied by more attention to the more subtle aspects of well-being of the children once they are born. Each mother was approached by the nurse of the ward on the first day after delivery, and neurological examination of her baby was offered. She received a questionnaire in which additional information was asked (for example, smoking during pregnancy, hereditary disease). The mother was invited to be present at the examination on the fourth postpartum day. This was possible because most women stay in the hospital for seven days after childbirth. During the procedure explanation was given to the mothers both voluntarily and on request. The mothers were informed of the results of the examination even if not normal. In that case, reexamination within a short period was arranged.

A traveling allowance for one adult was offered to the parents of the children selected for reexamination at 18 months. They were approached by letter, and if this appeared to be undeliverable, the help of the registrar's office was called in. In the case of refusal or failure to react, a personal call by one of the staff members was arranged. The follow-up at 18 months is still going on, but apart from one child who died from congenital anomalies, none of the 264 subjects due for examination has fallen out definitively. This includes 80 controls, who were told that there was no reason, other than scientific interest, for their coming to the hospital.

The main factors making this study possible were motivation of the staff, collaboration of the registrar's offices, and motivation of the subjects' parents. This aspect of longitudinal studies has been discussed by Dallas (1971), whose list of "ingredients in successful sample maintenance" is in almost complete agreement with ours (Table 9.2).

Change of Management over Time

The second objective of our study, early recognition and referral for treatment of children with neurological abnormalities, from a theoretical point of view, might influence the study in an improper way. Treatment

Table 9.2. Ingredients in Successful Sample Maintenance.

1. Resources
    a. Staff with clear-cut responsibility for this area
    b. Attractive, convenient physical facilities
    c. Transportation of patients to clinic
2. High Quality Work
    a. Accounting with respect to examinations due
    b. Information on current name and address of patients, tracing of movers
    c. Careful patient examinations at all levels and discussion of findings with parents
3. Proper Motivation
    a. "Selling study" required for patients
    b. Research use of data required for staff teamwork

Source: After Dallas, 1971.

hopefully influences the natural course of the disease and may thereby obscure the real extent of brain damage. But it is not so much the natural course of neurological abnormalities that interests us as their nature and severity in relation to pre- and perinatal circumstances.

More serious is the fact that the natural course of pregnancy, delivery, and neonatal period is altered by obstetrical and neonatological care, and this cannot in any way be avoided. Thus one of the main characteristics of a longitudinal investigation of pre- and postnatal development is that medical treatment is an essential variable. The question must therefore not be, does this or that complication of pregnancy contribute to the causation of brain damage in the child, but, does this or that complication, *treated in such or such a way,* contribute to the causation of brain damage? To some of the consequences of this principle referral is made above.

In long-term follow-up studies, the greatest problem is perhaps not even the fact of treatment as such, but the change in therapeutic schemes over the years. This is most clearly visible in the effect of changing neonatological practice on the survival of low birthweight children and on the proportion of brain-damaged children among the survivors at school age. Late sequelae can only be evaluated six to eight years post dato. In the meantime treatment in all probability has changed — for instance, because new diagnostic or therapeutic tools have become available, or because the *short-term* effects of treatment have induced new views. The results of long-term follow-up in this field, therefore, are necessarily outdated. Changes in social attitude may influence pregnancy outcome even more than do changes in medical management.

Thus the purpose of the project, the prevention of damage to the nervous system, will be served by short-term feedback and therefore by registration of neonatal neurological morbidity. This statement is subject to the condition that there be a correlation between neonatal neurological findings and late sequelae. This has been demonstrated by Prechtl in his earlier work. From the preliminary results it has appeared that follow-up is nevertheless necessary, as by far the majority (more than 80 percent) of neonatally abnormal children will recover. The interpretation in terms of clinical severity of neonatal abnormality depends largely on the late sequelae.

Scale of the Project

Large-scale studies, investigating several thousands of subjects, have several drawbacks, the most important being perhaps the lack of consis-

Table 9.3. Scale of Study.

	Large (5,000)	Medium (500–5,000)	Small (500)
Reliability of data	−	+	+ +
Statistical validity of results	+ +	+	±
Possibility of studying many variables	+	±	−
Adequate control group	+ +	+	−
Observer bias	− ?	±	+
Consistency of interpretation of examination	−	+	+ +
Staff motivation	−	+ +	+ +
Patient motivation	−	+	+

tency and reliability of data and the high attrition rate. On the other hand, very small studies lack the possibility of adequate control groups, as inevitable differences in other than study variables fail to be evened out (Table 9.3).

Medium-sized samples appear attractive because they lack most of the drawbacks of both large- and small-scale studies, although one disadvantage remains: the number of cases is too small for rare associations to become evident. Thus in our study it will be difficult to evaluate the significance of more than twenty to thirty pre- and perinatal variables. We hope to compensate for this by studying individual cases in depth. This explorative approach limits the validity of the results, but this will hopefully be balanced by the reliability and completeness of the data. A difficulty encountered in a relatively small project with frequent reexaminations carried out by a few investigators is the inevitable foreknowledge present when children with a notable obstetrical and/or neonatal history are reexamined. Preterm infants hospitalized for weeks in a neonatal unit before being examined at the gestational age of 40 weeks are not only seen in a different environment but are also marked as being more probably abnormal than term infants. This bias can only be overcome by a rigorously standardized examination technique, but even then some bias will remain present.

10 TWELVE-YEAR FOLLOW-UP STATUS OF LOW BIRTHWEIGHT INFANTS

Bengt Zachau-Christiansen
and Birgitte R. Mednick

The Danish prospective longitudinal perinatal project was begun in 1959 and is still in progress. The subjects for this project constitute a complete birth cohort; that is, all deliveries that took place at the State University Hospital of Copenhagen (Rigshospitalet) between 1959 and 1961 (N = 9,125). This paper describes a twelve-year follow-up study of a subsample of low birthweight (LBW) infants drawn from the cohort. The central purpose of the follow-up study is to compare the incidence of later mental retardation, reading disabilities, and emotional maladaptations of low birthweight infants with that of a randomly selected control group. In addition, the interactive influence of socioeconomic status (SES) on the relationship between low birthweight and the specified outcome variables is described. This study is a minor analysis presented as a context for the description of the perinatal cohort and as an illustration of the follow-up.

The Danish Perinatal Study was carried out under the guidance of Professors P. Plum and D. Trolle. In addition, Professors E. Rydberg, E. Brandstrup, and F. Fuchs gave expertise and support in the planning phase as well as during the data-collection phase. Professor B. Zachau-Christiansen and A. Villumsen, M.D., served as project directors and also carried out the medical examinations of the pregnant women and their children.

DESCRIPTION OF THE DANISH PERINATAL PROJECT

The first author was one of the original collaborators on the Danish project and played an active role in the planning as well as the initial data collection phase. During this phase, data on the pre-, peri-, neonatal, and one-year status of the subjects were collected (detailed description of the data collection is presented below). During the intervening years — that is, between the termination of the original data collection and the present time — a large amount of follow-up research has been done with this sample. The studies completed so far have involved specially selected subgroups of the cohort defined in terms of social and/or medical variables and followed up to various age levels (Kaad and Hesselholdt, 1976; Kyng, 1974; Lier and Michelsen, 1978; Mednick and Michelsen, 1977; Mednick et al., 1971; Kruse et al., 1975).

DESCRIPTION OF THE DANISH COHORT

The Danish Perinatal Project was begun in 1959 at the maternity department of the State University Hospital (Rigshospitalet) in Copenhagen. All deliveries (over 20 weeks gestation) that took place in this hospital between September 1959 and December 1961 were included in the study. A set of tightly controlled data collection procedures was employed by the original project collaborators (Zachau-Christiansen and Ross, 1975). The pregnant women were contacted and examined before delivery as early in pregnancy as possible, during attendance at the hospital's antenatal clinic. To evaluate and code the social, general medical, and obstetrical histories of the women uniformly, all prenatal examinations were done by the same physician. In addition to an obstetrician, midwives and midwife trainees were present in the delivery room and assisted in collecting the data describing the deliveries and the status of the neonates and mothers immediately after birth. In those cases where the general condition permitted, the live-born infants were again examined on the first and fifth day after delivery by one of three pediatricians. The first- and the fifth-day examinations included a physical examination and a thorough neurological assessment of the infant. Upon discharge from the hospital the mothers (or guardians) of the infants received a self-administered questionnaire related to the infants' developmental progress during the first year of life. Information concerning attendance to the free national infant health examination, intercurrent diseases, admission to hospitals and other institutions, and records of immunizations was also obtained. When the children reached their first birthday, the mothers were asked to bring them to the pediatric outpatient department of the State University Hospital for a special developmental examination. A team of three pediatricians conducted the follow-up examinations for all the surviving infants. Maximum effort was made also to include all surviving infants in the one-year follow-up. In cases where the parents were not able to bring the child to the hospital, home visits were arranged. All the information collected — the anamnesis of the pregnant women and the descriptions of the pregnancies, deliveries, and neonatal and one-year status of the infants — was precoded.

Representativeness

The Danish perinatal sample cannot be considered a representative sample of pregnant Danish women. The differences between this sample and the general Danish population of prospective mothers are related to (1) medical risks, (2) social background of subjects, and (3) the medical treatment to which the subjects were exposed.

Medical Risks. The Danish perinatal sample contains a higher than normal rate of problem pregnancies and deliveries. The State University Hospital, Rigshospitalet, is a unit of the University of Copenhagen and is also the country's largest center for medical research and progressive treatment of patients. It is therefore not surprising that a larger percentage of difficult births are referred to this hospital. During the period 1959 to 1961, the hospital system of Denmark was still so centralized that women from all the eastern parts of the country who were suffering grave complications in pregnancy or who were expected to present difficult deliveries would likely be referred to Rigshospitalet's obstetrical department. As an example of the elevated complication rate, the incidence of prematurity (that is, birthweight under 2,500 grams) was over 18 percent in the Danish perinatal sample, or about three times the incidence found in the general Danish population during the years in question.

Social Background. Women in the Danish perinatal sample experienced a higher rate of unwed motherhood and a lower average SES compared with representative samples of pregnant Danish women. This is likely due to the fact that Rigshospitalet is located in the center of the city and therefore draws a disproportionate number of patients from the poorer inner-city areas. In addition, there was a traditional tendency during those years to have unwed mothers from Copenhagen give birth at Rigshospitalet.

Medical Treatment. The quality of treatment received by pregnant women in the general population is known to vary as a function of such variables as SES, age of mother, area of residence, degree of wantedness of pregnancy, and so on (Kessner et al., 1973; Chamberlain et al., 1975; Pharoah, 1976). However, these factors did not influence the quality of treatment to which the subjects of the Danish perinatal sample had access. Irrespective of social or personal background, prospective mothers received prenatal care. During delivery, as well as during the postnatal period, all patients in the study sample were attended by highly trained medical personnel using the most advanced equipment available for the treatment of both mother and infant.

While the characteristics of the Danish perinatal sample influence the generalizability of incidence rates to the total Danish population, the data from the sample do present unusual possibilities for analyses of generalizable relationships between pre- and perinatal conditions and later outcomes in groups well defined in terms of social and medical variables. This type of follow-up research is especially facilitated in Denmark by the National Population Register. The register makes it possible for researchers to collect longitudinal data over the entire life of the subject irrespective of residence or name changes, and the like. Thus the methodological advantages inherent in prospective longitudinal research in general are further enhanced in the Danish Perinatal Project by increased continuity of data collection and a much diminished subject loss over time.

Comparability to American Samples

The white subsample of the American Collaborative Project is an analogous sample to the Danish cohort. That is, like the Danish cohort, the American sample possesses a greater incidence of mothers who are young, low SES, and at some medical risk when compared with representative U.S. samples (Niswander and Gordon, 1972). The comparability of the American and Danish studies has been further demonstrated by Mednick, Baker, and Sutton-Smith (1979).

Comparability of LBW Methods of Treatment: 1960 and 1980

The deliveries included in the Danish Perinatal Study took place between September 1959 and December 1961. Since 1960, the prognosis for LBW infants has improved significantly owing to the development of new neonatal treatments (Fitzhardinge and Ramsey, 1973; Rawlings et al., 1971). Implementation of new methods has led to significantly reduced risks associated with prematurity; for example, nonsurvival and long-term negative sequelae. Thus, data obtained prior to 1960 are likely to be limited in terms of their generalizability to the post-1960 or current period. The Danish study was initiated right at the time that the new methods were being introduced, and since the study was conducted within the context of a university hospital, it employed those progressive state-of-the-art medical intervention techniques that characterized the post-1960 practice. Thus the long-term correlates of low birthweight delivery in the Danish sample appear sufficiently analogous to the contemporary situation to be considered generalizable.

FOLLOW-UP OF LOW BIRTHWEIGHT INFANTS TO AGE 12

The total number of low birthweight infants (under 2,500 grams) in the Danish perinatal sample is 1,076. The selection of the sample for the twelve-year follow-up study was based on geographical convenience and socioeconomic representation. School districts within Copenhagen that, in the aggregate, represented the full SES range were selected. A total of 158 males and 191 females of the original Danish cohort were identified as attending one of the school districts at age 12. A control or comparison group (147 males and 147 females) was selected from same-aged children attending the same schools as the LBW children. A schooling control was deemed most appropriate since the outcome measures studied are school related. The birthweights of the children in the control group were not ascertained. However, based on population statistics, it is estimated that less than 6 percent of the control group would be classified as LBW infants. The presence of LBW infants among the controls means that differences observed between controls and LBW children may be viewed as conservative.

RESULTS

Comparisons of the LBW and Randomly
Selected Controls

Incidence of Mental Retardation. Table 10.1 shows the incidence of mental retardation for the LBW and control groups. The LBW group is further divided into subgroups on the basis of the severity of the original LBW condition (Table 10.2). For purposes of this study, mental retardation was operationally defined as the inability to function intellectually (or successfully) in the normal elementary school program. A total of 45 (13 percent) of the LBW group and 4 (1.4 percent) of the "normal" birthweight controls were described as mentally retarded. The difference is statistically and practically significant ($\chi^2_{df_1} = 25.92, p < .001$). Mental retardation was also significantly related to the severity of the LBW condition. The incidence of retardation ranged from 22 percent for children whose birthweight was less than 1,500 grams to 9.2 percent for children who weighed over 2,000 grams at birth ($\chi^2_{df_2} = 7.20, p < .05$). These results correspond to the findings generally reported (Drillien, 1964; Francis-Williams and Davies, 1974).

Reading Deficiency. In the analysis of reading deficiency only the subjects in the normal IQ range were included. Thus the mentally retarded children were excluded. No significant difference in reading deficiency was found between the LBW and control children (21.54 percent of the LBW children and 24.56 percent of the controls were found to be reading deficient). Others have found significant differences in incidence of reading deficiency between LBW infants and randomly drawn controls (Francis-Williams and Davies, 1974; Malmquist, 1973). It should be emphasized that had those children who were known to be incapable of

Table 10.1. Incidence of Mental Retardation for LBW and Control Groups.

Low Birthweight Group			Control Group		
Total	Number Mentally Retarded	Percentage	Total	Number Mentally Retarded	Percentage
349	45	13.1	294	4	1.4
		$\chi^2_{df_1} = 25.92, p < .001$			

Table 10.2. Incidence of Mental Retardation within LBW Subgroups.

LBW Subgroup	Total	Number Mentally Retarded	Percentage
≤ 1,500 g	45	10	22.2
1,501–2,000 g	97	16	16.5
2,001–2,500 g	207	19	9.2
		$\chi^2_{df2} = 7.20, p < .05$	

making normal progress in the mainstream curriculum been retained in the present analysis, the results would have paralleled those of Francis-Williams and Davies and of Malmquist. However, the purpose of this study was to distinguish LBW children who clearly possess scholastic achievement potential from those who do not. In this way it could be determined if, given "threshold" potential, there are any residual or persevering LBW effects on educational progress. It is clear that, severely retarded children aside, the LBW children evidence normal reading ability.

Behavior Disorders.   Children classified as possessing behavior disorders varied greatly in terms of degree of seriousness of the problem. Problems ranged from simple referral of the child to the school psychologist for a behavior problem to actual commitment in a mental hospital. Thirty-four (9.7 percent) of the LBW groups and eleven (3.7 percent) of the control group were found to have such behavior disorders. This difference is statistically significant ($\chi^2_{df1} = 10.0, p < .001$). In contrast to the findings related to mental retardation, the degree of severity of the LBW condition did not show a significant relationship to incidence of behavior disorders ($\chi^2_{df2} = 2.48$). Heightened incidence of behavior disorders during childhood among LBW infants has previously been reported by several researchers (Pasamanick and Knobloch, 1966; Drillien, 1964).

Interaction Effects of SES and Birthweight on the Outcome

In view of the frequently reported finding that the child-rearing environment significantly influences the rate and degree of recovery from perinatal traumas such as low birthweight (Drillien, 1964; Birch and Gussow, 1970; Sameroff, 1975), the incidence of negative long-term consequences was separately examined within and between each SES group (defined in terms of occupation of head of household). Assignment of the subjects to the different SES categories was according to the British five-category system (Classification of Occupations, 1950). Table 10.3 shows the SES distributions within each of the two samples and by birthweight subgroup within the low birthweight sample. Note that the LBW sample contains a disproportionately larger number of cases in the two lowest SES groups (IV, semiskilled, and V, unskilled workers) when compared with the control sample. Drillien (1964) has also noted that prematurity is more frequently noted in lower SES environments.

Mental Retardation. Table 10.4 shows the incidence of mental retardation for each SES group in the LBW sample. Since only four control subjects were classified as mentally retarded, no SES breakdown is presented for the control group. The table indicates that lower SES is associated with increased incidence of school-age mental retardation in the Danish perinatal sample ($\chi^2_{df4} = 13.59$, $p < .01$). To further test the independence of mental retardation from SES, the randomly selected control group was used as the basis for computing the expected frequencies of mental retardation for each SES group. That is, it can be assumed that if mental retardation were independent of SES, the distribution of mental retardation by SES membership would not differ from the SES distribution for the total control cohort. Table 10.5 shows that mental retardation is definitely associated with SES ($\chi^2_{df4} = 29.40$, $p < .01$).

The association of lower SES with increased incidence of mental retardation is relevant to the view presented by Sameroff (1979). Sameroff points out that it is possible to observe a significant negative impact of perinatal trauma on children's cognitive development during early childhood. This influence, however, tends gradually to decrease in significance and, in general, ceases to be observable at the time of school entry. The exception to this rule is constituted by perinatal traumas involving very high levels of organic damage. Sameroff also points out that during the same age period — early childhood — SES-related variables take on more and more importance as predictors of cognitive functioning. In effect, Sameroff is suggesting that if there is no excessive organic damage, improvement of cognitive functioning subsequent to experiencing perinatal trauma is likely so long as the child remains in an environment characterized as supportive, nurturant, and free from pervasively oppressive social conditions.

Results reported from mental retardation studies are congruent with the above. That is, since mental retardation represents a syndrome in

Table 10.3. Distribution of LBW and Control Samples by Socioeconomic Status (SES).

| | Low Birthweight Groups | | | | | | Total | | Control Group | |
| | 1,500 g | | 1,501–2,000 g | | 2,001–2,500 g | | | | | |
SES	N	%	N	%	N	%	N	%	N	%
I (high)	4	8.9	8	8.2	23	11.1	35	10.0	40	13.6
II	6	13.3	15	15.5	39	18.8	60	17.2	72	24.5
III	14	31.1	34	35.1	71	34.3	119	34.1	102	34.7
IV	9	20.0	21	21.6	40	19.3	70	20.1	47	16.0
V (low)	11	24.4	17	17.5	31	15.0	59	16.9	32	10.9
Unknown	1	2.2	2	2.1	3	1.4	6	1.7	1	0.3
Total	45	100.0	97	100.0	207	100.0	349	100.0	294	100.0

Table 10.4. Incidence of Mental Retardation for Each SES Group in LBW Sample.

SES	Number Mentally Retarded	N	Percentage
I	0	35	0
II	4	60	6.7
III	17	119	14.3
IV	10	70	14.3
V	14	59	23.7
Total	45	343*	13.1
	$\chi^2_{df4} = 13.59, p < .01$		

* Six subjects were excluded from this analysis owing to missing SES data.

which severe organic damage is likely to be involved and since such damage is more probable in the LBW group, the LBW group should contain more children with mental retardation. The magnitude of the relationship of SES to mental retardation provides support for the notion that SES-related factors are of critical importance for normal cognitive development. The data indicate that this effect may be powerful enough to impact intellectual outcomes significantly and positively even in cases where organic damage may be expected to be involved.

In view of the fact that low SES is known to be related to increased incidence of prematurity, one could imagine that within the LBW sample

Table 10.5. Frequencies of Mental Retardation for Each SES Group in LBW Sample.

SES	Frequencies	
	Actual	Expected*
I	0	6.13
II	4	11.04
III	17	15.62
IV	10	7.30
V	14	4.91
Total	45	45.00
	$\chi^2_{df4} = 29.40, p < .01$	

* Expected frequencies were computed by using the SES distribution of the randomly selected control group of 293 subjects.

the SES effect, at least in part, could be caused by the highest SES groups' having a disproportionately larger number of cases in birthweight group 3 (over 2,000 grams) and the lowest SES groups' having a higher number of cases in birthweight group 1 (under 1,500 grams). If this type of sample distribution were observed, the relationship between SES and the diagnosis of school-age mental retardation could be explained as being mediated by SES-related differences in severity of prematurity rather than by other SES-related factors such as environmental variations. Table 10.3 shows that the subjects in each SES group are approximately equally distributed across the three birthweight categories. A test for differences in the distributions yielded a nonsignificant $\chi^2_{df12} = 15.03$, n.s. Thus, the heightened retardation rate that covaries with lower SES is likely to be, in part, a function of environmental covariates of SES rather than differential distributions of severity of the original LBW condition between the SES groups.

This discussion does not present evidence relating to the factors mediating the SES-mental retardation relationship. Clearly the relationship may be mediated through genetic factors, environmental factors, or most likely through an interaction of both. It can be said, however, that the data presented do not contradict the very general notions concerning recovery from perinatal trauma presented above; growing up in an economically stable home characterized by middle- or upper-class conditions and values seems conducive to faster and more complete compensation for early organic trauma.

Reading Deficiency.   The group difference in reading proficiency between the LBW and control groups was not statistically significant. The data show a highly significant SES effect on reading deficiency ($\chi^2_{df4} = 38.63, p < .001$). In view of the lack of group difference based on birthweight, this χ^2 analysis for SES effects was performed by pooling the data from the two samples. Inspection of Table 10.6 shows that one exception to the general finding of lower SES's being associated with reading deficiency is presented by social group V in the control sample. An explanation for this exception has not at present been uncovered. The overall strong association between SES and reading deficiency is consistent with the findings of other authors (Rutter et al., 1966; Bronfenbrenner, 1974; Sameroff, 1979).

The pattern of findings produced by the analysis of the data on reading deficiency is also in accordance with Sameroff's hypotheses concerning the significant influences on children's cognitive functioning. Reading deficiency constitutes an etiologically more heterogeneous syndrome than mental retardation; and severe organic damage is in general a more

Table 10.6. Incidence of Reading Deficiency in LBW and Control Groups by SES.

	LBW Groups			Control Group		
SES	Number Reading Deficient	N	Percentage	Number Reading Deficient	N	Percentage
I	3	35	8.6	2	40	5.0
II	12	56	21.4	13	72	18.1
III	20	102	19.6	21	100	21.1
IV	15	60	25.0	31	45	28.9
V	14	44	31.8	4	32	12.5
Total	64	297*	21.5	71	289**	24.6
			$\chi^2_{df4} = 38.63, p < .001$			

* Forty-five LBW subjects were excluded because of mental retardation, and 7 LBW subjects presented missing data.
** Five control subjects presented missing data.

probable factor in the development of the latter syndrome. Thus, according to Sameroff, the birthweight effect on incidence of reading retardation should in this study be insignificant, and SES factors should be the more significant predictor of the child's functioning in reading (as indeed the data show). Again it must be emphasized that the finding of an association between SES and incidence of reading deficiency does not represent any basis for hypothesis formation about the more specific etiological relationships underlying the finding.

Behavior Disorders. Table 10.7 presents the incidence of behavior disorders in the two groups distributed by SES. The table shows a nonsignificant trend in the LBW group for decreasing SES to be associated with increases in incidence of behavior disorders. In the control group no systematic SES relationship may be observed. This trend in the data for the LBW group may again be seen as supportive of the general notion about the importance of a supportive middle- or upper-class environment for recovery from perinatal trauma.

SUMMARY

On the basis of the data presented, it may be concluded that when the total group of LBW infants is compared with the randomly selected

Table 10.7.   Incidence of Behavior Disorders in LBW and Control Groups by SES.

	Low Birthweight			Control		
SES	Number Behavior Disorders	N	Percentage	Number Behavior Disorders	N	Percentage
I	1	35	2.9	1	40	2.5
II	3	60	5.0	5	72	6.9
III	12	119	10.0	5	102	4.9
IV	8	70	11.4	0	47	0.0
V	9	59	15.3	0	32	0.0
Unknown	1	6			1	
Total	34	349	9.7	11	294	3.7

controls, higher incidences of mental retardation and behavior disorders were found among the LBW children. Obviously, if there is an association between birthweight and mental retardation, there will also be a relationship between birthweight and reading deficiency. However, when children diagnosed as unable to compete in the normal curriculum were eliminated from further analysis, incidence of reading deficiency was not related to birthweight. Analyses were performed with the purpose of estimating the interactive influence of SES on this pattern. In the case of the outcome variable — mental retardation — examination of the impact of SES was not possible in the control group owing to the small number of mentally retarded cases. The analysis of the distribution of mentally retarded cases as a function of the SES within the LBW group showed a relationship between decreases in SES and increased incidence of mental retardation. This result pattern is supportive of the well-replicated finding that birth traumas are less easily compensated for under disadvantaged environmental conditions (Drillien, 1964; Birch and Gussow, 1970; Sameroff, 1975). With one exception (for which no explanation readily presents itself) the data on reading deficiency showed a strong relationship between decreasing SES and increasing incidence of reading deficiency. This finding was interpreted as supporting Sameroff's notion of the relatively short-lived predictive significance of perinatal variables as compared with that of SES-related variables for children's higher cognitive functioning (that is, with the obvious exception of cases involving very severe and debilitating organic damage).

The findings resulting from separate examination of the incidence of behavior disorders for each SES group presented different results in the two samples. In the control group no systematic relationship between SES and incidence of behavior disorders was observed. In the LBW group a tendency was noted for lower SES groups to present higher frequencies of disorders. This result pattern was again interpreted to be supportive of the finding reported by other authors: perinatal traumas are less adequately compensated for in disadvantaged environments.

11 THE VALUE OF BIRTH COHORT STUDIES

J. W. B. Douglas

A birth cohort study sets out to describe in depth the characteristics of a generation that is making contact with contemporary medical, educational, and social services; experiencing contemporary living conditions; and absorbing contemporary attitudes toward life. Each generation carries the impress of these encounters, which help to determine its patterns of illness and levels of achievement. The entry of each new cohort provides potentialities for change; the extent to which it shows or fails to show change reflects the success or failure of our policies and our services and the dynamic state of our society.

From this it follows that birth cohort studies can make two types of contribution: scientific and administrative. The scientific contribution is the knowledge they provide on the natural history of disease, on the relation between the development of the individual and the environment in which one lives, and on the changing structure of society. The administrative contribution, which is mainly provided by comparisons between successive cohorts, is the monitoring of new services and new policies so as to show the extent to which these services and policies are reaching the sections of the population for which they were intended and are achieving their goals. Further, birth cohort studies make possible the examination of certain widely held beliefs and so may discourage precipitate and ill-judged political action.

Birth cohort studies should not be regarded as lucky dips from which useful information on any characteristic of a population can be drawn. On occasion they have been the only source of data urgently needed by government committees. But this is a fortunate by-product, and to use the studies as a source of current domestic statistics is to distort and detract from their real function. The proper use of cohort studies is to investigate the relation of events over time, and the particular advantage of birth cohorts is that the study of events can be pushed back to before birth.

THE 1946 BRITISH BIRTH COHORT STUDY

In Great Britain there have been three national birth cohort studies. The first, with which I have been concerned throughout, was the 1946 birth cohort, and the two later cohorts were the 1958 and 1970 ones. The 1946 study was taken as a template for subsequent birth cohort studies in 1958 and 1970, so it is relevant to consider how far its structure was determined by design and how far by outside forces, including the availability of money and staff. In other words, how good a template is it?

The 1946 study was mounted in response to a request from the Royal Commission on Population for answers to certain limited questions about maternity services and the costs of having children. When I started in October 1945 as director of the study, it was clear that a questionnaire inquiry was needed, though its size and scope would depend on who did the interviewing. The late Professor D. V. Glass, at that time a member of the Biological and Medical Committee of the commission, was in favor of asking health visitors (community nurses) to act as our agents. I first contested this proposal because I thought to give them an adequate briefing would be impossible and the quality of information would vary greatly according to the skill and degree of involvement of individual health visitors. There were, however, strong reasons for using them.

During the normal course of their duties, they visited more than 90 percent of the homes where there was a new baby. They had first-hand knowledge of maternity and child welfare services and access to records. They were distributed throughout Great Britain, and their numbers were such that even a large questionnaire inquiry would throw only a small burden on each health visitor. With their help a large national sample could be interviewed, whereas we would otherwise be committed to a smaller study that, although perhaps more detailed and accurate, would not be capable of providing a national description of maternity care. The clinching argument was the small size of our funds, which if used to pay commercial interviewers would have allowed us to collect only a few hundred interviews rather than the several thousand we needed.

The type of sample chosen was determined by limitations of money and time. There were obvious advantages in spreading the sample throughout the year — in taking, for example, six separate days as in the Scottish mental survey follow-up. But if the study lasted for more than two years, our funds (provided by grants from the Nuffield Foundation and the National Birthday Trust Fund) would run out. This meant that the information had to be collected in the first six months in order to have time to process it. Moreover students were the only source of coders, and they were available only in the summer vacation. The bulk of the questionnaires therefore had to be completed by the end of June 1946. For these reasons we decided to take a single week's births. This would yield 15,000 or so interviews, which was just within our resources to analyze. The week of March 3 to 9 was chosen as the earliest time we would be ready to go into the field.

At the end of 1947, when the book on maternity services (Douglas and Rowntree, 1948) was completed, we began to think about the possibilities of continuing to collect medical and social information about this group of children. As our funds were small we decided to cut down numbers in the sample to approximately five thousand, which we felt would be manageable. As we were interested in inequalities of opportunity, it was desirable to retain the whole of the relatively small nonmanual working-class group; otherwise we would be restricted when making comparisons between different educational levels. We also felt that agricultural workers had particular problems and decided to keep them as a complete group. We then took a random one-in-four sample of the remaining manual workers. This gave a total of 5,362 children, of whom approximately half had parents who were nonmanual workers. Illegitimate children and twins were excluded.

It is clear that a sample based on a single week's births carries many biases. Respiratory infections in early infancy, for example, are likely to be fewer among those born in the spring than in the autumn, and so are accidental burns, which are particularly likely to occur when the child is learning to walk: in the 1946 survey, this would have been in the spring and summer, when open fires were seldom used and the children less likely to be cooped up in the kitchen. The season of the year is also important in relation to the age of entering school. Those born between

April and August may have up to a year more primary education than those born between September and December, and the results of this discrepancy may show in later reading and attainment. As it is possible and not unusual to leave school at the statutory leaving age, the date of birth also affects job opportunities for early leavers. From this account it will be seen that any season of the year is likely to have both advantages and disadvantages; however, the advantages predominate for those born in the spring.

The choice of a complete week's births for the maternity survey sample was not arrived at by informed calculation but rather by the limitations of our resources and a guess that the numbers provided would be sufficient to allow regional comparisons and perhaps also comparisons between local maternity and child welfare authorities. The 13,687 in the original sample were in fact too few to give adequate information about any other than the most common illnesses and too few also for detailed local comparisons of morbidity. A much larger sample would have been required if we had wished to study either individual conditions or local peculiarities, and this would have been prohibitively expensive and administratively difficult. On the other hand, if the aim was to assess standards of care in different segments of the population or in different regions or to compare growth, test performance, or educational achievement, then a smaller sample was sufficient. The size of sample chosen for the follow-up, 5,362, still seems to me to have been just about right for our needs. It is small enough for frequent contacts to be possible and for complete checks of hospital admissions, qualifications, and the like, to be asked for without making excessive demands on local resources.

EVALUATION OF BIRTH COHORT STUDIES

If I were to repeat the 1946 study, I would take a six-day sample spread throughout the year. For the whole sample I would get minimal birth information and for the follow-up would divide each day's births into two random groups. One containing about seven thousand members would be followed up in detail; the other of equal size would be used as a control group to show up any biases introduced by the exposure of the main longitudinal sample to repeated interviews, examinations, and tests. The controls would also provide additional information at widely spaced intervals on major and checkable events such as accidents, hospital admissions, and school achievement. By spreading the sample over a year, the dangers of seasonal bias would be avoided. Moreover, the load of examinations and interviewing would be spread evenly, and this would make it reasonable to ask for frequent, perhaps yearly, contacts, whereas with our sample concentrated in one week we were only able to make two yearly contacts.

The fact that all three British birth cohorts are nationally based needs comment, as it might seem that locally based studies would be more satisfactory. There are two practical reasons for preferring a national coverage. First, losses through migration are so high and so selective in local studies that the sample rapidly becomes depleted and distorted. Second, when data are collected by local agents, it helps if the sample is widely spread so that the work is small for any individual health visitor, teacher, or other person involved. There is, however, another consideration that makes me feel national coverage is essential. I believe that the major scientific and administrative contributions will come from a comparison between cohorts. Since local boundaries change and local populations and industries alter, any method of sampling by area will prevent meaningful comparisons from being made between longitudinal studies set even a few years apart.

A frequent criticism of national surveys (Rutter and Madge, 1976) is that they are insensitive to local circumstances and do not provide local perspectives. This is true if we equate local with parochial; that is, when we are concerned with a small area only and do not wish to compare it with surrounding areas or to take account of migration into or out of it. If by local we mean regional, a national cohort provides opportunities to examine variations in, for example, educational achievement, employment, or medical care and can then be related to population movements between the regions.

Little is known about the relations between events occurring at different stages of people's lives. Most of our present theories on, for example, the importance of the early years in personality development are based on clinical and research studies that use remembered data. As Yarrow, Campbell, and Burton (1970) have shown — and indeed as we find in the 1946 study — memory is not only fallible but distorting. Moreover it distorts so as to confirm existing theories and beliefs. Yet these theories — based on fallible and distorted evidence — are often the source of costly and ineffective social action. It could be claimed that carefully checked retrospective data provide a cheaper alternative to longitudinal research. I do not believe this for the following reasons. First, obtaining an adequate sample for retrospective studies is difficult and expensive. Second, much retrospective data cannot be checked, as records were not taken or have been destroyed. Third, retrospective information on attitudes is worthless. Fourth, in retrospective studies the hypothesis to be tested is already known and there is danger of unintentional distortion of evidence to support or refute the hypothesis through selective gathering of data. Record linkage would provide answers to some of these objections, but in the present climate of opinion this is unlikely to be available within this generation, and it still holds that many of the records to be linked would be poor and in need of checking.

It has been suggested that secular trends make nonsense of longitudinal studies, but I think the reverse is true. As cohorts are by definition concerned with groups of the same age, each cohort will relate to a particular stage in a secular trend. For example, if we are studying bereavement, it is clear that the effects of the death of a parent, infant, or child today are very different from the effects even a generation ago, when loss was more prevalent and more expected. And the same holds, but in reverse, for divorce and separation.

Certain rather vague, rather Victorian, concepts such as the "cycle of transmitted deprivation" are important not because of their scientific content so much as that they concern aspects of society about which people now care and therefore about which governments are forced to act. When action is based on ignorance, it is likely to be unfortunate both in misdirecting resources, and in its impact on the individual. This is well shown in Packham's (1975) recent work on the history of child care. Birth cohort studies should make a unique contribution to the problem of the "cycle of disadvantage" because we can look at the extent to which disadvantage persists over generations, what this continuing disadvantage contributes to the total pool of disadvantaged, and the mechanisms of its transmission — that is, how it relates to the structure of the society in which families live.

New services are being set up and new policies implemented; if they are not adequately monitored, false and expensive conclusions may be reached that will determine the direction of our effort and expenditure. Many of us feel that the effectiveness of new methods can be validly tested only by using the techniques of clinical trials or agricultural experiment. But these techniques are seldom applicable to the assessment of new services, first because of the wide extent to which different sections of the population vary in using them, and second because of the long time scale over which assessments have to be made. An instance immediately to hand is found in the educational policies introduced in Britain during the last twenty years. If the level of academic performance rises, we will, in the absence of evidence to the contrary, attribute it to the beneficial effects of comprehensive education or to the early enrichment provided by play groups or nursery schools in deprived areas; and this will determine the direction of our future efforts and expenditure. Even if these conclusions seem to be supported by evidence from cross-sectional studies, we are still unable to relate specific types of education at one age to later performance. We need to be able to compare children going through the educational system before the new policies were introduced with groups entering at different stages during the implementation of these policies. Since the success of an education system is not shown by levels of qualification alone, we need to follow groups into adult life. Moreover, because internal movements of population may lead to profound changes in local levels of ability over relatively few years, and because of the great geographical mobility in the years between leaving school and marriage, we need to compare national populations or populations of large regional aggregates. That is to say, we need some form of national longitudinal study; and as the educational process starts at birth, I would say that we need a series of national birth cohorts.

I have mentioned education because the three existing cohorts of 1946 (wholly selective education with virtually no preschool), 1958 (partly comprehensive education and some preschool), and 1970 (wholly comprehensive with much preschool) can clearly make a contribution to what is now a national debate. The same considerations, however, apply to many other new medical and social policies and services and will continue to apply in the future. Comparisons between cohorts will not only show the effectiveness of policies and services but will also point to the reasons why they have failed in some sections of the population or unexpectedly succeeded in others.

My contention, then, is that a series of cohort studies spaced ten to fifteen years apart would provide the best and also the cheapest method of assessing the effectiveness of new policies. The point at issue is whether we wish to know to what extent new medical, educational, and social services are fulfilling the intentions of those who planned them. If we do, comparisons between cohort studies provide the opportunity to show relationships between the establishment of new services and later changes in health, growth, and behavior. If we need to know what benefits accrue, for example, from spending X million pounds on pre-school education and which sections of the population are receiving the greater benefits from this provision, comparisons between national cohorts will provide the best answers.

It may be objected that the answers will be long in coming, but this is the nature of the situation, and no quicker answers are worth having. It is usually necessary for governments to plan on inadequate evidence, and they should be prepared to provide the means to measure the effectiveness of their plans even if this requires a long-term investment.

SOME RESULTS OF THE 1946 BIRTH COHORT STUDY

I will now give a brief account of some results of the 1946 birth cohort study. Those of medical relevance are reported in Chapter 18. I am concerned here only with educational and social analyses. A selected list of published papers is given in the appendix to this chapter.

In the original maternity survey of 1946, I was struck by the variation in the services provided by different maternity and child welfare authorities and by the lack of information about the effect of these differences on local maternal and child morbidity. The diversity of local provision in Britain has been defended as providing natural experiments that can be used to see the effectiveness of different types of service. But if there is no assessment of the outcome, this defense is frivolous. Local variations were very evident in the provision of selective secondary school places. They were also noted by the Ministry of Education, who attributed them to differences in the local availability of independent schools and the unequal geographical distribution of ability (list 69, 1959). But these explanations are found to be false in the 1946 sample: indeed, geographical variation in the provision of selective school places accounted for approximately half of the social inequalities in secondary selection, after controlling for ability (Douglas, 1964). It was also argued by the ministry that when selective schools were in short supply, alternative courses would be provided in secondary modern schools and technical colleges. This, however, did not hold, and the adverse effects of local educational deficiencies on achievement have been cumulative as these young people grow older (Douglas, Ross, and Simpson, 1968). There is no reason to believe that the introduction of comprehensive education has fundamentally altered local differences in the quality of teaching or the overall level of educational provision, though it has made such differences more difficult to detect. Yet unless these geographical inequalities are removed, the social inequalities will remain, whatever type of secondary education we have, because those who value education for their children will move, if they can afford to do so, to areas where the services are known to be good. Where we live in Britain still influences our survival, health, education, and employment.

The 1946 group was among the last to go through a wholly selective system of secondary education; if we are to understand the subsequent changes, it is important to be able to look closely at the extent of support that the selective system gave or failed to give. A recent paper (Cherry, 1974) showed that the level of ambition, measured by preferences for jobs of low or high status, was influenced by the social classes from which the schools drew their pupils as well as by the types of family the individual pupils came from. For the same type of child the level of ambition is lower in schools that draw their pupils predominantly from the manual working class than in schools that have a more mixed or a middle-class catchment. This, however, applies only to secondary modern schools; in grammar schools the level of ambition is independent of the social composition of the school. In this sense the grammar schools in predominantly manual working-class catchment areas were giving support to their pupils no matter from what type of family they came.

Inequalities in the opportunities of men and women are of great current interest in Britain today. We have recently examined (Douglas and Cherry, 1977) the educational and vocational levels reached by men and women in the 1946 cohort. In the primary schools — that is, those taking children between the ages of 5 and 11 — the girls made higher scores in tests of ability and attainment than the boys and were described by their teachers as working harder and being more likely to benefit from admission to selective schools. However, the proportions of boys and girls selected were closely similar, and by 15 years the boys were making higher scores than the girls in all tests except verbal intelligence. This was so in each social class.

In the general certificate of education exams at "ordinary" level, the girls were less likely than the boys to fail completely, though they passed in fewer subjects and in particular gained few passes in math and science. There were no substantial differences in ages at which boys and girls left school; but girls of high ability were less likely than boys of similar ability to expect to enter full-time education after leaving the school.

Thus, our early expectation that boys would leave school with higher educational qualifications than girls has been confirmed. Although the age at which they left school was similar in both sexes, 14 percent of the boys had gained "advanced" level qualifications, but only 10 percent of the girls had done so. However, as many men as women entered courses at colleges or universities after leaving school, some simply to widen their qualifications at roughly the same level as their achievements at school and others to improve their levels. In this there were differences between boys and girls; the well-qualified girls on leaving school — that is to say, those with "advanced" levels — are just as likely to improve their qualifications after leaving as boys with "advanced" levels; but if the girls have lower qualifications — that is, "ordinary" levels rather than advanced — they are far less likely than the boys to improve them by further study. Part of these differences are explained by the fact that women start childbearing at an earlier age than men start families, and by doing so suffer a greater restriction of educational opportunity. But even if they have not started a family by the age of 25, women with "ordinary" levels are still less likely than men to improve their qualifications, and we feel that the explanation for this difference must lie in the types of job available to men and women.

One point emerged very clearly from this analysis; namely, that differences in the qualifications of men and women are not explained by lack of staying power of women who start courses or by their failure in exams. Once they have joined a course, women are more likely than men to be successful in the "key year" — that is, to complete the course and obtain their qualifications at the first attempt. Inequalities in the education of men and women are structurally determined by the schools they attend and by their employment prospects after leaving school.

Last, I should mention briefly one of our major current commitments — observations on the relation of achievement in a wide range of activities in adult life to events that have occurred at earlier ages and are likely to have caused disturbance or stress to individuals or their families. The early events we have recorded are numerous but relatively crude; for example, family disruption, death of siblings or parents, temporary separation from parents, frequent moves of home, deficiencies of parental care, serious or chronic illness, accidental injury, illegitimate pregnancies, broken marriages, and many others. Although this list is long, we unfortunately have no means of showing the immediate impact of these events on the individual — the circumstances in which they occurred or, when a loss was involved, the character of the personal bonds that were broken. Moreover, other events that were profoundly disturbing went unrecorded and may well not even have been known to the parents; for example, the death of a pet animal, difficulties at school, unreported assaults, or undiscovered delinquencies. Even with these limitations it is clear that the events we have recorded have had an important and cumulative effect on behavior in adult life. It is also clear that the outcome of a particular event in early life cannot be precisely forecast. In some individuals it may show itself in psychiatric illness; in others, in problems of marital adjustment, job instability, or unacceptable social behavior. Yet others have unexpectedly low educational achievement. There is thus no single dependent adult behavior to which early events relate. On the other hand, each type of adult behavior disturbance will show possible etiological associations with a great variety of early insults. If one were, for example, to predict psychiatric illness from early life events, many would be picked out who had no psychiatric history but had other behavior disturbances or illness. The outcome depends on the personality of the subjects and on the nature of the early insults and their sequels.

The variety of outcomes associated with the same type of early event could have been made clear only in a longitudinal study. In a retrospective study we would have been relating one of many possible outcomes to remembered early events, and the wider relationships would not have emerged.

The proportion of subjects who show later problems of behavior increases with the number of early traumatic events recorded, but even when the stack of events is high, there are many who show no apparent disturbance, at any rate up to the age of 26. We hope to examine the characteristics of these people and the strategies they have adopted in dealing with adversity. In particular, we intend to look at the variety of pathways that may be followed after the occurrence of a major disruptive event — pathways that may reinforce or alleviate the long-term effects.

12 SEQUENTIAL RESEARCH WITH SPECIAL REFERENCES TO THE SCANDINAVIAN PROJECT METROPOLITAN

Kaare Svalastoga

SEQUENTIAL RESEARCH — A TOUGH JOB

MacMullen (1977), in describing traveling problems in the Roman Empire, recently concluded that travels at that time were *time-consuming, expensive,* and *risky.* It so happens that his three adjectives are also applicable to sequential or longitudinal studies. They are almost by definition more time-demanding than other studies simply because they become more thrilling the longer you are willing to wait. They may not be more expensive per published page than other studies, but they need the attention of financing institutions for a long time, and their total cost will easily add up to some million crowns or at least ten times the cost of a cross-sectional study of the same sample size. Sequential research is also risky in the sense that its survival depends more than that of other research on a steady state of neutral or favorable attitudes among the general public, in the government, and in parliament.

It is therefore not surprising that the total number of cohorts that have been studied and reported on is rather modest (see Wall and Williams, 1970). The trail-blazing achievement in the social science field of sequential research is still more rare, being represented only by two men: Terman and Douglas.

Furthermore most longitudinal studies are based on small samples. Among those listed for the United States as of about 1970 by Wall and Williams, only one study comprised more than 10,000 individuals. This was Anderson and Maier's study of 34,000 pupils (1963). It may not be accidental that this study is the only one reported in which the authors themselves come out with warnings to future large-scale sequential researchers. According to Wall and Williams, they characterize their project as ambitious, expensive, demanding, difficult, and frustrating.

METROPOLITAN IN A TOUGHENING ENVIRONMENT

Among longitudinal projects in Scandinavia, the two Metropolitan projects — one in Stockholm and the other in Copenhagen — work with larger cohorts than most. If the size of a research project is given as $S = V \times N$, where S = size, V = variables per person, and N = number of persons, then each project has S values exceeding 5×10^6 — in other words, they are quite large enterprises.

It remains largely to be seen whether the Scandinavian Project Metropolitan, which studies the 1953 generation in Copenhagen and Stockholm, will be able to conquer the difficulties that are part of sequential projects and to achieve excellence. But one thing is certain: the Danish and still much more the Swedish studies represent an impressive array of objective and correctly timed information on the changing position of a person from birth to 25 years of age.

The Danish study defined its population as boys born in 1953 in the counties of Copenhagen, Roskilde, and Frederiksborg and in the cities of Copenhagen and Frederiksberg (Svalastoga, 1976). The Swedish study defined its population as persons of both sexes born in 1953 and living in Greater Stockholm on 1 November 1963 (Janson, 1975). Both cohorts could be said to be studied, at least in many instances, as total populations and could therefore be of considerable comparative interest to researchers working with samples of this or other cohorts close in age.

Project Metropolitan is the only Scandinavian research project that is both highly sequential and large scale. It includes about twenty years follow-up, about ten years for retrospective information, and is of size (N) between 10^4 and 2×10^4 both in Stockholm and in Copenhagen.

Sequential research in general is important because it comes closer than simultaneous or cross-sectional research in providing evidence for causal hypotheses not contaminated by errors of memory and also in providing noncontroversial dating of events in the life history of a person and his or her family of origin and family of procreation. Janson (1975) reviewed the history of this project, which in its origin and strategy is rather Scandinavian. I was one of many admirers of the British national cohort research that Douglas made famous. At the Scandinavian Sociological meeting in Helsinki in 1960, Gunnar Boalt, Gösta Carlsson, and I were present. We did not speak about sequential research then and there, but did so a few days later at Lojo (in Finnish, Lohja) in the environment of Helsinki, where Gösta Carlsson lived at the time.

One day we talked about the check on many findings in cross-sectional research that was possible by means of longitudinal research if such research was available. I agreed with the others about the desirability of longitudinal research but contended that because of large-scale internal migration a nationwide cohort study was the only usable strategy. Boalt then referred to his pioneer longitudinal study and pointed out that 94 percent of children studied in Stockholm in 1936 were still living there in 1949, or thirteen years later. We tentatively agreed to start cohort research in the four major Scandinavian capitals.

The Scandinavian Project centered on the capital regions of Scandinavia, assuming that the low out-migration observed for Stockholm was generally valid at least in Scandinavia, which could easily be verified for Copenhagen. Another characteristic property of the Danish project was its 100 percent maleness, as was also true of the early Swedish project. This characteristic was frequently met with criticism, although in my opinion it was a rational strategy to concentrate all effort on the most variable sex at the time (more criminals and more who-is-who material).

In 1961 a Nordic committee for sequential research was formed with representatives from all four larger Scandinavian nations. However, in Finland the study never got beyond the planning stage. In Norway the project was stopped by a popular Orwell 1984 scare. The project got itself launched in Stockholm and Copenhagen in 1965, and for about ten years considerable information was collected on the boys in Greater Copenhagen and on 15,000 boys and girls in Greater Stockholm. Then in 1976 both studies experienced a major setback. In Sweden the data law was interpreted for Carl Gunnar Janson in such a way that no further documentary data collection will be possible under the present law. In Copenhagen the project met with too strong competition in the Social Science Foundation and was forced to reduce its activity severely.

SURVIVAL

What are the conditions most conducive to survival for sequential research projects in Scandinavia today? If there was a new deal and we could start over again, where would it be most beneficial to place this kind of research? Would a university location, as at present, be the most desirable solution?

The time-consuming nature of sequential research in a world of high individual mobility strongly suggests that survival hinges on some kind of institutional association. Institutions tend to outlive individuals and give the chance to change and or expand the research staff.

Experience from Denmark in the 1970s seems to suggest that research institutions outside the universities may well provide a better environment for longitudinal studies than do the universities because they are less sensitive to waves of ideological fervor and can thus provide a more stable and more research-nourishing environment. One difficulty facing a sequential project more than a simultaneous project is that significant results demand much investment of time and work. As a consequence the number of research workers inside an average institution who are willing to opt for sequential research will tend to be severely limited.

It follows that we should expect researchers connected with sequential studies to experience severe difficulties in living up to the publish-or-perish norms, which, whether we like it or not, does obtain in both science and literary work. These problems may perhaps also be more easily coped with in the framework of a larger institution.

The present strong sentiment in Scandinavia against possible misuse of electronic data production has created a situation that the few sequential researchers cannot hope to change or make more research-tolerant in the immediate future, unless they can show that socially useful research results demand a more research-friendly attitude.

Project Metropolitan was originally designed to contribute to three problems: work career, marital adaptation, and deviant behavior. Among these three problem areas there can be no doubt that deviant behavior is the one most likely to receive both moral and financial support. The Metropolitan projects in both Stockholm and Copenhagen are in a favorable situation in that both the Swedish and the Danish leaders are well known as researchers in criminology. It would therefore seem that survival chances would increase by giving top priority to deviant behavior. It would of course be valuable if the two other areas, work career and marital adaptation, could also be given some attention because both these areas are in need of sequential research.

If the Scandinavian Metropolitan projects are compared to the major British and American longitudinal projects of social science content, one discovers that the latter studies have much better lived up to the rule that sequential researchers should publish their findings as they come and not sit and wait for something more interesting. On this point Metropolitan strategy in the past has not been conducive to survival. (This criticism is, as insiders know, to a large extent my own self-criticism.) It will probably be important for the future to consider carefully how a more up-to-date flow of information can be established.

13 SOME METHODOLOGY AND STRATEGY PROBLEMS IN LONGITUDINAL RESEARCH

David Magnusson

Most researchers can understand that longitudinal research involves many problems that do not arise in traditional cross-sectional research, be it laboratory experiments or field studies. However, the full implications of planning, performing, and reporting a longitudinal project cannot be foreseen by theoretical analyses alone. They must be learned through experience. The consequences of bad planning can be serious in cross-sectional studies, but in longitudinal research they can be disastrous. The need for foreseeing problems and handling them effectively is therefore much greater in longitudinal research. In this chapter a few problems met in longitudinal research, especially in large-scale studies of groups representative for ages, will be described and discussed against the background of experiences gained in a longitudinal project at the Department of Psychology, University of Stockholm.

TWO TYPES OF LONGITUDINAL PROJECTS

The distinction between two types of longitudinal projects with respect to their ultimate aims may be appropriate and fruitful; namely, between

192

what will be designated *descriptive* longitudinal projects and *problem-oriented* longitudinal projects. Each has its own characteristics with respect to the planning and carrying through of data collections and the analyses of the data obtained.

Descriptive Longitudinal Projects

Characteristic of a descriptive longitudinal project is that a certain variable or variables are studied as a function or functions of age. The parameters considered may be means, ranges, distributions, and intercorrelations (stability and change in patterns of correlations over time, longitudinal stability of single variables, and the like) for such variables as intelligence, achievement, interests, and so on (see Bayley, 1955; Block, 1971; Magnusson and Backteman, 1977a, 1977b).

Descriptive longitudinal studies imply the investigation of the same variable or variables over time. Once the decision has been made as to which variables are to be studied, they remain the same and are covered by data collected when the subjects reach certain ages. There are mainly two problems in this kind of research.

First, one and the same psychological variable, say an intelligence factor or anxiety, may (a) change its psychological content and/or (b) change its manifest expressions insofar as they can be studied by standardized tests, self-ratings, or ratings by others. This implies that using the same instrument or method for data collection does not guarantee that the same underlying psychological variable is actually studied. The same method for data collection applied to the same verbally defined variable may actually cover different psychological characteristics of the individuals at different ages. Therefore, the choice of data for investigating the variables under consideration at different stages of development is an important problem.

Second, there is the general problem involved in measuring change, whether it is a matter of choosing the relevant unit for developmental curves or a matter of interpreting and comparing patterns of correlations at different ages.

Problem-Oriented Longitudinal Projects

Problem-oriented longitudinal projects, rather than studying development for a given set of variables, are directed toward investigating a certain problem or set of problems by following individuals over a period of time. Such studies may concern the development of criminal behavior or the educational and vocational career. A problem-oriented longitudinal project implies the same main problems as those involved in descriptive projects; that is, the choice of appropriate methods for data collection, once the variables have been defined, and the choice of appropriate ways of measuring change. These problems will be even more accentuated in problem-oriented projects. Moreover, problem-oriented projects deal with variables that will not necessarily, and perhaps not very often, be the same at different ages. They cannot be chosen once and for all. A problem-oriented longitudinal project, then, requires very careful planning and a heavy work load not only from the beginning but also at every new stage, in order to ascertain which variable should be investigated and which methods are the most effective. The demands on the care and sophistication of the data analysis are also heightened considerably, since, for one matter, we are faced with different kinds of data for different variables at different ages.

THE ÖREBRO PROJECT — A PROBLEM-ORIENTED LONGITUDINAL PROJECT

In 1965 the first data were collected in a problem-oriented longitudinal research project called the Örebro Project, from the name of the town in central Sweden where it is being performed.

Main Purpose

In very general terms, the aim of the project is to study how an individual's life-situation as an adult, as it can be described by others and is experienced by the individual, has its roots in a developmental process in which potential person factors interact with physical, social, and psychological factors in the environment.

This general formulation of the purpose had to be broken down into more specific terms to be useful for steering the planning and performance of the project. From the start, data collection and data treatment have been concentrated on a few problem areas, of which the main ones are the following:

1. The predictive value of early indicators of possible maladjustment,
2. The stability of single adjustment symptoms or patterns of symptoms and sequences of changes (see Magnusson and Backteman, 1977a, 1977b),
3. The educational and vocational career and its impact on the life-situation (see Dunér, 1978; Ekehammar, 1977, 1978),
4. The developmental process underlying criminal behavior among boys (see Olofsson, 1971),
5. The stability of overachievement as a personal characteristic and its long-term consequences for the adult life-situation (see Bergman and Magnusson, 1979; Magnusson, 1976a, 1978),
6. The role of norms and values in the adult life-situation (see Henricson, 1973),
7. The relation of neglect, isolation, and rejection at the age of 11 to the adult life-situation (see Zettergren, 1977).

Other studies have also been performed, such as one concerning creativity and its relation to adjustment at school.

Two Crucial Concepts: Extrinsic and Intrinsic Adjustment

Two major aspects of individual development and the life-situation have played a crucial role in the planning and carrying through of the investigation and in the planning of future research; namely, *extrinsic* and *intrinsic* adjustment.

Extrinsic adjustment refers to the degree of agreement between an individual's factual behavior and achievement on the one hand and the demands and expectations directed at him, as a consequence of his roles in family life, working life, social life, and so on, on the other. We mean the individual's way of dealing with his potential capacities in relation to the demands from his environment, completely divorced from the positive or negative value we might like to attach to such an adjustment. Extrinsic adjustment is the individual's life-situation as it can be observed and evaluated by others.

Intrinsic adjustment refers to the individual's own perception of and satisfaction with his family life, working life, social life, and so on. Thus intrinsic adjustment is the individual's life-situation from his own point of view.

Subjects

In view of the project's purpose, it was desired that the sample of subjects should be as representative as possible for the age group. In order to minimize sampling problems as well as the crucial problem of dropout during the following-up stages and to permit a more intense investigation of environmental factors, it was decided to study a complete age group in one local area, rather than to take a representative sample of individuals from all over the country. Such a strategy also makes the planning and performing of the data collections less expensive and less time-consuming.

The final decision was to perform the study in Örebro, a town in Sweden with about 100,000 inhabitants, with a differentiated school system at different levels, and with a heterogeneous industrial structure. Data from the project have shown that the socioeconomic standard there is somewhat higher than the average for Sweden.

Two age groups of pupils from the Örebro school system formed the subject groups of the project, one consisting of the pupils born in 1955, the other of those born in 1952. The first of these age groups has been our *main group,* and the second our *pilot group.* Each of the groups consisted from the beginning of about 1,000 boys and girls.

The number of pupils for whom data are available for different age levels and the number who have been followed over different time intervals are presented for the main group in Table 13.1.

The start populations of the pilot and the main group were defined as those who attended the local schools in the spring of 1965, when the first data collection took place. This means that institutionalized children were excluded from the investigation.

Variables

As underlined in the introduction, the developmental process in which an individual's adult life-situation has its roots is regarded as a continuous interaction between person factors and environmental factors. Physical, social, and psychological factors in the environment are highly influential. The interaction is bidirectional; the individual is an active agent in the process and affects his or her environment in many ways. These statements are fundaments in an interactional model of behavior (see Endler and Magnusson, 1976; Magnusson, 1976b; Magnusson and Endler, 1977). The interactional view leads to the conclusion that it is essential to

Table 13.1. Sizes of Groups for Which Data Exist for Different Grades and Combinations of Grades, Main Group.

Grades	Boys	Girls	Total
Total grade 3	515	510	1,025
Total grade 6	543	557	1,100
Total grade 8	600	590	1,190
Total grade 9	609	578	1,187
3, 6, and 8	421	440	861
3, 6, not 8	31	27	58
3 and 6	452	467	919
6 and 8, not 3	81	65	146
6 and 8	502	505	1,007
8, not 3 or 6	94	83	177
3 and 9	418	431	849
3 and 11	264	234	498
3 and 12	102	85	187
9 and 11	358	306	664
9 and 12	141	114	255
3, 6, 8, 9, 11, and 12	101	85	186

investigate both person and environmental factors to understand the developmental process in which an adult's life-situation has its roots. Once this conclusion has been formulated, it seems obvious. Even so, it has not had the impact one might expect on actual research strategies for investigating development.

On the person side, one of the basic principles behind the planning of strategy in the present project has been to study both psychological and somatic variables. Too much research on development has failed to consider the inevitable, continuous interaction between psychological and somatic factors in the individual development process. Obviously the character of the data collected on psychological variables in a certain situation may be strongly affected by the somatic status of the person in that situation. A good example is motivation; if this is studied at puberty in psychological terms only, without considering the individual's somatic status, one may be grossly misled.

Totally, a large number of person characteristics have been covered through various methods of data collection. The variables can be separated roughly into (1) person variables of trait character with subdivisions into (a) psychological and (b) somatic variables and (2) adjustment variables with subdivisions into (a) intrinsic and (b) extrinsic adjustment variables. This categorization, which is used below to present the variables studied for the main group, is arbitrary. Some of the variables could be classified both as trait and as adjustment variables, for example.

For a full description of the variables covered and the methods used for data collection the reader is referred to Magnusson (1978) and Magnusson, Dunér, and Zetterblom (1975).

Data Collection

Since the start of the project, large-scale data collections have been performed regularly on the subjects of the whole main group at ages judged to represent essential stages in development; that is, 10, 13, 15, and 16 years. Data for specific variables were collected at appropriate stages. For example, data relevant for the study of the educational and vocational career were collected each time the subjects had to make a choice as to what educational program to follow.

Sample investigations have been performed in two main studies. Data for somatic variables were collected for a sample of about 225 boys and girls. In a study of aspects of social neglect and/or mobbing, a sample of 90 boys and girls has been analyzed intensively. One study involved a close examination of dropout from school. In these cases the appropriate data could be obtained for only one individual at a time. Data collection for the whole group would have been too expensive. The data collected fall into the three categories shown in Tables 13.2, 13.3, and 13.4.

Follow-up in Adult Life

The primary aim of the project is to study the interaction between an individual's person characteristics and environmental factors in development and to see how this interaction leads to his or her adult life-situation. This means that the final information is not available until adulthood and that criterion data have to be collected at that age. The main issues of the project can be properly elucidated only when we have data on the life-situation of our subjects as adults.

Life-Situation Investigation.   Our subjects were 25 years of age in 1980 and almost all of them passed through the educational system and have taken their place on the labor market. A follow-up study covering the

Table 13.2. Basic Data on Total Groups.

Area	Methods for Data Collection
Domestic background, domestic situation	Parental questionnaire
Intrinsic adjustment, satisfaction, etc.	Pupil questionnaire
Classmate relationships	Sociometric methods
Extrinsic adjustment: behavior	
in school,	Teacher ratings
at home,	Parental questionnaire
in society	Public records
Intelligence, knowledge	Tests and grades given on report cards
Attitudes and values	Semantic differential

NOTE: The data have been collected on pupils at the ages of 10, 13, and 15 years (grades 3, 6, and 8).

life-situation of our subjects is being conducted for performance at that point in time.

The life-situation can be seen from two angles, both of which are being studied in the follow-up in adulthood:

1. The life-situation in terms of *factual conditions* and states: somatic status, work, education, family life, leisure activities, cultural activities, and so on,
2. The life-situation in terms of *subjective experience*: satisfaction with respect to work, family life, leisure activities, and so on.

Table 13.3. Data on Subprojects and Applying to *Total* Group.

Area	Age*	Methods for Data Collection
Norms	15	Situation inventory
Symptoms (girls)	15	Questionnaire
Criminality (boys)	16	Questionnaire, situation inventory
Study and vocational decisions	13–19	Questionnaires, Semantic differential
Goals, values in life	18	Questionnaire

NOTE: School start is at age 7. Grades 1–9 are in comprehensive school. In grade 3 most children are 10, in grade 6 they are 13, and in grade 9 they are 16. Upper secondary school (gymnasium) has three grades; the students are 17–19 years old.

Table 13.4.   Data on Special Problems Collected during Subprojects and Applying to Random Samples from Total Group (Used When Expensive Methods Are Necessary).

Area	Age	Methods for Data Collection
Social relations (N = 90)	10–12	Interview, etc.
Biological variables (N = 225)	13–15	EEG, hormone analysis, ossification measurements, physical achievement capacity
Dropout problems	16–17	Interview, questionnaire

Extensive and Intensive Data.   Two kinds of extensive data — that is, data for the total main group — are being collected; namely, (a) data from public records and (b) inventory data. Data of the first kind have proved very useful in other studies. In regard to inventories, our experience of earlier data collections indicates that our subjects are willing to answer these, even when considerable time has passed since they left school.

Intensive data are being collected for groups of individuals either drawn at random to be representative of the total group or defined by some criterion related to a particular problem. In studying these cases, all extensive data can be used as well as data that have been collected on a group for some specific aim. These data collections are also being performed by instruments that have to be administered individually, such as interviews.

Investigation of the Total Group.   The total group of subjects is fairly representative of the total age group in the country. It will be of interest in itself to describe the life-situation, with respect to different aspects of extrinsic and intrinsic adjustment, for a whole group with this composition. One central question to be dealt with using the data on the total group is the role of educational and vocational career in the life-situation.

Studies of Specific Groups.   Right from the early planning stages, the collections of data have been steered by an interest in certain main aspects of adjustment and development, criminal behavior, norms and values, educational and vocational career, and so on. During the course of the project, other problems not formulated originally have attracted attention and become a focus of interest.

One strategy for studying specific problems within the general frame of reference is to study groups of individuals defined by criteria relevant for the problem in question. This strategy can be fulfilled in two ways: (a) by defining a group of subjects who, at an early age, say 11, meet the criterion and then following them until adult life and (b) by defining a group of adult individuals and looking at them, in an absolute sense or in relation to the total group, in terms of appropriate variables at different stages of development.

In another strategy the interest is directed not toward groups but toward variables and their cross-sectional and longitudinal relationships.

Using the two main strategies, we put into focus the following five subprojects as we plan the follow-up in adult life:

1. *Socially neglected and mobbed children.* The life-situation at home, at school, and during leisure time of fifteen boys and fifteen girls who were isolated, neglected, or mobbed in their school classes was studied when these children were 10 to 11 years of age. As a control, the life-situations of the same numbers of popular boys and girls and of randomly chosen boys and girls were investigated. The follow-up data hitherto collected on these ninety pupils have been reported by Zettergren (1977, 1980). What is now planned is a specific follow-up of these boys and girls at the age of 25.

It must be important to learn more about the possibility of good adjustment in adulthood for boys and girls who have been socially neglected, isolated, and mobbed during school years. The cases where development has been more successful or more positive than expected should be particularly worth investigating. Interest is focused on (a) actual incidents in the individual's life, (b) life circumstances after school, (c) attitudes and values expressed by the individual as an adult, and (d) the description and evaluation given by the adult individual of his or her actual situation at the age of 11 and of what has happened to him or her from early age to adult life.

2. *Overtly criminal boys and men.* A follow-up in adulthood will be made of the boys who were overtly criminal at the age of 15 to 16. This study will also include men who are registered in public records for criminal acts as adults without having done so at the age of 15 to 16 according to our data. The follow-up will enable us to test the prediction models for criminal development that have been evolved in the project.

3. *Overachievement, overconformity, and type-A behavior.* During recent years, particularly in the context of research on stress in working life, much interest has been devoted to a certain personality type, char-

acterized by type-A behavior (see Friedman and Rosenman, 1974). Related to type-A behavior — though not identical — is overachievement; that is, achievement above that expected for a given intelligence. Two results of interest for this issue have been obtained in the project: (a) The measure of relative achievement — that is, the difference between actual and predicted achievement — is a fairly stable personal characteristic for both boys and girls from age 10 to 16. (b) A strong correlation exists between relative achievement and urinary adrenaline output in a stressful examination situation in boys but not in girls (see Bergman and Magnusson, 1979; Magnusson, 1976a, 1978). These findings led to the formulation of a series of follow-up studies designed to illuminate the long-term consequences of an habitual overachievement pattern of behavior and of sex differences in this respect.

In this context we shall also investigate the group of individuals who had what may be called an overconformity pattern of behavior at an early age. There are some indications in our data that overconforming boys and girls show below-average intrinsic adjustment — that is, lower satisfaction, lower self-confidence, and so on.

4. *Predictive value of early indicators of maladjustment.* One of the main questions in the project has been the predictive value of early symptoms of possible maladjustment; for example, exaggerated aggressiveness, strong anxiety, strong inhibitions, and so on. To what degree are such symptoms indicators of deep disturbance, with long-term consequences for the individual's extrinsic and intrinsic adjustment in adult life?

5. *Reliability and validity of retrospective data.* One of the follow-ups planned will provide unique possibilities for studying the reliability and validity of retrospective data. Such data are used to a large extent as bases for far-reaching conclusions, both in research and in practical contexts — for example, in guidance, admissions, and placement — without their value in such connections having been investigated sufficiently.

SUCCESSIVE AGE COHORTS

As described, we follow subjects of two age groups, those born in 1952 and those born in 1955. The first one constitutes our pilot group and the second our main group. The strategy of using two age groups differing by at least a few years in age was chosen for several reasons. It has obvious advantages with respect to resources and scientific outcome.

Performing a longitudinal project implies a series of theoretical, methodological, strategical, and practical problems (see, for example, Baltes and Schaie, 1973; Brim and Kagan, 1980). The outcome of the project is dependent upon the effectiveness with which the problems have been foreseen and handled from the beginning and at each stage of the project. A mistake at any stage of a longitudinal project will have much more serious and far-reaching consequences for the researcher than a mistake in a laboratory experiment. It is not possible to start anew, and the effects of a single mistake will follow and influence the project to its end. However, even with very careful planning it is not possible to foresee and handle all the problems — for example, dropout, choice and construction of instruments, or environmental conditions — in the most effective way. Important lessons are learned at every stage of a longitudinal project. It would have been of great value if the information thus gained had been available from the beginning.

By using two age groups of which the first serves as pilot group, it has been possible to gain experiences and information that have been invaluable for planning and performing data collections and data analyses on the main group. Besides experience of the local environmental conditions for our project, in physical, organizational, and personal respects, the pilot group has given us pilot data for comparison with data on the main group, as well as the possibilities of pretesting our instrument, testing our preliminary hypotheses and predictions, and separating age effects from temporary environmental effects.

Panel Data

Following a group of individuals over time with successive collections of data will introduce two kinds of possibly irrelevant variance in data. First, we may have a test-training effect. The subjects get used to the instruments, and the extent to which individuals direct their interest to problems in different domains of experience and knowledge is influenced by the content of tests and inventories with which they have had to work. Second, the circumstance that the individuals are conscious of being the subjects of special interest may affect the information they deliver in different types of data both positively and negatively. Both these effects can be linear and interaction effects. By using more than one age group on which the collection of data starts at different ages, it is possible to estimate, to some extent at least, the linear effects of testing the same group successively.

Testing of Instruments

Instruments for data collection may be geared specifically to the nature and aims of a given project. This has been the case within the Örebro Project. To cover essential areas in the educational and vocational career and in the development of criminal behavior, for example, we have constructed new instruments, mainly inventories. Pretesting such instruments on the pilot group, composed of the same types of subjects from the same local area under the same environmental conditions, provides especially effective information as to how the instruments should be reconstructed before using them on the main group.

Testing of Hypotheses

Our project does not aim at testing a certain personality theory for development. Nor has the data collection been steered by one and the same general personality theory. At each stage of the project, the variables to be covered have been formulated, and the choice of methods for data collection and analysis has been made with regard to the specific aim of of the subproject. Moreover, the psychological knowledge and the theoretical analyses available for the specific problem area have been taken into consideration. Data from the pilot group have made it possible to evaluate the effectiveness of the original set of hypotheses and predictions and to revise them for the main group.

Separating Age Effects and Environmental Effects

Personal variables of central interest in longitudinal projects may be influenced, sometimes very strongly, by environmental factors. These factors may be specific for some individuals, but they may also hold for the whole group. They may be linear or interactional. In a static society these factors would not need to be considered in the collection and analyses of data, since they would be the same for the next generation and would be part of the general development of all individuals. However, our society is characterized by rapid and important changes in cultural factors such as norms, values, modes, and ideologies, as well as in the labor market, in attitudes toward higher education and work, and so on. Strong changes in the environment in respects essential for the behavior of individuals and groups must thus be taken into account.

It is important to separate general age effects from environmental effects, which can be done most effectively by studying different age groups composed in the same way and living in the same local environment. A good example can be taken from the area of educational and vocational career. From the time when the subjects in our pilot study were about 13 years of age and had to make their first choice in their educational career to a few years later, the situation in the labor market has undergone dramatic changes. The fact that we had data from two age groups differing by three years gave us the possibility of observing the effects of these changes on the willingness and interest to go on to higher education, among other things, and of estimating the strength of these effects.

REPRESENTATIVE SAMPLES — ADVANTAGES AND PROBLEMS

The definition and choice of the sample or samples of individuals to be studied depend on the purpose of the project. The individuals who form the age groups in the Örebro Project are supposed to be representative for the age groups. Thus they represent a wide range of intelligence and social background. The advantage of studying data on groups thus defined is obvious; we would hardly have been able to reach our aim as effectively with a selected group. For example, data for basic variables for the total group form the frame of reference for the interpretation of data for any given subgroup, which may be defined in terms of one or a set of characteristics and studied in specific respects. However, when the interest is in data for the total groups of individuals, using a group of individuals with such a wide range of intelligence and social background creates serious methodological problems. These must be considered and dealt with in planning the data collection and data analyses. One such problem concerning the methods for data collection is discussed here.

In our studies of the whole set of age groups, we have used inventories to cover important aspects of the development. Inventory data usually contain systematic and unsystematic variance caused by the existence of irrelevant factors. Well-known effects of this type are those designated as social desirability, acquiescence, and so on. Such factors may influence data in a linear way and in an interactional way as well.

We have had to face and eliminate the problem that individuals differing in intelligence and/or in other personality variables related to social background, for example, may interpret our instructions, questions, and alternatives in procedures for data collection differently, thus introducing an irrelevant variance of unknown size in our data. When reliable data are available for intelligence or other variables that we want to control, we can do so by statistical methods, partial regression analysis, and covariance analysis, for example. However, if no special considerations have been taken, irrelevant factors may influence even highly reliable measures. There are strong reasons to analyze possible sources of irrelevant variance carefully due to the fact that we have unrestricted groups of individuals and to try to avoid these sources as far as possible.

The problem is not unique to our project or to other longitudinal projects; it holds true for all research using unrestricted samples of individuals. In all these cases it is fundamental to consider carefully possible sources of irrelevant variance.

Minimum Level of Intelligence

The first problem in choosing inventories or constructing new ones for data collection at a certain age level is the minimum level of intelligence among the subjects. The items should be *understood* by everyone, including the least intelligent individuals. For many groups it is therefore necessary to formulate instructions, items, and alternative answers in very simple, concrete terms. In inventories in which the subject has to mark one of a number of alternatives, even subjects with a very low level of intelligence can mark one alternative without understanding its meaning. It might be difficult to ascertain to what extent this is the case, if the problem is not given special consideration. Since it is obvious that it is essential for all subjects to understand the instructions, questions, and alternatives, pilot studies can be used to see if they do so before the main data are collected.

Control of Intelligence Level and Social Background as Irrelevant Factors

However, it is not enough that all the subjects understand the instructions, questions, and alternatives. They should also understand and interpret them in the same way and in the way that the researcher has intended. Because of differences in intelligence and/or social background, individuals may understand and interpret instructions, questions, and alternatives differently, thus answering different questions.

One way of avoiding this problem, to some extent, is to formulate the instructions, questions, and alternatives in very simple, concrete terms, which hopefully have the same meaning for all subjects. However, even if this strategy is possible to carry out in some cases for some limited purposes, it is not sufficient for avoiding the effects under consideration. As soon as we want to cover variables that have to do with attitudes, values, norms, and the like, we cannot avoid formulations that can be interpreted differently by subjects with different intelligence and/or different social background. And in most cases we still have the effects of social desirability and acquiescence. Thus there is an obvious need for data to be collected for important variables with methods by which the factors I have described are minimized.

In our project the problem was especially relevant when we wanted to study such areas as norms and norm conflict among teenagers and criminal behavior among boys. Inventories covering such areas would be especially sensitive to the irrelevant factors we wanted to avoid. Traditionally in studies of norms, for example, the subjects have to answer a series of general questions concerning their own, their peers', or their parents' views. In an attempt to improve the control of irrelevant factors right from the start of the collection of data, we have chosen another procedure, which is described below.

Situation Inventories

In a subproject on norms and norm conflicts among teenagers, we were interested in elucidating the questions of whether there is *one* teenage culture or distinct subcultures and of how norms and evaluations of teenagers are related to norms and values of peers and parents, as they are experienced and estimated by the youngsters. The study included two main parts, one in which the evaluations and expectations by the youngsters were investigated, and one in which their behavior intentions were studied. The intention was to minimize as much as possible the effect of differences in intelligence and social background in understanding the instructions and questions.

The following ten situations, each involving the breaking of a specific norm, were formulated in concrete, verbally simple terms:

1. Tomas is walking down the aisle in a department store. He has no money, but he is longing for sweets. There is a whole shelf

with sweets; it is unguarded and he is tempted to steal a box of candy.

2. Björn has never smoked hashish. One day he meets some friends in town and they say that they have hashish. They ask if he wants to try, but he is hesitant.

3. On his way to school Kalle meets some friends who are free from school and want to do something fun together. Kalle is tempted to play hookey.

4. Magnus has to be home at a certain time every evening. One evening he meets some friends in town and they are going out to the country. They won't be home until very late. Magnus is tempted to go with them, but he hesitates over staying out that late without permission.

5. It is exam time, but Johan has not had time to prepare himself. It is important for Johan to succeed. He has a cheat-sheet with him. He hesitates over whether to use it.

6. In his class Anders has a friend who is using drugs. Anders is worried about him and thinks that he needs help to stop his abuse, but the friend doesn't want any help. Anders hesitates over whether he should tell the school medical officer or nurse about his friend.

7. Leffe meets some friends one evening and they have lots of beer and wine. He has never been drunk, but the others are drinking heavily. He feels a bit dizzy. He is afraid that he will drink so much that he will get drunk.

8. Per has been dating a girl for some time. One evening he is at her place when her parents are away. They like each other very much, but Per is not certain whether they should use the opportunity to have sexual intercourse.

9. Bo's friends loiter about town every evening. They usually stand talking at the street corner or sit in a café. Bo finds himself hanging out with them more and more often. He wants to be part of the gang, but he hesitates over whether to loiter about town every evening.

10. Lars's parents have forbidden him from going to "parent-free" parties. He is invited to that kind of party and wants to go. All his friends are going but he hesitates over whether he should go and disobey his parents' orders.

For each situation the subjects had to answer five questions:

1. If your peers found themselves in the same situation as Tomas, what do you think they would do? My peers:

    ____ 1 would absolutely not   ____ 5 would perhaps
    ____ 2 would probably not   ____ 6 would probably
    ____ 3 would perhaps not   ____ 7 would definitely
    ____ 4 I am not sure whether
          they would

               take a candybox (shop-lift).

2. To be quite honest, what would you do in such a situation? I myself:

    ____ 1 would absolutely not   ____ 5 would perhaps
    ____ 2 would probably not   ____ 6 would probably
    ____ 3 would perhaps not   ____ 7 would definitely
    ____ 4 am not sure whether I
          would

               take a candybox (shop-lift).

3. What do you believe your parents think you would do? My parents think that I:

    ____ 1 would absolutely not   ____ 5 would perhaps
    ____ 2 would probably not   ____ 6 would probably
    ____ 3 would perhaps not   ____ 7 would definitely
    ____ 4 I am not sure whether
          they think I would

               take a candybox (shop-lift).

4. How do you think your parents and your peers would react if they found out that you had shop-lifted? My parents:

    ____ 1 would probably not   ____ 4 would probably
          worry.   disapprove.
    ____ 2 would perhaps not   ____ 5 would definitely
          worry.   disapprove strongly.
    ____ 3 I don't know how they
          would react.

    My peers:
    ____ 1 would probably not   ____ 2 would perhaps not
          worry.   worry.

_____3 I don't know how they   _____5 would definitely
       would react.   disapprove strongly.
_____4 would probably
       disapprove.

5. Have you yourself shop-lifted?
    _____1 Never   _____4 4–10 times
    _____2 Once   _____5 More than 10 times
    _____3 2–3 times

This strategy has the advantage of directing the interest toward norms in terms of true-to-life *acts* instead of directing it toward the abstract content of verbal statements. Defining norms and norm breaks in terms of specific acts in given situations may reasonably be assumed to provide a greater probability (a) that the subjects understand easily, precisely, and similarly to which norm a possible break refers, which in turn implies (b) that they are taking a stand concerning the same norm break.

The data from such an inventory can be used just as data from traditional inventories are used; that is, by summing scores across situations to arrive at a sum score of behavior intentions and estimated intentions among peers and parents. However, besides the advantageous psychological and methodological effects mentioned above, the type of data obtained from situation inventories is especially useful for analyses in the interactional frame of reference. During recent years the interest in personality research has been devoted to the person-by-situation interaction in which behavior develops, both in learning process over time in a series of situations and in a specific, actual situation (see Endler and Magnusson, 1976; Magnusson, 1976b). In the interactional model of behavior, the continuous bidirectional influence of personal and situational factors has been the focus of much debate and research.

One central assumption in an interactional model of behavior is that the characteristics of individuals are to be sought in their specific patterns of stable and changing behaviors across situations of different kinds. In that frame of reference the question of the existence of one homogeneous teenage culture was investigated in the following way, with the use of latent profile analysis for the treatment of data.

Latent profile analysis categorizes individuals in homogeneous groups on the basis of their profiles; in this specific case, on the basis of their profiles of behavior intentions across situations. The method has the advantage of not requiring any specific type of distribution of data or linearity in the relationship among variables. The advantages and weak points of the method have been discussed by Mårdberg (1973), among others.

In Figure 13.1 the outcome of the analysis is presented. It is indicated that we can separate five subgroups of individuals, each with its own specific, characteristic profiles of behavior intentions across a number of relevant norm situations. The meaningfulness of the grouping of individuals in these five subgroups has been investigated by testing predictions about the relationships between subgroup identity and other psychological characteristics. The calculations show that the subgroups differ in predictable ways with respect to other variables at the same age, and sometimes even at the early age of 10. Differences in cross-situational profiles for behavior intentions thus reflect different lifestyles.

INFORMATION AND COMMUNICATION IN LARGE-SCALE LONGITUDINAL RESEARCH

The success of longitudinal research is dependent upon the cooperation of individuals not only on each testing occasion but also continuously. Forming and maintaining cooperative relations to the subjects are thus imperative.

For a number of years our data collections concerned children and were performed in homes and in schools. This fact entailed the necessity of continuous cooperation with pupils, parents, teachers, and school authorities. Much work has therefore been devoted to information and communication with these groups. Measures taken in this context have been chosen with respect to the group and problems involved.

A Reference Group

A central role in the planning of every stage of the data collections has been played by a reference group, which was formed at the beginning of the project and has served during the whole period of data collections in the school system of Örebro. The composition of the group has been surprisingly stable, affected only by changes in professional positions of single members.

The reference group has consisted of one member from the Swedish Board of Education, one member from the local board of education (the chairman), the head of the local school system, one school principal, one

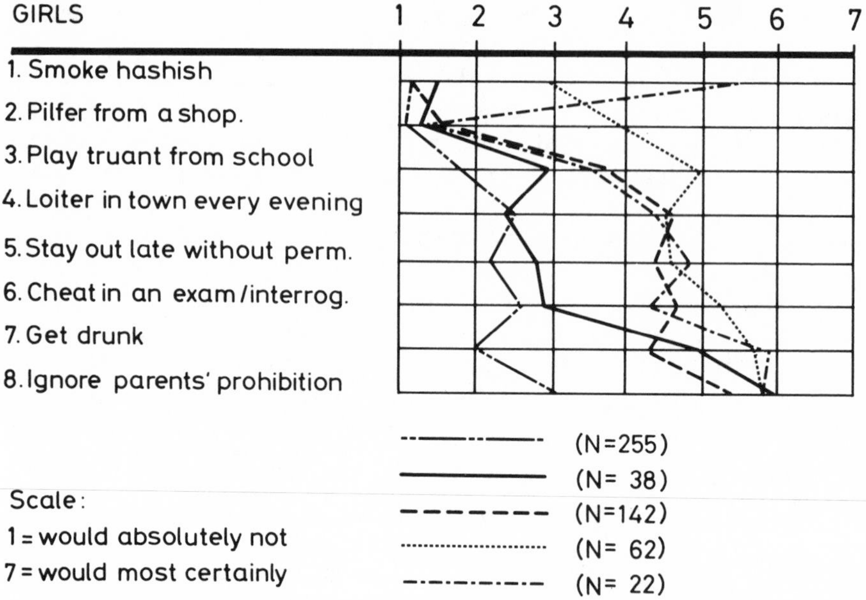

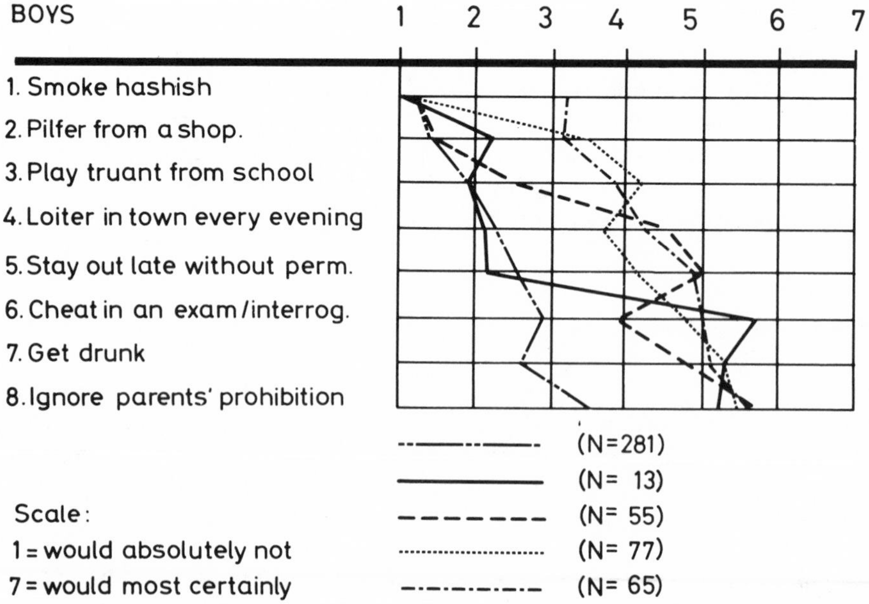

GIRLS

	1	2	3	4	5	6	7

1. Smoke hashish
2. Pilfer from a shop.
3. Play truant from school
4. Loiter in town every evening
5. Stay out late without perm.
6. Cheat in an exam/interrog.
7. Get drunk
8. Ignore parents' prohibition

------··------ (N=255)

───────── (N= 38)

── ── ── ── (N=142)

·············· (N= 62)

─·──·──·──·─ (N= 22)

Scale:

1 = would absolutely not

7 = would most certainly

BOYS

	1	2	3	4	5	6	7

1. Smoke hashish
2. Pilfer from a shop.
3. Play truant from school
4. Loiter in town every evening
5. Stay out late without perm.
6. Cheat in an exam/interrog.
7. Get drunk
8. Ignore parents' prohibition

------··------ (N=281)

───────── (N= 13)

── ── ── ── (N= 55)

·············· (N= 77)

─·──·──·──·─ (N= 65)

Scale:

1 = would absolutely not

7 = would most certainly

Figure 13.1. Profile Groups Based on Teenagers' Own Behavior Intentions in Grade 8. (Source: Henricson, 1973, Figure 10, p. 64.)

member of the parent-teacher association, and one teacher from each of the three main grade groupings in the school system.

At an early stage of the planning of each data collection, the preliminary material that was to be distributed was discussed in meetings with the reference group. The contact with administrative representatives made it possible to discuss administrative limitations and ways to handle them properly. Representatives of the teachers and parents provided essential information about attitudes and reactions toward the form and content of our methods. Members of the reference group participated very actively and constructively and played a substantial role in the success of the data collections.

Parents and Teachers

Besides exerting a direct influence on the procedures and instruments for data collection, the reference group provided a direct contact with school authorities, teachers' organizations, and the parents' organization. Information to the single individuals who became involved as subjects, parents, or teachers was also an important part of the project. Continuous written information was given to parents in connection with the parts of the data collections that did not concern internal school variables. All teachers were also informed beforehand, in close cooperation with the school authorities. On each data collection occasion, one member of the research group was present at each school, ready to answer questions from teachers and to present supplementary information. Besides giving them information in the instructions accompanying different collections of data, pupils were regularly invited to comment upon and discuss whatever they wished concerning the specific procedure and its content.

The Press

In a large-scale data collection running over a rather long period of time, there are many possibilities for misunderstandings and conflicts. Stories are told and rumors circulate about procedures and about the specific or general content of certain instruments. There are many examples of how such things have caused serious trouble in longitudinal projects.

The press can play an important role in this area. It is the duty of the press to observe and scrutinize what is going on in society and to present its findings to the public. However, it has happened that the press has published information about research projects that has been based on false facts or misunderstanding of facts, whereupon chances of fulfilling the projects have been severely damaged. Such incidents have led to a critical and suspicious attitude toward the press among researchers in the behavioral and social sciences. Many researchers have tried to avoid giving the press access to their instruments.

We took the initiative to cooperate closely with the two local papers, a cooperation that has functioned very effectively during the whole period of the project. The editors of the papers were given full information about each stage of the project, including all tests and instruments, and each paper appointed a special member of its staff to follow the project in cooperation with the researchers. We have continuously distributed material about the project to the papers for publication. We have done so prior to the extensive data collections and we have contributed short articles about results that we judged could be published without affecting further data collections.

The cooperation with the press has been very successful. In no way have the papers misused our information; on the contrary, they have supported us in their regular publicity. We have also seen cases where the journalists, since they have had access to full information, have been able to inform parents who have contacted them that the information they had received from their children about what was going on was not correct. The fact that we have been able to collect data from more than 2,000 subjects over a period of thirteen years without any serious conflict or negative public debate is certainly due to a high degree to our cooperation with the press.

Comments

Handling information and communication problems has taken more time and resources than expected. However, this work is a necessary precondition for good results in large-scale longitudinal research, and here it has obviously been worthwhile. A few figures can be presented to illustrate the trust with which parents and pupils have supplied us with information, even if it has sometimes been of a very personal character.

In the first stage of the project, the parents were asked to fill in an inventory, and 98 percent of them did so. In 1975 a data collection took place for the pilot group, when the members were 23 years of age. Among those who had left school at the age of 16 seven years earlier, without going on to higher education, 84 percent answered the inventory, and among those who had graduated from the gymnasium four years earlier, 93 percent answered.

Such a high rate of participation would not have been obtained if a considerable amount of time and other resources had not been devoted to analyses and discussions of information and communication problems in the planning stages and thereafter. It is indicated that the subjects place a high degree of trust in the project. Such trust is a necessary condition for the effective carrying through of a longitudinal project. In such projects, the researcher is forced to handle carefully the problems connected with spread of information to and communication with all parts involved. This fact should be observed by all those who, from the outside, advocate bureaucratic control of the ethical aspects of scientific work.

14 PSYCHIATRIC EPIDEMIOLOGICAL STUDIES IN ICELAND

Tómas Helgason

The purpose of this chapter is to review some of the findings in a retrospective psychiatric study of a birth cohort and a more prospective follow-up study of the same cohort as well as to consider the methodological problems inherent in the studies. The studies are biographical in their approach and limitations since they involve the collection of both recorded data and data memorized by a number of individuals as well as the verification of the latter. The advantage of this method is that health information is collected on every member of the cohort during his or her life span from all available sources.

Ideally the collection of data starts with information on the mother's health during pregnancy and a history of the individual's birth and possible complications during this period. From then on the growth and the development of the person should be followed during childhood and adult life until senescence. Provided adequate records are available, it should be possible to reconstruct and summarize the psychiatric-medical history of any individual and assess whether he or she has had a psychiatric illness or not. But such records are only exceptionally available for persons who have reached an advanced age. Therefore a compromise has to be made between the ideal and the obtainable. Furthermore, the amount of information required, especially about the early life, depends on the purpose of the study. If it is etiological, the necessity is obvious, but if it is limited to the more descriptive epidemiological approach, such information is of less importance when the main focus of interest is on comparing the morbidity between various social and demographic groups.

A considerable proportion of psychiatric disorders are not seen by psychiatrists. These are often, but not necessarily, the so-called minor disorders. The factors that determine whether a patient sees a psychiatrist are far too often of a nonmedical nature. These may be of an environmental, physical, or social nature relating to the accessibility of the service or the social stigma attached to seeking psychiatric assistance. The advent of new therapeutic techniques may work both ways, either by increasing or by decreasing the demand for service. If a new technique is relatively simple to apply and resembles other techniques applied by general practitioners, the latter will probably attempt to treat more patients without referral to a psychiatrist. On the other hand, the patients will be referred if the patient and his or her doctor believe in the efficacy of the specific psychiatric treatment.

It is necessary to combine information from general practitioners and other key informants in the community with information from hospitals and psychiatrists to improve the epidemiological data necessary for evaluation of the psychiatric morbidity in the population. The uniformity of the data can to some extent be secured by having the same psychiatrist collect them and evaluate the mental health of all the probands. Ideally the same psychiatrist should interview all the members of the cohort. This is difficult in a large cohort followed over a lifetime. Longitudinal studies are of either a prospective or a retrospective nature, or a combination of both. Certain characteristics of the population can be followed in retrospect, and from then on the population can be followed either continuously or at certain intervals. The studies reviewed briefly here are of the combined type; that is, a birth cohort has been followed retrospectively from the age of 13 to 15 years until the age of 60 to 62 years and then followed up until the age of 74 to 76 years and finally until the eightieth birthday of every member of the cohort.

METHOD AND MATERIAL

The cohort was selected and investigated according to the principles of Klemperer's (1933) "biographical" method. This method is not applicable except under special external circumstances. Given these circumstances, as in Iceland, the method is most effective and should give information for the determination of disease expectancy as reliably as possible in retrospective investigations. The essentials and main advantages of the method are as follows:

1. The initial probands are an almost unbiased sample of children in the population to be investigated; that is, persons who have not entered the usual manifestation period of the major psychoses.
2. The health of each individual is investigated as thoroughly as possible during his or her life span or until the individual has passed the manifestation period of the disorders to be investigated.

The only bias in the sample itself is that all the probands belong necessarily to one age group, selected by the fact that those alive at the time of the investigation have passed the manifestation period. Therefore, it is not possible to draw the primary material by random sampling in many age groups; a suitable number of probands born during one year or as few years as possible have to be obtained, possibly by including every person born in these years. This very selection is most helpful in collecting the necessary information about the probands. It makes possible the search of all official registers and hospital files, whereas this work would have been practically impossible if the initial study were carried out for the same number of persons drawn completely at random.

Information is collected on each proband, living or dead, to find all those who may have been sick or abnormal during the observation period and to find out what they have suffered from, when their illness started, how long it lasted, and how severely they were affected. Furthermore, information is collected on social status, family, and other aspects that might affect the health and development of the individual.

It is obvious that information on mild disorders in persons who died forty years ago may be missed. Information on such disorders could only be obtained with complete certainty in a prospective investigation where every minor illness was registered at the time of its occurrence from early adolescence until old age. The difficulties inherent in such a project are evident. The second best choice, when an exploration of a long period is necessary, is a retrospective investigation involving the collection of as much information as possible. The results obtained from such a study concerning minor disorders will have to be regarded as minimal figures.

In longitudinal studies such as this one, it is essential to compromise between two standpoints if the investigation is to achieve its purpose. On the one hand, the probands of the cohort have to be born so long ago that those still alive at the time of the investigation have passed the manifestation period of the diseases to be investigated. Because one of the main purposes of the present investigation was to find the disease expectancy for manic-depressive psychoses, the probands should preferably have been born seventy to seventy-five years before the time of investigation. This condition is also desirable in the investigation of the risk of senile dementia and other diseases that do not make their appearance until one reaches an advanced age. On the other hand, it is important for the reliability of the information obtained that the number of probands who died long ago not be too large.

In compliance with these considerations, it seemed most appropriate to select probands who were born sixty years before the first study was carried out, although about one-fourth of the probands who were in the age range of 13 to 15 years in 1910 would have died by 1957, when the study began. It could be expected that there would still be many persons alive who had known the dead probands well enough to give reliable information on their health. It was also considered more valuable to obtain information about major diseases appearing when the probands were in their fifties than to try to concentrate on minor disorders among those who died at an early age.

Klemperer (1933) and Fremming (1951) selected their probands from birth registers, but only persons who had reached the age of 10 or more were included in the psychiatric survey. The Icelandic study was intended to proceed in the same way. But unfortunately some of the parish records that contained the necessary birth registers had been lost by fire. Therefore the only way to obtain a complete sample of the population in the necessary age group was to draw the names of the probands from the population census registers. The census register from 1910 contained all the necessary identification data on each person. This register was therefore used to draw the sample; that is, all Icelanders born in Iceland during the years 1895 to 1897 and living there on 1 December 1910. The probands were thus 13 to 15 years of age at the beginning of the observation period. As the sample includes all Icelanders of a certain age group alive on a certain date, there is no question about the national representativeness.

The primary sources of information about the probands' health were the general practitioners who had been taking care of them. For the dead and emigrated probands, information was also collected from relatives and acquaintances of the probands as well as from various key informants in each community. Some probands were approached directly, either in writing or personally, and a number of probands who were still alive, especially those with more serious psychiatric problems, had been seen in psychiatric consultation. The information thus obtained was amplified and verified by searching the files of all general and special hospitals in the country, the files of the State Disability Insurance Board, the files of nursing and old age homes, the police records, the files of clinics for alcoholics, and the files of a psychiatrist who had been in practice in Iceland during thirty years of the first forty-seven years of the observation period.

The first stage of the study (Helgason, 1961, 1964) covered forty-seven years; that is, the period from 1 December 1910 to 1 July 1957, when the probands still alive were at the age of 60 to 62 years. Owing to the very extensive sources of data, it was possible to acquire knowledge of 99.4 percent of the 5,395 probands alive on 1 December 1910, sufficient to determine whether they had had mental disorders or not, and most often to diagnose what sort of mental disorder it was.

The second stage (Helgason, 1973, 1979, 1980) of the study covers a period of fourteen years from 1 July 1957 to 1 July 1971, when the probands still alive were at the average age of 74 years. The information in the second phase of the study was collected in very much the same way as during the first stage, except that by this time a psychiatric register had been established comprising those who had been seen by a psychiatrist in Iceland from 1908 on and those who had been admitted to departments of neurology or internal medicine and nursing homes after 1960 and assigned psychiatric diagnoses.

The third stage of the study involves a follow-up of all the members of the cohort until the age of 80. A fourth phase (Helgason, 1979), which has just started, is aimed at identifying the children of the members of the cohort and studying the mental disorders among these in relation to those of their parents.

The material for the first stage of the study comprises all Icelanders born from 1895 to 1897 who were still alive in Iceland on 1 December 1910, a total of 5,395 probands. During the period 1895 to 1897, 7,209 children were born alive in Iceland (Stjórnartíðindi, 1896–1989). Thus 74.8 percent of the birth cohort survived in Iceland until the age of 13 to 15 years.

Only 0.2 percent of the probands of the study could not be traced after 1910. And with regard to another 0.4 percent, it was not possible to obtain sufficient information of psychiatric relevance except that they had been functioning socially. Thus it was possible to trace 99.8 percent of the cohort and to secure relevant data on the health of 99.4 percent.

During the period 1910 to 1957, 27.8 percent of the probands died, while 0.8 percent disappeared alive from observation (Table 14.1). The emigration was minimal — 4.5 percent — during this period.

During the second stage of the study, 0.7 percent of those alive in 1957 could not be traced, and 26.9 percent died before 1 July 1971 (Table 14.2). Thus almost one-half of the original cohort was still alive and available for follow-up in the third phase of the study. In the second stage of the study those who had emigrated were excluded.

Demographic data collected to which the morbidity can be related include age at death or disappearance from observation, causes of death, birthplace, migration, residence at the beginning of the observation period and at the various cross-sectional dates, occupation, social class, and marital status.

The morbidity in the study is expressed as disease expectancy, incidence during certain age periods, and lifetime prevalence. Disease expectancy is defined as the probability of an individual of a given age developing a specified disease at some time during his or her life or previous to a certain later age, provided that the individual survives the manifestation period of the disease or to the specified age. Incidence refers to the number of new cases in the cohort during a specified period of time. Lifetime prevalence is the number of active and previously active cases in the population alive at a certain point in time. If there is no excess mortality among those contracting the disease under study, the lifetime prevalence should be the same as the disease expectancy; other-

Table 14.1. Distribution of Birth Cohort of Icelanders Alive in Iceland at Age 13 to 15 Years (in 1910) According to Sex and Survival until Age 60 to 62 Years (in 1957).

	Male (%)	Female (%)	M+F (%)
Not traced	0.2	0.2	0.2
Disappeared alive 1910– 1957	0.8	0.8	0.8
Deceased 1910–1957	30.7	24.8	27.8
Alive at age 60–62 years	68.3	74.2	71.2
Total	100.0	100.0	100.0
Total no. of probands	2,729	2,666	5,395

Table 14.2. Distribution of Birth Cohort Whose Mental Health Had Been Studied until Age 60 to 62 Years (in 1957) According to Sex and Survival 14 Years Later (in 1971).

	Male (%)	Female (%)	M+F (%)
Emigrated before 1957	2.5	4.6	3.6
Not traced	0.2	1.2	0.7
Deceased 1957–1971	32.5	21.7	26.9
Alive in 1971	64.8	72.5	68.7
Total	100.0	100.0	99.9
Total no. of probands	1,864	1,979	3,843

wise, the disease expectancy will be higher than the lifetime prevalence, provided the case finding among the deceased is as efficient as among those alive.

Disease expectancy is thus an age-corrected expression of morbidity, independent of mortality in various groups at various times. Therefore it is suitable for comparison of morbidity. For methods of calculation of disease expectancy the reader is referred to the main report on the studies (Helgason, 1964).

Here the morbidity is calculated for broad diagnostic groups only. These are, in the results from the first stage of the study, functional psychoses (schizophrenia, manic-depressive psychosis, and psychogenic [reactive] psychoses), neuroses, alcoholism and drug abuse, organic mental disorders, and other functional mental disorders (personality disorder, intellectual subnormality, and unspecified mental disorders). In the results of the second stage, the incidence of organic mental disorders and functional mental disorders, depressive or other, is given.

RESULTS

During the first stage of the study, which was purely retrospective, 1,543 probands were identified with mental disorders occurring before the age of 60 to 62 years or before the proband's disappearance from observation. The available information was sufficient to assign a diagnosis to the majority of these probands. Only 5.8 percent of them could not be given a specific diagnosis and were labeled unspecified mental disorder, which probably is most often some form of personality disorder. Besides this group, another 7.4 percent of the probands had mental disorders whose diagnostic category was uncertain. In Table 14.3 they are included with the group at that time thought to be most likely. Table 14.3 comprises only main diagnosis; it is therefore possible to add the expectancy of developing different forms of mental disorders to obtain a total estimate of developing a mental disorder before the age of 60 to 62 years, which is probably slightly higher for women than for men. Women have a higher expectancy of developing functional psychoses or neuroses before the age of 60 to 62 years, whereas men have a much higher expectancy of developing alcoholism. With regard to the other disorders, the difference between the sexes is not significant. Within the group of functional psychoses, manic-depressive psychosis is the most frequent according to the results of the studies, followed by psychogenic psychoses. Manic-depressive psychosis and psychogenic psychoses are more frequent among women than among men.

The disease expectancy varies according to sociodemographic factors, as shown in Tables 14.4 and 14.5. However, it is not possible to decide from this study whether the mental disorder or the sociodemographic status is the antecedent factor. It has to be borne in mind that in the present study the sociodemographic variables are classified according to

Table 14.3. Expectancy (Percent ± Standard Error) of Mental Disorder until the Age of 60 to 62 Years According to Sex and Main Diagnosis.

	Male (%)	Female (%)	M+F (%)
Functional psychoses	3.57 ± 0.39	6.19 ± 0.50	4.89 ± 0.32
Neuroses	9.50 ± 0.68	18.04 ± 0.86	13.89 ± 0.56
Alcoholism and drug abuse	8.98 ± 0.59	0.89 ± 0.19	4.91 ± 0.31
Organic mental disorders	2.55 ± 0.34	3.45 ± 0.39	3.02 ± 0.26
Personality disorders	2.35 ± 0.29	2.36 ± 0.29	2.35 ± 0.21
Intellectual subnormality	3.11 ± 0.33	2.74 ± 0.32	2.93 ± 0.23
Unspecified mental disorders	2.41 ± 0.36	1.67 ± 0.29	2.03 ± 0.23
Total	32.47 ± 1.00	35.34 ± 1.03	34.02 ± 0.72

Table 14.4. Expectancy (Percent ± Standard Error) of Mental Disorder until the Age of 60 to 62 Years According to Social Class and Main Diagnosis.

	Social Class I	Social Class II	Social Class III
Functional psychoses	4.23 ± 0.64	3.89 ± 0.49	6.00 ± 0.53
Neuroses	14.29 ± 1.19	11.76 ± 0.88	15.41 ± 0.89
Alcoholism and drug abuse	6.78 ± 0.79	4.49 ± 0.52	4.34 ± 0.44
Other functional mental disorders	1.81 ± 0.42	5.50 ± 0.58	10.92 ± 0.64
Organic mental disorders	2.12 ± 0.47	2.71 ± 0.42	3.69 ± 0.43
Total	29.23 ± 1.49	28.35 ± 1.18	40.36 ± 1.11

the probands' own achievements. Thus it is obvious that disorders which have developed at an early age and impair social achievements will result in the probands' low socioeconomic status and their remaining unmarried. According to Table 14.4, the expectancy of alcoholism tends to be highest in social class I, whereas the expectancy for all other disorders tends to be highest in social class III. In these tables intellectual impairment, personality disorders, and unspecified mental disorders are taken together as other functional disorders. Their common factor is that they have developed at an early age and characterize the person for most of his or her life. These disorders explain the much higher total expectancy

Table 14.5. Expectancy (Percent ± Standard Error) of Mental Disorder until the Age of 60 to 62 Years According to Marital Status and Main Diagnosis.

	Never-Married	Ever-Married
Functional psychoses	8.39 ± 0.86	3.85 ± 0.33
Neuroses	14.04 ± 1.22	13.86 ± 0.63
Alcoholism and drug abuse	4.81 ± 0.64	4.94 ± 0.36
Other functional mental disorders	13.89 ± 0.95	4.96 ± 0.36
Organic mental disorders	4.03 ± 0.62	2.70 ± 0.28
Total	45.16 ± 1.53	30.31 ± 0.80

of developing a mental disorder in social class III. The morbidity pattern is slightly different among men and among women, as the expectancy of neuroses among women tends to be slightly higher in social class III than in the other social classes, whereas among men it is highest in social class I.

The expectancy according to marital status is calculated only for those who have remained single during their life and for those who are or have been married. The divorced and widowed are thus included with the married under the heading "ever-married." The expectancy for alcoholism and neuroses is fairly similar among the never-married and among the ever-married, whereas the expectancy of functional psychoses and especially of the other functional mental disorders is much higher among the never-married than among those who have married. Again, a large proportion of the difference in the total expectancy of mental disorders is explained by the much higher expectancy of unspecified and personality disorders and intellectual impairment among those who have remained single during their life. In connection with the organic mental disorder, it should be remembered that epileptics, who most often have developed their disease at a young age, are included in this group, which probably explains the higher expectancy of organic mental disorders among the never-married in comparison with the ever-married.

The lifetime prevalence at the cross-sectional date of the first stage of the study is shown in Table 14.6. At the probands' average age of 61 years, the total lifetime prevalence of mental disorders was 30.9 percent,

Table 14.6. Lifetime Prevalence of Mental Disorder (Percent ± Standard Error) According to Sex and Main Diagnosis at Age 60 to 62 Years.

	Male (%)	Female (%)	M+F (%)
Functional psychoses	2.74 ± 0.38	4.95 ± 0.49	3.88 ± 0.31
Neuroses	9.50 ± 0.68	18.04 ± 0.86	13.90 ± 0.56
Alcoholism and drug abuse	7.46 ± 0.61	0.61 ± 0.18	3.93 ± 0.31
Other functional mental disorders	7.78 ± 0.62	6.37 ± 0.55	7.05 ± 0.41
Organic mental disorders	1.88 ± 0.31	2.37 ± 0.34	2.13 ± 0.23
Total	29.36 ± 1.05	32.34 ± 1.05	30.89 ± 0.75

probably slightly higher among women than among men. The lifetime prevalence comprises those who have had a mental disorder at some time during their life, but are not necessarily ill at the time of the study. The lifetime prevalence of disorders that have an excess mortality is lower than the disease expectancy, whereas the prevalence of disorders without excess mortality is the same as the lifetime prevalence.

The second stage of the study included those of the original cohort who were alive in 1957 in Iceland at the age of 60 to 62 years. Information was collected on this group until their death or until they reached the age of 74 to 76 years; that is, over a period of fourteen years. Besides giving an epidemiological description of the mental disorders occurring during this period of life, this part of the study provided answers to the question of whether those with previous functional mental disorders were more prone to develop age-related organic mental disorders than were probands without a mental disorder. During this period 534 new psychiatric cases were identified. About 55 percent of these were diagnosed as organic mental disorders related to cerebrovascular disturbances or degenerative processes in the brain occurring with advancing age. Of functional disorders identified during this age period, depressive syndromes were most common, accounting for almost one-fourth (22.6 percent) of all new cases identified. In addition to the new cases with depressive syndromes, 173 cases that had previously had a psychiatric diagnosis with depressive or other symptoms were now classified as depressive. Thus, 8 percent of the probands who had reached the age of 60 to 62 years had a depressive illness after this age and before the age of 74 to 76 years. More than one-half of these cases had at some time been seen by a psychiatrist or admitted to a hospital.

The incidence of organic and functional mental disorders during this period is shown in Table 14.7. In spite of allegedly intensive case identification during the first stage of the study, sixty-two cases were identified during the second stage, which actually had an earlier onset. These are considered here as having an onset at the age of 61. The incidence of organic mental disorder rises with age, especially after the age of 70, whereas the incidence of functional disorders other than depressive decreases after this age. The sum of the incidence rates or disease expectancy is 16.7 percent for men and 16.5 percent for women. By adding these rates to the expectancy rates calculated from the results of the first stage of the study, the overall expectancy of a person at the age of 14 developing a mental disorder before the age of 75 years can be estimated to be 49.2 percent for men and 51.8 percent for women. But it could be maintained that it was more correct to calculate the incidence rate only

Table 14.7. Expectancy (Percent ± Standard Error) of Mental Disorders Developing for First Time in Population Aged 61 to 74 Years According to Sex and Main Diagnosis.

	Male (%)	Female (%)	M+F (%)
Organic mental disorders	10.67 ± 0.80	8.46 ± 0.69	9.49 ± 0.52
Depressive mental disorders	3.36 ± 0.46	4.11 ± 0.48	3.75 ± 0.33
Other functional mental disorders	2.66 ± 0.39	3.91 ± 0.46	3.30 ± 0.30
Total	16.69 ± 0.95	16.48 ± 0.90	16.54 ± 0.65

for the previously mentally healthy probands. If this is done for the age group 61 to 74, the incidence rates are approximately 27 percent for men and 28 percent for women instead of 16.7 and 16.5 percent, respectively, thus inflating the estimate of the overall disease expectancy by 10 percent.

Besides new cases identified during the second stage of the study, a number of previously diagnosed cases were assigned a new main diagnosis, most often an organic mental disorder. Table 14.8 shows that similar proportions of previously mentally healthy probands and probands who previously had a functional mental disorder were diagnosed as having organic mental disorder during the age period 61 to 74 years. On the other hand, a similar proportion of previously organic cases were now given a main diagnosis of functional mental disorder. Almost 30

Table 14.8. Distribution of Mental Disorders Occurring from Age 61 to 74 Years According to Diagnosis before Age 61 Years.

Diagnosis at Age 61–74 Years	Diagnosis before 61 Years of Age				No. of Probands
	None (%)	Organic (%)	Functional (%)	Total (%)	
None	78.8	12.5	29.5	63.0	2,315
Organic	11.8	75.0	13.0	13.5	497
Functional	9.4	12.5	57.5	23.5	865
Total	100.0	100.0	100.0	100.0	3,677

percent of the probands who had previously had a functional mental disorder were not assigned any diagnosis after the age of 61. These were mostly probands with an earlier diagnosis of neuroses. These results do not give any support to the notion that people with functional mental disorders are more prone to develop organic mental disorders with advancing age.

Tables 14.9 and 14.10 show the distribution of patients identified during the follow-up in the second stage of the study according to social factors, compared with those without mental disorder. There are proportionally more unmarried and fewer married patients with functional disorders than in the general population, which reflects the findings from the first part of the study, whereas the marital status among those with organic syndromes is fairly similar to that of the general population and not very different from that of those without mental disorders. A greater proportion of patients with organic or functional disorders than of persons without mental disorder belong to social class III. More probands without mental disorders belong to social class II, whereas a similar proportion of patients and probands without mental disorders belong to social class I.

Table 14.11 compares the outcome of those having a diagnosis of mental disorder during the age period of 61 to 74 years with the outcome of those without such a diagnosis. An excess proportion of deaths and disability is found among those with organic mental disorders and also, but to a lesser extent, among those with functional mental disorders. Disability is defined as a reduction in working capacity that would entitle a person to social security benefits; that is, a disability rating of more

Table 14.9. Comparison of Marital Status among Probands with Psychiatric Diagnosis and without Psychiatric Diagnosis from Average Age 61 to 74 Years.

	Single (%)	Married (%)	Widowed (%)	Divorced (%)	Total (%)	No. of Probands
Organic mental disorders	20.5	50.9	23.5	5.0	99.9	497
Functional mental disorders	27.4	41.8	24.5	6.2	99.9	865
Without mental disorders	18.6	53.8	24.1	3.5	100.0	2,315
Total	20.9	50.6	24.1	4.4	100.0	3,677

χ^2 52.59, df = 6, p < 0.001

Table 14.10. Comparison of Social Class among Probands with and without Psychiatric Diagnosis from Average Age 61 to 74 Years.

	Social Class I (%)	Social Class II (%)	Social Class III (%)	Total (%)	No. of Probands
Organic mental disorders	23.7	31.0	45.3	100.0	497
Functional mental disorders	21.3	31.3	47.4	100.0	865
Without mental disorders	22.2	37.0	40.9	100.1	2,315
Total	22.2	34.8	43.0	100.0	3,677
		χ^2 16.03, df = 4, p $<$ 0.01			

than 50 percent. Psychiatric disability is higher among women, both among those with organic and those with functional disorders, while a greater proportion of men are deceased in both illness groups. The high mortality among men with functional mental disorders is mainly accounted for by the alcohol abusers, almost exclusively a male disorder in this cohort. Of the group without mental illness, 63.5 percent were still

Table 14.11. Comparison of Outcomes among Probands with and without Psychiatric Diagnosis Registered during Age Period 61 to 74 Years.

	Psychiatric Diagnosis				No Psychiatric Diagnosis	
	Organic (%)		Functional (%)			
	Male	Female	Male	Female	Male	Female
Not disabled	28.7	30.5	39.6	46.9	60.5	66.3
Psychiatric disability	23.1	27.6	11.5	21.8		
Other disability	8.8	6.9	8.1	9.4	10.0	12.5
Dead	39.4	35.0	40.8	21.8	29.4	21.2
Total	100.0	100.0	100.0	99.9	99.9	100.0
No. of probands	251	246	407	458	1,155	1,160

SOURCE: Data from Helgason, 1980.

alive at the average age of 74 years and not disabled, while 43.5 percent of those with functional mental disorders were still alive and not disabled, and only 29.6 percent of those with organic mental disorders were still alive and classified as not disabled.

In the first stage of the study, suicide accounted for 3.4 percent of the deaths. In the second part, it accounted for 1 percent of the total number of deaths, whereas in the third part of the study, only one proband had committed suicide out of approximately 600 deaths. Almost 90 percent of the probands who had committed suicide had been mentally ill. From these data, the expectancy of committing suicide before the age of 75 years can be estimated to be approximately 2 percent for men and 1 percent for women.

DISCUSSION

I have attempted to make the case finding in the study of this birth cohort as intensive as possible. This has been done by seeking information on each proband individually from a number of sources where he or his family may have applied for treatment or assistance. One of the major sources of information has been the present or the last general practitioner taking care of a proband. This practitioner obviously has not been taking care of the proband during the whole observation period, and therefore it is quite possible that he or she has incomplete information on the proband's state of health prior to registration on the practitioner's list. This was borne out by experience during the first stage of the study, when a number of cases were identified through sources other than the general practitioners, who under these circumstances added information on the proband's state of health at the cross-sectional date of the study. The coverage with regard to the identification of psychoses and the more severe form of other mental disorders is probably fairly good. But it is beyond doubt that it has not been possible to identify all cases of minor illness, especially those occurring during the earlier part of the observation period. This is clearly borne out by comparison of the lifetime prevalence of these disorders among those still alive at the cross-sectional date of the study with that among the deceased. Therefore, lifetime prevalence among the probands alive at the age of 60 to 62 years has been taken as the best estimate for the disease expectancy for neuroses and unspecified mental disorders. Also, in the follow-up part of the study a number of cases were identified that had developed during the observation period of the first stage and should therefore have been identified earlier.

On the other hand, the long observation period, as well as the follow-up during the second stage of this study, makes it unlikely that many cases have been misidentified as psychiatric. In the first stage of the study, some cases were marked as uncertain in view of limited information. Those who survived until the follow-up period, when further information was collected, proved during the second stage of the study to be psychiatric.

In the second stage of the study, the cases were identified through other psychiatrists, general practitioners, and hospital records. The proband or his family thus had to decide if he was ill enough to consult a physician. Only exceptionally were cases identified through other sources, contrary to what had to be done in the first stage of the study, when cases were also identified through key informants, family members, or by interview with the probands themselves. Therefore it is possible that cases remain unidentified in the population where the initiative to seek treatment or other forms of assistance has not been taken.

Clearly, then, the estimates of disease expectancy presented here are presumably minimal figures. The total disease expectancy for men and women is fairly similar, although slightly higher for women. But the morbidity pattern is different for the sexes, especially with regard to neuroses and alcoholism. Neuroses are twice as frequent among women as among men, while alcohol and drug abuse is ten times more frequent among men than among women. The sum of the expectancy of developing either neuroses or alcoholism is almost equal for men and women. Further, the expectancy according to social class and marital status is similar for neuroses and alcoholism. This finding has been used as epidemiological evidence for the hypothesis that alcoholism and neuroses may have a common etiological factor (Helgason, 1970).

Apart from the difference between the expectancy of neuroses and that of alcoholism, the fact that women have higher expectancy of functional psychoses is accounted for by manic-depressive psychosis and reactive depressive psychosis.

Disorders other than neuroses and alcoholism occur most frequently among those who belong to the lowest social class and among those who have never been married. Compared to the probands without mental disorders during the age of 61 to 74 years, more patients in this age group are either single or divorced and belong to social class III. When evaluating these results, it must be considered that a personality disorder, mental subnormality, or psychiatric illness contracted at an early age, or for that matter any illness contracted at an early age, impedes the possibilities of an individual's climbing the social ladder or getting married. Therefore, the frequency of mental disorders is higher among probands socially isolated and with low social status. But it is also likely that the stress related to poverty, social isolation, and low social status predisposes one to the development of mental disorders.

With regard to the outcome among the probands who have survived until the age of 74 to 76 years, it has already been pointed out that alcohol abuse undoubtedly contributes to the higher mortality among men than among women with functional mental disorders. Conversely, the higher frequency of neurosis may explain why more women are disabled for psychiatric reasons at this age. It may be pointed out here that mortality is the only epidemiological criterion considered in this study in which neuroses and alcoholism differ markedly. The lower ratio of physical disability among psychiatric patients is probably more apparent than real. These patients may be as physically handicapped as the others, although mental illness accounts for the major part of their disability.

SUMMARY

In a study of a birth cohort of 5,395 Icelanders followed from the age of 13 to 15 years until the age of 74 to 76 years, 2,077 cases of mental disorders were identified. On this basis, the expectancy of developing a mental disorder before the average age of 75 years is estimated to be about 50 percent, similar for both sexes. The expectancy of committing suicide before this age is 2 percent for men and 1 percent for women.

V EXAMPLES OF LONGITUDINAL RESEARCH:
Populations at Risk

15 CHILDREN OF SCHIZOPHRENIC MOTHERS: *The Danish High-Risk Study*

Sarnoff A. Mednick, Fini Schulsinger, and John J. Griffith

The research program for the Danish high-risk study of schizophrenia was first formulated in 1960 (Mednick, 1960) and operationalized in Copenhagen in 1962. This study was the first of its kind. It has provoked a number of similar enterprises in various parts of the world.

METHODOLOGY OF HIGH-RISK STUDY

The high-risk method involves the prospective follow-up of individuals who have characteristics that are empirically predictive of eventual psychological breakdown. The most commonly used characteristic has been parental schizophrenia. It should be pointed out that the *risk* model is used only because of its efficiency. A superior research design would assess and follow an entire unselected birth cohort. However, in view of the fact that only 1 percent of such a population would become schizophrenic, a fairly large cohort would be required in order to yield an appropriate number of schizophrenics. Because the critical predisposing factors that this design hopes to ascertain can be detected only by intensive individual assessments, smaller cohorts with higher yields of schizophrenics are desirable. This is the reason we turned to children with chronically schizophrenic mothers, where the risk of schizophrenia is as high as 16 percent.

After the high-risk subjects are identified and intensively assessed (typically along with controls), they are followed for an appropriate period until some level of decompensation is observed in some of the subjects. The life data and individual characteristics of the decompensated subjects are then examined to find characteristics that distinguish them from their more fortunate cosubjects. If these distinguishing characteristics can result in efficient and reliable discrimination, and if generalization to the population as a whole is feasible from the high-risk subjects, then we shall have devised an assessment battery that can be administered to an unselected population of children to identify a target group for intervention research. (For further elaboration, see Mednick and Lanoil, 1977.)

Rationale

When we compare this research methodology with the typical study that observes characteristics of patients already schizophrenic, we find certain advantages in the high-risk design:

1. When they are first examined in the study, the high-risk children typically have not yet experienced such aspects of the schizophrenic life as hospitalization or drugs. These factors do not color their reactions to the test procedures.
2. Since at the time of the examination no one knows which of the high-risk subjects might become schizophrenic, the data are relieved of much of the tester bias.
3. The information we gather in such research tends to be current and not exclusively retrospective.
4. The data are uniformly and systematically obtained.

A more complete statement of the rationale of the high-risk design may be found in Mednick and McNeil (1968).

Procedure

Having presented the rationale of this design, we will now briefly describe the manner in which the project was conducted. In 1962 we intensively examined 207 children who had mothers whose schizophrenia was typical and severe and would be agreed upon as being typical and severe both in Europe and in the United States. We also assessed 104 low-risk control children who had had no member of their immediate family hospitalized for mental illness for three generations. This was determined by reference to the National Psychiatric Register, which maintains a central file for every psychiatric hospitalization in the Kingdom of Denmark going back to 1916.

Table 15.1 presents the characteristics of the high-risk and low-risk groups at the time of their initial assessment in 1962. Note that we attempted to match for their having been reared in a children's home. Note also that the average age of the samples was 15.1 years. They ranged from 9 to 20 years of age. Studies of 3-year-old and 10-year-old high-risk samples are currently underway.

Table 15.2 presents a list of the procedures and examinations that all subjects experienced. During the examination, the examiners did not know whether a subject was a high-risk or a low-risk individual.

Table 15.1. Characteristics of Experimental and Control Samples.

	Control	*Experimental*
Number of cases	104	207
Number of boys	59	121
Number of girls	45	86
Mean age*	15.1	15.1
Mean social class**	2.3	2.2
Mean years education	7.3	7.0
Percentage of group in children's homes (5 years or more)†	14%	16%
Mean number of years in children's homes (5 years or more)†	8.5	9.4
Percentage of group with rural residence††	22%	26%

* Defined as age to the nearest whole year.
** Scale runs from 0 (low) to 6 (high) and was adapted from Svalastoga, 1959.

† We only considered experience in children's homes of 5 years or greater duration. Many of the experimental children had been to children's homes for brief periods while their mothers were hospitalized. These experiences were seen as quite different from the experience of children who actually had to make a children's home their home until they could go out and earn their own living.

†† A rural residence was defined as living in a town with a population of 2,500 persons or fewer.

Table 15.2.   Experimental Measures, 1962 High-Risk Assessment.

1. Psychophysiology
   a. Conditioning-extinction-generalization
   b. Response to mild and loud sounds
2. Wechsler Intelligence Scale for Children (Danish adaptation)
3. Personality inventory
4. Word association test
5. Continuous association test
   a. 30 words
   b. 1 minute of associating to each word
6. Adjective check list used by examiners to describe subjects
7. Psychiatric interview
8. Interview with parent or rearing agent
9. School report from teacher
10. Midwife's report on mother's pregnancy and delivery of subject

Preliminary Findings on Sick-Group Characteristics

Following the intensive examination in 1962, an alarm network was established in Denmark so that most hospital and all psychiatric admissions for anyone in this sample would be reported to us. The number of reports of serious psychiatric or social breakdowns reached twenty in 1967. Very brief summaries of their case stories are given in Table 15.3.

We then looked back to our data from 1962 to find characteristics that distinguished those who suffered breakdowns from carefully matched high-risk (HR) and low-risk (LR) controls. The most important characteristics distinguishing the sick group from the controls are given in Table 15.4. We shall call attention to a few of these characteristics:

1. The sick group suffered considerably more early separation from their parents than did the two control groups.
2. Rather than the classic textbook picture of the preschizophrenic child, the sick-group subjects were disciplinary problems, domineering and aggressive in their classroom behavior.
3. While a number of psychophysiological variables predicted to their sick-group status, the one that was the best discriminator was the rate of recovery from momentary states of autonomic imbalance.
4. The sick group evidenced considerably more pregnancy and delivery complications.

Table 15.3. Descriptions of Sick-Group Conditions.

Male, born 16 March 1953; extremely withdrawn, no close contacts, 2 months' psychiatric admission following theft, currently in institution for boys with behavior difficulties, still performing petty thefts.

Female, born 19 January 1943; married, one child, extremely withdrawn, nervous, evidence of delusional thinking, pulls her hair out, has large bald area.

Female, born 29 March 1946; promiscuous, highly unstable in work, no close contacts, confused and unrealistic, psychiatric admission for diagnostic reasons, recent abortion, some evidence of thought disorder.

Male, born 1 July 1946; under minor provocation had semipsychotic breakdown in army, expresses strange distortions of his body image, thought processes vague, immature.

Male, born 2 May 1944; severe difficulties in concentrating, cannot complete tasks, marked schizoid character, marginally adjusted.

Male, born 3 June 1947; lonely in the extreme, spends all spare time at home, manages at home only by virtue of extremely compulsive routines, no heterosexual activity, marked schizoid character.

Male, born 1 October 1953; no close contact with peers; attends class for retarded children; abuses younger children; recently took a little boy out in the forest, undressed him, urinated on him and his clothes, and sent him home.

Male, born 17 January 1954; has history of convulsions, constantly takes antiseizure drug (Dilantin), nervous, confabulating, unhappy, sees frightening "nightmares" during the day, afraid of going to sleep because of nightmares and fear that people are watching through the window, feels teacher punishes him unjustly.

Female, born 18 March 1944; nervous quick mood changes, body image distortions, passive, resigned, psychiatric admission, paranoid tendencies revealed, vague train of thought.

Male, born 14 March 1952; arrested for involvement in theft of motorbike, extremely withdrawn, difficulties in concentration, passive, disinterested, father objected to his being institutionalized and consequently he is now out under psychiatric supervision.

Male, born 19 October 1947; level of intellectual performance in apprenticeship decreasing, private life extremely disorderly, abreacts through alcoholism.

Male, born 20 January 1944; severe schizoid character; no heterosexual activity; lives an immature, shy, anhedonic life; thought disturbances revealed in TAT.

Female, born 25 May 1947; psychiatric admission, abortion, hospital report suspects pseudoneurotic or early schizophrenia, association tests betray thought disturbance, tense, guarded, ambivalent, current difficulties somewhat precipitated by sudden death of boyfriend.

Table 15.3. Continued

Male, born 13 August 1950; sensitive, negativistic, unrealistic, recently stopped working and was referred to a youth guidance clinic for evaluation, is now under regular supervision of a psychologist.

Male, born 28 May 1947; history of car stealing, unstable, drifting, unemployed, sensitive, easily hurt, one year institutionalization in a reformatory for the worst delinquents in Denmark.

Female, born 1 June 1945; psychotic episode; one year of hospitalization; diagnoses from 2 hospitals: (1) schizophrenia, (2) manic psychosis.

Male, born 3 September 1946; severe schizoid character; psychotic breakdown in army, preceded by arrest for car thievery; now hospitalized.

Male, born 28 January 1953; perhaps borderline retarded, psychiatric admission for diagnostic reasons, spells of uncontrolled behavior.

Male, born 23 June 1948; repeatedly apprehended for stealing, severe mood swings, sensitive, restless, unrealistic, fired from job because of financial irregularities.

Female, born 5 July 1941; highly intelligent girl with mystical interests, very much afflicted by mother's schizophrenia, TAT reveals thought disorder, receiving psychotherapy.

An interesting sidelight with respect to the perinatal events noted in item 4 is the fact that the high-risk group that had not suffered breakdown evidenced fewer perinatal difficulties than did the low-risk control group. This finding suggested to us that perhaps there is a special interaction between the genetic predisposition for schizophrenia and pregnancy and delivery complications. It was almost as if a complication-free pregnancy was needed for a high-risk subject to fare well. The paper reporting the findings (Mednick, 1970) mentioned that there was a marked correspon-

Table 15.4. Distinguishing Characteristics of Sick Group.

1. Lost mother to psychiatric hospitalization relatively early in life
2. Teacher reports disturbing, aggressive behavior in school
3. Evidence of associative drift
4. Psychophysiological anomalies
   a. Markedly fast latency of response
   b. No signs of habituation from response latency evidence
   c. Resistance to experimental extinction of conditioned GSR
   d. Remarkably fast rate of recovery following response peak
5. Serious pregnancy and/or birth complications suffered by 70% of sick group

dence between the pregnancy and birth complications and the deviant electrodermal behavior. Almost all the electrodermal differences between the groups could be explained by these perinatal difficulties in the sick group. The perinatal difficulties in the low-risk group were not as strongly associated with these extreme electrodermal effects. This finding further suggested that pregnancy and delivery complications trigger some characteristics that may be genetically predisposed.

THEORY

A minitheory has guided but not dominated this longitudinal project. The theory, first published in 1958, suggests that the syndrome of schizophrenia is an evasion of life, learned on the basis of physiological predispositions (Mednick, 1958). It suggests that the combination of exposure to an unkind environment, possession of an autonomic nervous system (ANS) that responds too often and too much, *and* an abnormally fast rate of autonomic recovery provide an aptitude for learning evasive avoidance responses. If an individual is to become schizophrenic, he must possess both the ANS responsiveness *and* recovery characteristics. If an individual is rapidly, exaggeratedly, and untiringly emotionally reactive, he may become anxious or even psychotic but will not tend to learn schizophrenia unless his rate of recovery tends to be very fast. It also seems likely that an extraordinarily reactive ANS will require only moderately fast recovery, while an extraordinarily fast rate of recovery will require only moderate reactiveness. Both very high reactiveness and very fast recovery will result in a very heavy predisposition for avoidance learning and hence for schizophrenia.

DIAGNOSTIC ASSESSMENT, 1972

From an earlier study by Niels Reisby (1967) at the Copenhagen Psykologisk Institut, we could estimate that at the average age of 25 years — that is, in 1972 — we should expect to be able to diagnose approximately half the eventual schizophrenics in the high-risk group. Thus at that time we initiated an intensive assessment of the high- and low-risk samples. The central goal of this reassessment was the establishment of a reliable diagnosis and an evaluation of the samples' current life status.

Table 15.5.   1972 Follow-up Results with 1962 Samples.

	High-Risk (N = 207)	Low-Risk (N = 104)
Full assessment complete	173	91
Home interview only (social worker)	10	6
Not yet contacted (parent objected or the subject could not be located)	6	2
Living abroad	6	0
Deceased	10	0
Subject refused	6	5

Procedure

The 1972 assessment consisted of psychophysiological and cognitive tests, a social interview, and, most important, a battery of diagnostic devices. The diagnostic devices included a 3¼-hour clinical interview by an experienced diagnostician, a full MMPI, and psychiatric hospitalization diagnoses and records, where they existed. Both the Current and Past Psychopathology Scales (CAPPS) and the Present Status Examination (PSE), 9th edition, were completed by the interviewer. Computer diagnoses were obtained from the PSE and CAPPS materials. Details of the assessment have been published (Mednick, Schulsinger, and Schulsinger, 1975; H. Schulsinger, 1976).

Table 15.5 presents information on the results of our follow-up contacts with the subjects. Ten of the high-risk subjects have died in the course of the follow-up: seven by suicide, two by accidental causes, and one by natural cause. None of the low-risk subjects has died. This is a dramatic difference, which we shall explore further in future papers. Of the ten, six died before the assessment began; three of the other four took part in the assessment. Thus, of the 201 high-risk subjects available for the assessment, 91 percent took some part in the interview (10 had only a home interview by the social worker). Of the low-risk subjects 91 took part in the full interview and 6 took part in the home interview. Thus, 93 percent of the low-risk group has taken some part in the interview.

Table 15.6 presents identifying information on those who completed the full interview. The groups seem to be well matched with each other

Table 15.6.   Identifying Characteristics of High- and Low-Risk Subjects Participating in Full Interview, 1972.

	High-Risk	Low-Risk
Number — full interview	173	91
Mean age at 1962 assessment	14.9	15.1
Mean social class	2.1	2.4
Number males	97	53
Number females	76	38

and with the total original sample with respect to age, sex, and social class.

Reliability of the Diagnosis

The diagnosis of schizophrenia made by the interviewer is based on the presence of Bleuler's primary symptoms: thought disorder, autism, ambivalence, and emotional blunting, as well as Bleuler's secondary symptoms: delusions and hallucinations. For a diagnosis of schizophrenia it was not necessary that all these symptoms be observed at the time of the interview; they might also be drawn from the case history. In two separate papers (Mednick, Schulsinger, and Schulsinger, 1975; H. Schulsinger, 1976), detailed descriptions of the tests of the reliability of the diagnoses have been reported. For our purposes here, it is sufficient to say that across the two computer-derived diagnoses, the MMPI (analyzed blindly by Professor Irving Gottesman) and the clinical diagnosis, as well as an independent diagnosis arrived at by two Danish psychiatrists listening to the audiotape of the entire interview for ten subjects, a rather excellent diagnostic agreement was achieved. (We wish to thank Drs. Lise Hauge and Raben Rosenberg for their work on the reliability tests.)

The interview was, in part, coded in the form of a rather extensive series of questions. A very significant portion of these questions refer to symptoms of mental illness. It is interesting that one of the Danish psychiatrists listening to the audiotapes of these interviews had almost perfect agreement with the interviewer's codings of the CAPPS items. The codes for these items range from 1 to 6. In 91 percent of the items his coding was no more than one unit different.

Another indication of the reliability of the coding and diagnoses may be found in the two important measures of severity of illness resulting from the interview. At the conclusion of the CAPPS interview form, the interviewer is required to rate the severity of illness on a scale from 1 to 6. Ratings of 5 and 6 occurred only for those who were diagnosed schizophrenic. This rating correlated .70 with a rating of severity derived from the PSE.

RESULTS OF THE 1972 ASSESSMENT

Premorbid Characteristics of Diagnosed Schizophrenics

Seventeen of the high-risk subjects (nine men and eight women) received a diagnosis of "schizophrenia" by consensus on two of the following diagnostic methods: PSE, CAPPS, and clinical diagnosis.

In an initial overview of the data we noted that the high-risk subjects who became schizophrenic were significantly characterized by the following premorbid factors (in comparison with the other high-risk subjects):

1. Their mothers evidenced a more severe course of illness.
2. The schizophrenics had been separated from their parents and many placed in children's homes quite early in their lives.
3. Perinatal difficulties for the schizophrenic group were greater than for the other groups.
4. Schoolteachers reported that the schizophrenics were extremely disturbing to the class, easily angered, violent, and aggressive.
5. The autonomic nervous system recovery rate as measured in 1962 was found to predict schizophrenia very well, especially for persons suffering symptoms of hallucinations, delusions, and thought disorder.

Sex Differences in Factors Predisposing to Schizophrenia

In considering these preliminary reports, one factor seemed extremely striking. We were sensitized to the factor of sex differences in high-risk children by Dr. Helen Orvaschel (1976). Almost all the findings listed above have been cited in the literature as being especially responsive to sex differences in schizophrenics. Gardner (1967) and Sobel (1961) have reported that the degree of the mother's illness, for example, affects the level of schizophrenia in females but not in males. Rosenthal (1962) has commented on the higher concordance for female monozygotic schizophrenics than for males. Male discordance in monozygotic twins with schizophrenia is twice as great as for females. Although there are some sampling problems in these twin studies, such information might suggest that schizophrenia in females is more genetically determined and that schizophrenia in males has a heavier environmental weight.

With respect to the pregnancy and delivery complications, in our more recent high-risk study, focusing on perinatal factors (Mednick et al., 1971), we have found differential sex effects of perinatal complications. It is also well known that males are more vulnerable to pregnancy and delivery difficulties. Finally, aggressive school behavior has been shown by Watt et al. (1970) to be associated with later schizophrenia in men but not in women.

In view of the fact that almost all the preliminary findings mentioned above are highly sex dependent, we determined to conduct separate analyses of these variables for males and females.

Hypotheses to Be Examined

The analyses of the factors potentially predispositional to schizophrenia were conducted separately for male and for female HR individuals. It was hypothesized that:

1. The *seriousness of illness* of the mother (as indicated by early onset) would be of significance for both sexes, but would be more important for women.
2. *Separation from parents* during early life would be important for both sexes.
3. *Pregnancy and birth complications* would increase the probability of the development of schizophrenia in both sexes (because of the male foetus's greater vulnerability to perinatal stress, we hypothesized greater effects for males than for females).
4. *ANS recovery and responsiveness* would be involved in the development of schizophrenia.

In summary, we hypothesized that for female HR individuals the development of schizophrenia would be especially related to early onset of the schizophrenic mother's illness. In males we hypothesized that the perinatal variables would be especially predictive. In both sexes ANS factors and early separation were hypothesized as predispositional to schizophrenia.

METHOD OF STATISTICAL ANALYSIS: PATH ANALYSIS

While a practical goal of this statistical analysis is to develop identifying characteristics of children who will later become schizophrenic, an underlying hope is progress toward an understanding of the etiology of schizophrenia.

Methods have been developed in the field of genetics and used extensively in the field of economics that allow for hypothesized causal models to be stated in mathematical form in a way that allows their agreement with observed covariances to be examined. So although we can never completely validate or prove a "causal" statement, we can examine its expected consequences by examining the goodness-of-fit of hypothesized covariances (that is, generated under a hypothesized model) to observed covariances.

In this analysis we are operating with variables that span the lifetimes of the individuals involved. We begin with the seriousness of the schizophrenia of the mother, examine perinatal factors, consider the intactness of the individuals' homes, and see all this in the light of their socioeconomic status during rearing, the functioning of their autonomic nervous system, and their sex. We know that many of these independent variables are intercorrelated. For example, the earlier the onset of illness of the mother, the more separation from the mother the child experiences. Other, less obvious intercorrelations also exist in these data. Therefore, multiple analyses of individual independent variables in relationship to the dependent variable, schizophrenia, run the risk of repeatedly rediscovering a single or few common findings. Therefore, we chose a model in which all the interrelationships are estimated simultaneously and all other intercorrelations are taken into consideration. We also foresaw the possible problems inherent in mediated effects. Thus, the seriousness of the illness of the mother might not have any direct effects on her child's development of schizophrenia but may have its effect mediated by the resulting disruption of the child's home life. For these and other reasons, we chose a statistical technique that could estimate both the direct and the mediated effects; that is, Jöreskog and von Thillo's (1972) maximum likelihood estimation procedure for structural equations (LISREL). LISREL is a special case of Jöreskog's (1970) earlier analysis of covariance structures and is an advanced form of path analysis. It is a statistical tool that has great advantages for the analysis of data from longitudinal projects.

Definition of Constructs

In the Jöreskog LISREL path analysis important factors are represented as constructs. The constructs are not directly measured but are defined by indicators. These indicators of a construct go through a process that may be seen as roughly analogous to the development of communalities in factor analysis. These "communalities" then represent the construct. Rather than relate the individual and relatively unreliable indicators to one another, the constructs are interrelated. This serves to reduce some of the lack of reliability inherent in any individual indicator of a construct. For example, as indicators of the construct "separation from parents" (separation) in the first five years of life, we used three indicators from the first five years of life: (1) amount of separation from the father, (2) amount of separation from the mother, and (3) amount of time the child spent in children's homes. For the construct "age of onset of mother's schizophrenia" (mother's onset) we used two indicators: (1) age at first appearance of symptoms and (2) age at first psychiatric hospitalization. Thus, when we are interrelating separation and mother's onset we are interrelating two constructs rather than individual indicators.

Indicators of the Constructs

Table 15.7 lists the constructs and their indicators. Certain of the constructs may require more explanation.

Age of Onset of Mother's Schizophrenia (Mother's Onset). Age of onset of schizophrenia is a rather good indicator of the seriousness of the condition. The mother's age at the beginning of symptoms was taken from her hospital case record. Her age at first hospital admission was taken from the Risskov Demographic Institute's Psychiatric Register.

Pregnancy and Birth Complications (PBCs). The scale has been described in previous publications (Mednick, 1970; Mirdal et al., 1974). It is based on weights assigned by obstetricians and pediatricians to the

Table 15.7. "Early Factors" Constructs and Their Indicators.

Construct Name	Indicators
Mother's age at onset of illness	Age at first appearance of symptoms Age at first hospitalization
Parental separation (first five years of life)	Amount of separation from father Amount of separation from mother Amount of time in children's home
Pregnancy and birth complications (PBC)	Number of complications Weighting for most severe complication Total weighted score for all complications
Autonomic nervous system (ANS) (recovery × responsiveness)	Percentage of electrodermal responses × recovery rate (conditioning) × recovery rate (tests for conditioning) × recovery rate (extinction testing)
Socioeconomic status	Caretaker's occupational title (see Svalostoga, 1959)
Schizophrenia (in the high-risk child)	*Factors* Hallucinations and delusions Hebephrenic features Thought disorder

various pregnancy and delivery complications noted by Danish midwives in their reports.

ANS (Recovery × Responsiveness). In the preceding discussions of the theory, we have indicated that if an individual is relatively autonomically unresponsive, fast recovery will result in that much less of an aptitude for avoidance learning. Conversely, a highly sensitive ANS will not lead to schizophrenia if not associated with fast recovery. Thus the theory specifies an interaction effect that can be most simply expressed mathematically, in a single score, as a *product* of recovery rate and responsiveness. "Responsiveness" was taken as the percentage of measurable responses in the entire 1962 electrodermal examination. Mean recovery rates were taken from conditioning, tests for conditioning, and extinction testing. The distribution of recovery rates in the high-risk group evidenced kurtosis. This was due to a small group of the *most* schizophrenic high-risk subjects who had the very fastest recovery rates. These outliers (who will be the subject of special study) resulted in highly exaggerated correlations between recovery rate and the outcome variables (such as hallucinations and delusions). Before producing the recovery responsiveness products, we transformed the recovery rates by a square root transformation that reduced kurtosis to an acceptable level. The intercorrelations of recovery rates and the three product scores were .90, .86, and .92; the intercorrelations of the percentage responses with the three product scores were .73, .70, and .68.

Schizophrenia in High-Risk Children. The diagnostic interview took about 3¼ hours and consisted of a rather extensive series of symptom descriptor items. These items were subjected to factor analyses that yielded (among others) four factors that described the schizophrenia symptoms of the high-risk children (see Table 15.8). The four factors were named (1) hallucinations and delusions, (2) "hebephrenic" features, (3) thought disorder, and (4) autistic features.

RESULTS OF PATH ANALYSIS

We shall express the results of the path analysis in two ways. First, by means of path diagrams we shall present the significant direct effects; then by means of bar graphs we shall consider the sum of the direct and indirect effects of the hypothesized predispositional variables on the outcome, schizophrenia.

Path Diagrams

Figure 15.1 presents the path diagram for men. Significant path coefficients (and their probability levels) are indicated. Note that "PBCs" have no direct effect on "schizophrenia"; their effect is mediated by the ANS construct. Childhood separation and the ANS construct are directly related to later schizophrenia in high-risk men, as hypothesized. Also as hypothesized, the ANS factors are rather well predicted by PBCs. Childhood separation is predicted by an early age of onset of the mother's schizophrenia, which does not evidence a direct relation to schizophre-

Table 15.8. Indicators of the Schizophrenia Construct: Symptoms Defining the Four Factors.

A. Hallucinations and Delusions
1. Hears voices or sounds, sees, feels, smells, or tastes something with no apparent source outside of himself (CAPPS, 227)
2. Auditory hallucinations (CAPPS, 228)
3. Visual hallucinations (CAPPS, 229)
4. Level of preoccupation with hallucinations and delusions (PSE, 95)
5. Acts upon delusions and hallucinations or expresses them in public with strangers (PSE, 96)
6. Systematization of hallucinations and delusions (PSE, 93)
7. Concealment of hallucinations and delusions (PSE, 94)
B. "Hebephrenic" Features
1. Silliness — laughs or giggles in a foolish way (CAPPS, 239)
2. Retardation — lacks emotional expression (CAPPS, 240)
3. Speech disorganization — shows impairment in form of speech; aimless, no logical connection, irrelevant (CAPPS, 248)
4. Denial of illness (CAPPS, 251)
C. Thought Disorder (items from diagnostic interview)
1. Train of thought tends to shift or drift spontaneously
2. Thought sequences are unrelated
3. Quality of transition between ideas, themes, and topics is impaired.
D. Autistic Features (items from diagnostic interview)
1. Emotionally impoverished
2. Frankly psychotic defenses
3. Autistic, withdrawn, no eye contact, no emotional contact
4. Autistic — empathy only regarding own affects

nia. The LISREL computer program calculates a multiple R of .62 for the prediction of schizophrenia by these predispositional variables for the high-risk men.

Figure 15.2 presents the path diagram for women. In this path diagram the only construct that is significantly directly related to the development of schizophrenia is the age of onset of the mother's schizophrenia. The pattern for women is quite different from that seen in Figure 15.1 for men. The ANS construct (a reliable predictor for men) is not significantly related to schizophrenia in women, nor is childhood separation. Comparison of the path diagrams strongly suggests that some aspects of the etiology of schizophrenia are quite different in high-risk men and women. The multiple R for the prediction of schizophrenia for women is .49.

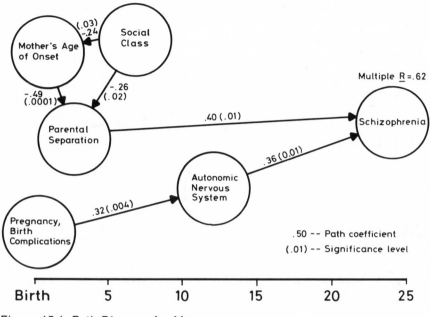

Figure 15.1. Path Diagram for Men.

Direct and Indirect Effects

Before leaving the path diagrams, note that in these reported relationships socioeconomic status (SES) is included and consequently held constant. SES has no direct, significant relationship with the construct schizophrenia. It does, however, influence schizophrenia via the mother's age of onset (in men and women) and amount of childhood separation (in men). The indirect effect of SES on schizophrenia via separation may be calculated by simply multiplying the two relevant path coefficients (.26 × .40), yielding an indirect effect of .104. Note that we have earlier observed a similar interaction of social class and separation experience in relation to breakdown (Stern, Mednick, and Schulsinger, 1974).

By adding the direct and indirect effects onto schizophrenia, the total effect of each construct in this path diagram can be calculated. Figure 15.3 presents a bar graph depicting the total direct and indirect effects of each of the constructs on the construct schizophrenia.

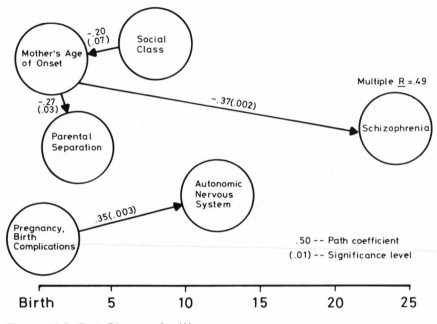

Figure 15.2. Path Diagram for Women.

DISCUSSION OF PATH ANALYSIS RESULTS

From the lives of our high-risk subjects we have chosen a small group of childhood variables to explore their relationship to the subjects' current diagnosis of schizophrenia. These early factors seem to relate to the development of schizophrenia quite differently for men and women.

In interpreting these results we must keep in mind the fact that for women, schizophrenia tends to have a later onset (greater incidence for women of the age of 35, Yolles and Kramer, 1969). This assessment took place when the subjects ranged from 20 to 30 years of age; the results for the later-onset women may be different.

Aside from this age factor we cannot suggest other serious reservations regarding these findings. Perhaps, in some cases, the 1972 interviewer learned about the separation factor (and even something about the mother's age of onset) while talking to the subjects. It seems rather unlikely, however, that this would affect her coding of the schizophrenia symptoms listed in Table 15.8. It seems even more unlikely that her ratings would be influenced differently for men and women. At the time of the interview (and in fact to date) the interviewer was totally blind

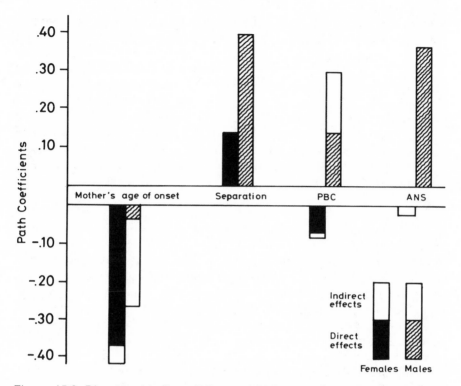

Figure 15.3. Direct and Indirect Effects of Childhood Constructs on Schizo-phrenia Construct.

regarding the perinatal and psychophysiological data. It should perhaps also be pointed out that at the time these early variables were recorded, there was no information available regarding who, among the high-risk subjects, would become schizophrenic.

It does not seem overly imprudent to begin to accept the possibility that these four factors have some relationship to the development of schizophrenia in these high-risk individuals. The interpretation of the meaning of these results, some of which were rather unexpected, may be less straightforward.

Early Detection

Our initial aim is the identification of factors that might be useful in the early detection of individuals in the general population who are at high risk for schizophrenia. With respect to this aim, these four early factors are worthy of some consideration and testing. However, it should be pointed out that we have demonstrated only that they predict reliably within a group of children born to schizophrenic women. The level of separation from the parents experienced by these children is unusually high. In a general population, this factor may not account for as high a proportion of the variance as it does for these high-risk families. The variable, age of onset of the mother's schizophrenia, is also not generally and directly applicable to population studies. Perhaps when we understand better what role the mother's early onset plays in her daughter's schizophrenia, some hypotheses regarding predictive measures may be suggested.

The ANS construct (the product of recovery and responsiveness) is an individual measure that is more promising for utilization in early detection in general populations. It has been a central variable in the theoretical framework of our research for the past twenty years. It predicted quite well the 1967 psychiatric breakdowns; almost all published studies with schizophrenics (with one exception, Maricq and Edelberg, 1975) have supported the hypothesis of faster ANS recovery for schizophrenics (see Mednick, Schulsinger, and Schulsinger, 1975). Interestingly enough, almost all of these studies have been carried out on *male* schizophrenics. Our path analysis suggests that these reported results would not replicate with female schizophrenics. A senior member of our research group, Peter Venables, has repeatedly failed to find ANS differences between female controls and female schizophrenics (personal communication). The ANS measures would seem to be a useful addition to an assessment of risk in a male general population.

Interpretation of Findings

It is the fate of longitudinal researchers continually to be presenting interim results. Now we must await the next wave of schizophrenic breakdowns. In addition to those inevitable developments and changes in our subjects over the years, we also face the problem of analyzing literally lifetimes of data. In this case we are slowly and more or less systematically (but certainly slowly) analyzing the individual and life-event factors related to the outcome — schizophrenia. This analysis is very much in progress. Thus, this report must be understood as interim also for the same reason. We now will attempt to transmit to you our reflections on the meaning of these results. These reflections will suggest our strategy for future data analyses. We present these reflections very tentatively for each of the early factors that were shown to relate to the construct — schizophrenia.

Mother's Age of Onset.   Figure 15.3 depicts the direct and indirect effects of mother's age of onset on the construct of schizophrenia for both men and women. Note that although there is a strong tendency for "onset" to relate to schizophrenia in the males, the relationship is almost completely mediated by "separation." Sons of "early-onset" women have an especially heightened risk of becoming schizophrenic themselves. This relationship seems to be almost completely explained by the separation from parents that follows the mother's early onset of illness.

In the women, the "onset" variable also has an important relationship to later schizophrenia. However, in the case of women the indirect effects are negligible. This simply means either that the effect is actually only direct or that the critical mediators were not included in this path analysis. We examined correlation matrices including some early-childhood variables and "onset" for the male and female high-risk children. Early onset of the mother's illness is associated mildly and significantly with the girls' evidencing low verbal IQ, disturbed and peculiar word associations and continual associations, and adult thought disorder. Curiously enough, in males none of these relationships is observed. For the males, mother's early onset is better related to adult characteristics associated with a diagnosis of "psychopathy." Our findings have led to the following tentative reflections related to the mother's age of onset:

1.   Perhaps the seriously ill mother is genetically transferring some language deviation to her daughters and not to her sons. This sex-linked transmission is, of course, a possibility that we must contrast with an identification-learning hypothesis. We must relate the seriousness of the daughter's illness to the amount of contact she had with her mother. The course of illness for the HR parents and their children is currently being compared.

2.   The earlier development of language behavior in girls than in boys and the fact that girls tend more to identify with their mothers may combine to differentially influence the associative and verbal responses of daughters of severely schizophrenic women. Maccoby and Jacklin (1974) suggest that this childhood advantage of girls in the acquisition of language behavior probably exists only before the age of 3. In future analyses this suggestion may help us to pinpoint possible critical periods of development for further intensive analysis. Careful analysis of our

case files should enable us to estimate the amount and closeness of the contact between the mothers and their children at various age levels as well as the relation between the child's age at the time of mother's breakdown and the child's adult diagnostic status.

3.   It is also possible that the more seriously schizophrenic mothers pass on some specific characteristic to both their daughters and their sons. But perhaps this characteristic predisposes to schizophrenia only in the daughter because of differences in the manner in which society deals with the two sexes. We shall return to this thought when we discuss the ANS construct.

4.   In male high-risk children, "onset" is not directly related to schizophrenia. As mentioned, inspection of the case material for the boys indicates that for them, "mother's early onset" is significantly associated with adult symptoms of psychopathy. We know that the schizophrenic mothers (in this sample) tend to mate with criminal men (Kirkegaard-Sørensen and Mednick, 1975; see also Lewis et al., 1976). We intend to examine the possibility that for the most early-onset schizophrenic women this tendency is even stronger. If this is true, it might explain the heightened psychopathy of the sons who have early-onset mothers (Schulsinger, 1972; Hutchings and Mednick, 1974). It might also suggest hypotheses regarding the mother-daughter findings.

Separation in Childhood (0 to 5 Years).   Early separation from parents is highly and significantly related to later schizophrenia for male, but not for female, high-risk children. The path coefficient for the females is in the same direction as for the males but is not statistically significant. Differences between the girls and boys in *amount* of separation are minimal and not statistically significant.

Walker, Cudeck, Mednick, and Schulsinger (1980) have examined the relationship between parental absence and scores on eight factor-analytically derived clinical symptom scales for the high-risk subjects. The association between parental absence and schizophrenic symptomatology as measured by the Walker et al. scales was stronger for males than for females. Their analysis also revealed, however, that this association is mediated by the variable of institutional care provided to many of those children whose parents are absent. High-risk boys who were separated from their mothers but placed with relatives or normal foster parents tended to do much better than those who were institutionalized. These recent findings suggest the following tentative reflections related to separation in childhood:

1.   The amount of separation experienced by the boys (but not by the girls) is related negatively to their social class status. It is possible this social class factor may mean that the treatment of boys separated from their parents is of a different (poorer) quality than the treatment of girls. We shall attempt some modest examination of this possibility by interviewing individuals who worked in these children's homes in the forties and fifties. We must also check to see whether reasons for selection of children to be placed in children's homes are different for the two sexes. We do have some suggestive evidence, for a subsample of the HR group, that children's home placement is partly dependent on preplacement infant characteristics (Herrmann, 1973).

2.   Perhaps the reason early separation is a more important variable for boys than for girls is that boys experience more "separation anxiety." While the research evidence on this issue is far from unequivocal, Maccoby and Jacklin (1974, p. 196) suggest that where sex differences exist, "boys cry more when the mother or father leaves the room; and at the early age of 9 to 10 months they are more likely to crawl quickly after the mother if she moves into an adjacent room." Perhaps the boys in this study (because of their sex-linked immaturity) did suffer a stronger separation reaction than did the girls. This may have, in some way, been involved in the chain of events leading to their eventual schizophrenia. Unfortunately, our longitudinal project does not contain reliable data concerning the children's reactions to their separation from their parents. The high ANS reactiveness of the boys who eventually became schizophrenic could suggest that separation from their parents may have produced a relatively strong emotional reaction.

Walker et al. (1980) have offered two additional alternative explanations for the differential effects of parental separation on males and females:

One possible explanation is that males are exposed to greater stress in both familial and institutional settings. Thus, it may be that the quality of the schizophrenic mothers' interactions with sons and daughters differs. Perhaps schizophrenic mothers are harsher or more inconsistent in their treatment of sons. There is evidence that normal parents are less protective and indulgent with male children (Block, 1973). However, there is little research on the specific behavior of schizophrenic mothers relative to male and female offspring. Along the same lines, the institutional treatment of males may be qualitatively different from that experienced by females. Interviews with the individuals who had been directors of the Danish institutions at the time these children attended lend support to the hypothesis that the boys' institutions were more stressful than the girls' institutions.

An alternative explanation for our findings would be that high-risk males are constitutionally more vulnerable to environmental insults than high-risk females. Thus the presence of a psychotic mother and the experience of institutionalization may constitute more traumatic events for high-risk males. Again, there is little information in the literature on sex differences in vulnerability to stress among high-risk children. However, there is one study reported by Rutter (1970) in which the male and female offspring of adult psychiatric patients were compared. He found that familial discord and disruption were associated with antisocial disorders in boys but not girls. In a recent review of the literature on childhood psychopathology, Eme (1979) concludes that there is evidence not only for greater male vulnerability to biological stressors, but also psychological stressors.

PBC Factors

The high-risk boys suffered slightly more serious and a greater number of perinatal complications than the girls (not statistically significant). This direction of results is in keeping with our expectations. For boys there is a large significant relationship between PBCs and later schizophrenia (see Figure 15.3). The relationship for the girls is actually negative (not statistically significant). For the boys, most of the PBC-schizophrenia relationship is mediated by an ANS-schizophrenia relationship, which is not found in the girls.

There is evidence that females' electrodermal responsiveness is related to their menstrual cycle (Bell, Christie, and Venables, 1975). One could suggest the hypothesis that the lack of a relationship between ANS factors and schizophrenia for the females is due to a menstrual cycle–related lack of reliability of the ANS measures in the females. (We failed to note menstrual data in 1962.) Note, however, that the PBC-ANS relationship is at least as strong in the females as it is in the males. ANS responsiveness was as reliable as the males'. ANS reactiveness and recovery are reliably related to PBCs in the girls, but this increased reactiveness is not associated with an increased risk of schizophrenia.

ANS Factors

We have observed unexpected sex differences in the relationship between ANS factors and schizophrenia. These differences are puzzling; we offer some observations related to sex differences in ANS-relevant emotional behavior.

Maccoby and Jacklin (1974) suggest that if there are sex differences in *amount* of emotionality, they are very small. The self-reported lower fearfulness of boys is almost certainly explained by their unwillingness to admit their fears and anxieties. Boys are much more defensive than girls and conceal and avoid such emotions more than girls do. For a boy to admit emotionality is to admit a weakness and to risk being called a "sissy." Girls "are simply more willing than boys to admit that they feel anxious" (Maccoby and Jacklin, 1974, p. 186). It is not unfeminine to admit being afraid. Under some conditions and in some social circumstances, emotionality in women may be seen as a positive, feminine attribute. In males it is often regarded with considerable suspicion; it is not masculine.

Little girls are freer to express fear and to cry when disappointed without being judged a sex-role deviant. "Parents show considerably more concern over a boy being a 'sissy' than over a girl being a tomboy" (Maccoby and Jacklin, 1974, p. 362). Perhaps girls have less need than boys to avoid expressing fear or anxiety. In that case perhaps little girls need *not* learn deviant ways of thinking and behaving to avoid emotional expression.

Little boys tend to learn that they must avoid emotional expression. The little boy who has an extremely reactive ANS may often be pushed by parents, guardians, teachers, and peers to suppress this emotionality. Thus, any response (such as irrelevant thought or bizarre behavior) that will avoid an encounter with a potentially emotion-provoking stimulus (such as an approaching person) will be reinforced and quickly learned. Fast ANS recovery will ensure a relatively powerful reinforcement for such an avoidance response and will increase the probability of its being elicited. The repetition of this learning sequence over the years could produce an effective screen of avoidance behavior that will function to isolate the schizophrenic and support his withdrawal.

What about the female schizophrenics? This discussion implies that (not being influenced by the ANS factors) the women should develop a less withdrawn form of schizophrenia. The clinical picture for the male schizophrenics is dominated by withdrawal, isolation, thought disorder, and hallucinations. The women evidence serious thought disorder, but are frequently quite promiscuous and socially "active." The fact that schizophrenic women become married three times as often as schizophrenic men (Forrest and Hay, 1972) probably has many explanations, but in any case it does testify to less avoidant, withdrawn behavior than is the case for male schizophrenics. Forrest and Hay express some suspicion regarding early onset diagnoses of schizophrenia in women. They report it has been their experience that "almost every female patient first admitted under the age of 20 years with a presumptive diagnosis of schizophrenia later has this diagnosis revised to personality disorder or manic-depressive illness" (Forrest and Hay, 1972, p. 55). This statement is probably too extreme for most clinicians to accept.

These reflections suggest two related notions that may repay some consideration by investigators. First, perhaps the condition we call schizophrenia takes a different form in men and women; second, perhaps the etiology is, in part, different for men and women.

Most investigators (including ourselves) have until now neglected to consider the *possibility* of sex differences in the schizophrenics. Frequently, an area of research that has almost exclusively studied male schizophrenics is reviewed (with no mention of the sex variable) and the conclusions generalized to all schizophrenics. These analyses suggest that we may explain more variance if we consider the sexes separately.

Additional Maternal Characteristics

Talovic, Mednick, Schulsinger, and Falloon (1980) analyzed the psychiatric hospital records of the mothers of high-risk children to determine whether any of the maternal characteristics were predictive of later breakdown in their children. They found two variables that appeared to distinguish independently those children who suffered schizophrenic breakdown from those who did not: (1) one of the psychotic episodes of the mother was precipitated by and occurred within six months of childbirth ($\emptyset = .54$, $R^2 = .29$) and (2) the mother was unstable in her relations with men ($\emptyset = .29$, R^2 increment $= .09$). These two variables account for 38 percent of the variance in a multiple regression equation.

Talovic et al. (1980) demonstrated that early parental separation, which might be associated with puerperal psychosis, was not the factor responsible for this relationship: the childbirth that preceded the mother's psychotic episode involved only the siblings of the index child. It also appeared that even though mothers who suffered from puerperal psychosis tended to become ill earlier than other mothers, age of onset did not account for all the prognostic significance of the puerperal psychosis variable.

The mother's instability in relations with men proved to be related to three other factors: antisocial behavior, irregular work history, and drug or alcohol addiction.

Talovic et al. (1980) note that "the independence of these two factors (r = .01) suggests that perhaps they are each 'explaining' separate subgroups of the schizophrenic children. It will be interesting to explore the possibility that these subgroups have differing symptom and outcome characteristics which might meaningfully relate to the maternal symptoms."

Verbal Associative Disturbances

To determine whether premorbid verbal associative disturbance was characteristic of those high-risk subjects who later experienced breakdown, the single-word and continuous-association test behaviors of these individuals, which were measured in 1962, were analyzed. Griffith, Mednick, Schulsinger, and Diderichsen (1980) found that the high-risk individuals who later became schizophrenic did not manifest premorbidly more deviant associative responses than the other high-risk subjects. In fact, they did not produce premorbidly a significantly greater number of deviant responses than the low-risk subjects.

Griffith et al. (1980, p. 129) "considered the possibility that this lack of observable associative disturbance prior to onset of schizophrenia was due to the subjects' awareness of the peculiarity of their thoughts, which they might have hidden by screening of inappropriate responses. However, . . . they did not exhibit longer latencies to a greater extent than the high-risk subjects who did not become schizophrenic."

Although the findings reported by Griffith et al. (1980) appear to suggest that learning theories of associative disturbance cannot be called upon to account for the development of schizophrenic thought disorder, a learning theory approach that incorporates the autonomic responsiveness and recovery paradigm may assist in clarifying the processes involved in the development of affective disorder and other characteristics of the schizophrenic syndrome.

The next clinical assessment of the high- and low-risk groups will undoubtedly reveal additional cases of schizophrenic breakdown. This will increase the number of cases in our index group and will allow us to continue our analysis of the premorbid characteristics of those who later become schizophrenic, as well as to extend the tests of our hypotheses concerning sex differences in etiological factors in schizophrenia.

16 THE MAURITIUS PROJECT

Fini Schulsinger, Peter H. Venables,
Charles Yip Tong, Cyril Dalais,
and Sarnoff A. Mednick

The previous chapter by Mednick, Schulsinger, and Griffith described a prospective longitudinal study of children of severely schizophrenic mothers. The general aim of this project was the early detection of variables that alone or in combination with other variables were characteristic for the individuals who eventually developed schizophrenia. The hypothesized variables were psychosocial and biological. The latter comprised certain autonomous nervous system (ANS) variables, which supposedly were part of the constitution of the child. Children with the highly responsive and fast-recovering ANS were hypothesized to develop schizophrenic thought disorder under certain bad psychosocial circumstances.

This study began in 1962. Five years later, in 1967, the twenty first psychological breakdown subjects — the sick group — showed the following characteristics from the 1962 assessment when compared with matched controls from the high-risk and the low-risk sample:

1. Mother lost to psychiatric hospitalization relatively early in life;
2. Teacher reports disturbing, aggressive behavior in school;
3. Evidence of associative drift;

4. Psychophysiological anomalies:
    a. Marked fast latency of response,
    b. Response latency shows no signs of habituation,
    c. Resistance to experimental extinction of conditioned GSR,
    d. Remarkably fast recovery rate following response peak;
5. Pregnancy and/or birth complications suffered by 70 percent of
    sick group (against 15 percent of high-risk well control group and
    30 percent of low-risk control group).

In 1968 we did not know about the correlations between the outcome
of schizophrenia and the ANS deviance. We knew it only for the psychological breakdown group — the twenty sick subjects who might or
might not become schizophrenics. But we were extremely preoccupied
with the fast-recovery findings. We learned from Ax and Bamford (1970)
that the fast autonomic recovery was also found in chronic schizophrenic
patients.

In 1968 the World Health Organization in Geneva published a technical
report on neurophysiology in psychiatry (WHO, 1968) in which the 1962
Copenhagen high-risk study was described and recommended as a good
model for international research because it applied culturally independent
measures (GSR) as well as culturally dependent variables, such as school
behavior, family constellation, and so on.

Also in 1968, the little island country of Mauritius in the Indian Ocean
became an independent nation after hundreds of years with French and
subsequently British colonization. Mauritius became a member country
of WHO. The leading Mauritian psychiatrist, Dr. A. C. Raman, suggested
that WHO initiate mental health research in Mauritius in order to stimulate the development of this field.

WHO, in turn, suggested that the Copenhagen high-risk researchers
examine the possibilities of carrying out a prospective longitudinal high-
risk study in Mauritius along the patterns of the 1962 Copenhagen study.
As described in greater detail by Schulsinger et al. (1975), we found the
infrastructure and the attitude of the Mauritian society encouraging
enough. We proposed to WHO a project that eventually could form the
basis of cross-cultural comparisons with the Danish study or other ones.
But we did not want to carry out a replication of the Danish study. In
Denmark we operated with an empirical risk factor; namely, severe
schizophrenia in the mother. Later studies have shown this empirical
risk factor to have a large genetic component. It was hypothesized that
part of the risk would show itself as ANS characteristics.

Heavily influenced by the 1967 results for the sick group in Copenhagen, we proposed for the Mauritius project a prospective longitudinal study designed to test the ANS characteristics as proper variables in young children who developed schizophrenia as adults, no matter whether they had schizophrenic parents or not. Approximately 90 percent of schizophrenics have nonschizophrenic parents.

We selected a representative population of 1,800 3-year-old Mauritian children. To test this specific hypothesis of ANS variables as predictors of adult schizophrenia, we would have to follow the 1,800 children for at least twenty-five to thirty years. Not knowing the problems of stability or sample attrition in a small developing country, we felt it was an adventurous enterprise. To counteract these risky aspects of the project, we decided to perform it as part of a general survey and follow-up of 1,800 3-year-old children in a developing country with regard to personal and social development and health. The following is an ultrabrief review of the project from its actual beginning in July 1972 up to the present.

METHODS AND RESULTS

The 1,800 children were almost all from two neighboring municipalities, and on the day of examination were between 3 and 3¼ years old. The two municipalities were representative for Mauritius with regard to ethnic composition and rural/urban residencies.

The program for these 1,800 children consisted of:

Social description in connection with a home visit,

Brief pediatric examination, including blood and urine analysis,

Testing of psychological development according to Piaget's principles,

Psychophysiology (as in the Copenhagen project),

EEG (possible for only approximately 1,100 children),

Obstetrical history (quality varied — information obtained on approximately 60 percent).

From these 1,800 children, 200 were selected for an intensive prospective study on the basis of their ANS recovery and ethnic group (Hindu, Muslim, Creole). There were three psychophysiological recovery groups: 112 fast recoverers, 28 nonresponders, and 60 normal recoverers. Half of each group was selected for a two- to three-year nursery school experience. For each school child, a child of the same sex, ethnic group, municipality, and psychophysiological characteristics was designated as a community control child. The project ran two nursery schools, one in each of the two municipalities.

Originally we planned to subject the school children to various types of preventive interventions — in natural as well as arranged situations. We thought of stimulating them and rewarding them for giving up the tendency to withdraw in conflict situations. We expected such behavior in the fast recoverers, based on information from school teachers in the old Copenhagen study. However, we never managed to introduce such programs. The main reason was shortage of funds for skilled researchers to carry out the study on location. But the nursery schools themselves were of an unusually lucky kind. Danish pedagogues worked with bright young Mauritians who were offered a two-year intensive course to become preschool teachers. The atmosphere was enthusiastic and the children were offered a lot of activities involving physical and mental stimulation and also a lot of creative activities.

Weekly and monthly behavioral observations on the children were made by the teachers and by external observers. The 100 control children who did not attend the schools — the so-called community controls — were seen approximately every six months for the standard psychophysiological assessment. During the two years of nursery school activity the psychophysiological laboratory, under the guidance of Peter Venables, also collected a substantial amount of normative data on healthy Mauritians of various sex and age groups.

Controlled Study of Nursery School Effect

At the end of two years of nursery school attendance, a controlled experiment of the possible nursery school effect was carried out in the following way:

Every morning one child from each school and his or her matched community control were picked up and brought to a neutral site. The children were dressed uniformly and observed by a staff who did not know which ones were the school children and which the community controls. Neither did the staff know anything about their original psychophysiological status. These latter conditions were kept secret from everybody in the nursery schools during the whole period.

A number of behavioral observations were now carried out. Before the observations started, the children waited some time in a playground with swings, sandpit, and the like, giving them an opportunity to mix socially. The observation took place in a special room where there were areas with toys and equipment laid out. Each child's behavior was rated over an eight-minute period. The rating system used employees' counts of behavior, such as number of times a child played with a particular toy, changed toys, approached adults, and so on. The various aspects of behavior were timed. These timed aspects included:

Watching — when a child watched a peer or adult while not otherwise interacting,

Positive interactions — when a child talked, played cooperatively, and helped or accepted help from a peer,

Constructive play alone — when a child played constructively with a toy or toys by himself or herself.

Figure 16.1 compares the autonomic high-risk and the autonomic low-risk groups who experienced the nursery schools with the psychophysiologically matched community controls who did not experience the nursery schools. For convenience of comparison all three sets of data are placed on the same figure. Please note, however, the grossly different

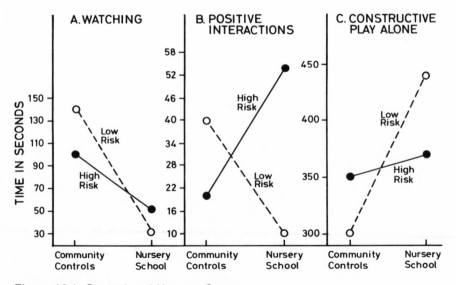

Figure 16.1. Control and Nursery Groups.

scales of time used in the three figures. Note that both autonomic high-risk and autonomic low-risk groups decreased their inactive watching after having attended the nursery schools. The low-risk (community) children were relatively high in positive interactions and watching. After the nursery experience they reduced both of these activities to the benefit of indulging in constructive play. The autonomic high-risk (community) children tended not to engage in positive interactions but were high in constructive play. It is perhaps gratifying that the greatest effect of the nursery school experience for the autonomic high-risk children was their increase in positive social interactions (at the expense of time spent in isolated, inactive watching).

Interpretations of the Findings

We offer the following interpretations of these results:

The psychophysiological selection criteria are correlated with specific characteristic behaviors before the influence of the nursery school.

The nursery school experience affects the social and play behavior of the children.

The nursery school affects behavior in the children differentially as a function of the psychophysiological characteristics used in selection.

What is most encouraging is the fact that the largest change for the autonomic high-risk group was an increase in positive social interactions. This increase was observed in a situation where they were thrown in with peers and adult observers who were unknown to them. In terms of the interventive goals of this project, these results are rewarding.

A potentially interesting finding is that of the high level of constructive play shown by both school and community samples of the short-recovery children. Venables et al. (1978) discuss this finding in the context of other researchers' interpretations with regard to hippocampal dysfunction and to attention. They indicate some possibility that the short autonomic recovery time is associated with "openness to the environment." This openness, again, may be associated with creativity, which furthermore is associated with schizophrenia. The nursery school experience over two years may have helped the child to achieve more voluntary control over the development of his attention, which may be protective against schizophrenia.

CONCLUSION

First, we found that the hypothesized criterion of high risk for adult schizophrenia was meaningful. Children with fast autonomic recovery behaved differently in certain situations than children with normal recovery.

Second, we found that two years' experience of a good nursery school had a positive effect on all children, but the type of effect was dependent on whether the child had fast autonomic recovery.

Third, these findings could hardly be achieved by using designs other than the prospective longitudinal design.

Fourth, we believe that the success of a project like ours in a developing country is due to the fact that the Mauritius society was just entering into a phase of industrialism. The women began more and more to work outside home. Our project activated a (maybe preconscious) need of nursery schools and public interest in preschool education. We believe that failures of projects in developing countries may sometimes be caused by a lack of conscious need of the project in question. At least preschool education has become a generally recognized field in Mauritius. After our use of nursery schools for scientific purposes, the Mauritian government and some municipalities have continued to create facilities in this area on their own, with minimal expert assistance from outside.

Thus, our longitudinal research in the mental health field has enjoyed maximum cooperation and facilitation from the Mauritian population and from the Mauritian authorities.

VI LONGITUDINAL RESEARCH: *Implications and Recommendations*

17 LONGITUDINAL RESEARCH IN THE WHO EUROPEAN REGION PROGRAM

André E. Baert

The World Health Organization European Region comprises thirty-two countries with a total population of about 850 million people. The geographical, social, economical, political, and historical diversity explains the wide variety of mental health problems found in the region and the wide range of approaches needed to tackle them.

MAJOR OVERALL MENTAL HEALTH PROBLEMS IN THE WHO EUROPEAN REGION

The care of the mentally ill has traditionally been the responsibility of the public authorities, mainly because in the past these patients were considered dangerous. As a consequence there are still more than one million people in mental hospitals in the WHO European Region. A quarter of the establishments have more than a thousand beds, and the large size of these mental hospitals leads to impersonal custodial regimes,

The views expressed in this text do not necessarily represent the decisions or the stated policy of the World Health Organization.

lack of privacy, and absence of social and intellectual stimulation. Although the trend in most WHO member countries in the European Region toward community-oriented delivery of mental health care continues, the pace of this development varies, and the process is nowhere complete.

As the European Region faces the demographic phenomenon of an absolute and relative increase in its older population, there is a growing demand for various types of medical and social care for chronic patients. Information collected in pilot studies in some European countries indicates that about 20 percent of the population may have recourse to mental health services in the course of a lifetime and that every third hospital bed is used for a patient suffering from a mental disorder.

Mental health legislation has not kept up with changes in mental health care and is sometimes in dissonance with other social legislation. Many countries still do not adequately formulate the mental health component in their national health policies, and the monitoring and management of mental health care are frequently unsatisfactory.

Effects of excessive alcohol consumption appear at an earlier age, while the aggregate level of alcohol consumption is increasing together with multiple drug misuse. The annual alcohol consumption in the European Region varies from an equivalent of about 0.5 liter of pure alcohol per capita to 16 liters. The number of deaths by suicide is of the same magnitude as those from road traffic accidents, each estimated at about 100,000 in 1974.

The concept of mental health stresses its public health and social aspects rather than linking it only to mental diseases and to psychiatry as a separate specialty that can be applied only in special institutions. There is steadily increasing evidence that such behavior patterns as smoking, overeating, excessive use of alcohol and drugs, extended exposure to psychosocial stresses, loneliness, and even sedentariness are common factors in certain noncommunicable diseases such as arteriosclerosis, hypertension, lung cancer, and various other forms of physical illness, as well as increased dependence on mental health care (Commission of the European Communities, 1978). In spite of the enthusiasm of some investigators, technologies for primary prevention have failed, and huge public health campaigns are insufficiently assessed or evaluated.

THE LONG-TERM MENTAL HEALTH PROGRAM
OF THE WHO EUROPEAN REGIONAL OFFICE

At its twentieth session in 1970 and at its twenty-third session in 1973, the WHO Regional Committee for Europe approved proposals for a long-term program in mental health covering the years 1970 to 1980, with projections up to 1983. The six detailed objectives selected are:

1. The strengthening of the *mental health component* within national health policies,
2. The promotion of *community mental health* care and its integration with other community services,
3. The promotion of mental health in specific *high-risk groups and situations,*
4. The prevention of *alcohol and drug dependence,*
5. An improvement in the *training* of mental health workers and administrators,
6. The development of primary prevention programs.

Accordingly, a number of subprograms were developed as a coherent series of studies, working groups, symposia, publications, training courses, and conferences together with direct assistance to countries in the form of courses, consultantships, fellowships, and expert advice, where appropriate, and with a network of pilot study areas in selected member countries.

THE NEED FOR PRIMARY PREVENTION
AND PROGRAM EVALUATION

The energetic development of medical technology has actually increased the prevalence of a variety of chronic illnesses and handicaps because it allows us to prolong life. This is turn has created a greater need and demand for medical services, giving rise to an ever-increasing spiral of demands for and needs of services. There is increasing awareness among decisionmakers that the cost spiral must be stopped and that society could be better served by devoting more effort to research on methods of primary prevention. The change in attitude from medication to mental health promotion has increased the demand for further knowledge about psychosocial factors, the influence of the environment on health, and the effects of changes in lifestyle on the use of medical services and on drug consumption.

One important line of research on prevention is concerned with early detection of populations at risk and the development of intervention techniques to reduce the probability of morbidity in these populations. The prospective longitudinal approach is most suitable for the elaboration of methods of early detection. A large representative sample of a population is studied intensively early in life and then followed until some members of the population sample develop a morbid condition under study. By going back to the original assessment, it is possible to identify the individual and environmental characteristics that distinguish those who later succumb to the illness or deviation in question from those who do not. Such research has a contribution to make in understanding the causation of mental illness and in planning research on promotion of mental health.

Apart from being a basic research tool in psychiatry, education, and somatic development, the prospective longitudinal approach is vital for assessing and evaluating the impact of all health programs, including those devoted to mental health. It may be suggested that no major national mental health program should be launched without providing, within the allocated budget, for an evaluation employing the prospective longitudinal method. However, it is for their administrative as well as for their scientific value that such studies are essential. As Douglas (1976) pointed out, the question is whether we wish to know to what extent the new medical, social, educational, or other services and programs fulfill their stated objectives and intentions.

Prospective longitudinal studies develop methodologies for conducting population surveys, for continuous population monitoring and defining catchment populations, for characterizing distinguishable subgroups of the population in terms of risks and of special needs for services, and for identifying social and environmental determinates of such special needs. Both at the national and at the international level, such methods need a degree of standardization as well as validity.

One of the main difficulties in health planning and in assessing the effectiveness of health services is the lack of population-based information. The population-based prospective longitudinal approach offers, potentially, a unique opportunity to obtain serial pictures of the state of a population's health and to relate this information to social and environmental conditions. However, the survey conducted by the WHO European Office (Mednick and Baert, 1981) has revealed many pitfalls and potential hazards in such work. These can be avoided, however, by careful preparation and efficient administration. Among the problems are the following:

There is a tendency to collect much data that remain underanalyzed or even unused. A data librarian is necessary to correct this problem, and the complexity and volume of the raw data — often a wilderness of unretrievable information — usually make it essential to use computer storage for subsequent multivariate statistical analysis. The funding of such services should be foreseen and allowed for in the planning stages of any project.

Frequently the sample being studied far outlives the contractual time (and even on occasion the life) of the investigators. It is important, therefore, to ensure that guaranteed funding of a project is sufficiently long-term to eliminate much of this danger. Staff must have security if they are to be recruited and retained.

The heart of the longitudinal approach lies in the opportunities it presents for successive follow-up and reexamination; and these in turn depend on careful preliminary long-term planning and long-range funding. If successive examinations cannot be made either because of lack of staff able to carry them out or because of lack of subjects willing to participate in them, then the whole study is jeopardized. Thus planners must not seek to minimize costs if this means maximizing the project's risk of failure. If the cohort is no longer representative of the population being studied, then all may have been wasted.

Prospective long-term research in the mental health field is by its very nature interdisciplinary. This fact in itself seems to inhibit the interest of individual disciplines and administrative departments. It follows that cooperation between disciplines and departments is important at the earliest planning stages and also that the contribution from each discipline and department should be clearly defined. A single scientist or departmental head should act both as a reference point for those with the same interest and as a coordinator of that interest with the other disciplines concerned in the study.

Ethical issues should be identified and taken seriously from the inception of any project. It is desirable also that any longitudinal study have an advisory group of senior scientists, paid as consultants, who are independent from the funding agencies and from the study itself.

Because these studies are usually of a transdisciplinary nature, funding may be by different government departments, by different research councils, or by other grant-giving bodies, each contributing part of the whole. This complexity adds to the importance of not underestimating the number and appropriate level of experience of the administrative staff who will service any project. The organization, financing, and administrative structure of a longitudinal study must be given a combination of stability and supervision; here also adequate tenure of staff and guaranteed financing are crucial to success. Ideally, population-based prospective longitudinal studies should be an intrinsic part of any long-term public health measure (for example, a community mental health program or a health education program on drugs, alcohol, and smoking) so that their impact on consequent planning and adjustment of policy can be assessed.

As many longitudinal cohort studies exist in Europe, it was felt that a coordinated description of them would advance the goal of establishing common methodology, terminology, and criteria and stimulate further studies. This survey of prospective longitudinal research may serve as an introduction to the subject for those responsible for evaluating health and social action as well as for those engaged in research on primary prevention.

18 THE CONTRIBUTION OF LONG-TERM RESEARCH TO SOCIAL MEDICINE

J. W. B. Douglas

When discussing the contribution of long-term research to social medicine, I shall limit myself to those problems that in my opinion could not be solved by cross-sectional studies or by studies using retrospective data. Moreover, I shall mainly be referring to work based on the 1946 birth cohort and using comparisons between the three British birth cohorts of 1946, 1958, and 1970. This is, of course, only one of many types of long-term research that can contribute to medical knowledge; but it is a type with which I am familiar and which has been particularly productive in recent years.

THE NATURAL HISTORY OF DISEASE

It is often difficult to test hypotheses or accepted beliefs in medicine because the very existence of such beliefs alters people's perception of their own medical histories and makes it difficult for research workers themselves to avoid concentrating data collection in areas or within samples that are likely to support their hypotheses (Ferguson, 1918). These perils are largely avoided in longitudinal studies where observations are not subject to distorted recall and there is a wide range of information on living conditions and the changing circumstances of individuals' lives that makes it possible to seek explanations in areas for which data are not usually available. Moreover, it will usually be true that the data were collected before the hypotheses were formulated or, alternatively, before it had been decided to test them. For example, if it were suspected that hairdressers, through their contact with dyes, ran particular risks, it would be an easy matter in a large longitudinal study to identify those who, at various points in their lives, had been hairdressers and to compare their health records with the rest of the cohort population or with matched controls. In this way it might be possible to confirm or refute the original hypothesis; even if numbers were too small to give a definitive answer, the main structural considerations that should guide any future study designed to assess the hazards of this particular occupation would be apparent. The 1946 study provides a number of examples of the way in which preexisting hypotheses may be examined.

A recent study by Menkes (1977), based on a clinical sample, suggested that learning disorders were excessively high among children who had not been breastfed. However, the sample was poor and the information on breastfeeding based on recall, so it seemed likely that a replication using a better sample and better data would not support this conclusion. An examination of the 1946 birth cohort by Rodgers (1978), however, shows that the wholly bottle-fed had lower reading scores at 15 than the wholly breastfed. This difference was not eliminated, though it was substantially reduced, after removing the effect of a large number of other factors such as social class, schooling, parental attitude, and birthweight, which were known to be related on the one hand to the type of infant feeding and on the other to reading ability. Rodgers was unable to find any factor or combination of factors that would remove the positive correlation between bottle feeding and low attainment. Thus, against expectation, Menkes's conclusion was confirmed. However, the 1946 data do not provide the means to reach conclusions about the mechanisms by which bottle feeding is associated with intellectual impairment. It could be related to the content of bottle feeds — for example, protein or lipid concentration or osmotic load — or to less easily defined factors such as the greater burden of early infection among the bottle-fed or the relative strength of the emotional bonds associated with different types of feeding. It is also possible, though unlikely, that some as yet unidentified environmental factor is responsible.

With the growing realization of the vulnerability of small infants, there is considerable interest in the relationship between the type of feeding in infancy and adult levels of blood pressure and blood lipids. A study of this relationship in a subsample of the 1946 cohort is now nearly completed, though it is too early to comment on the results.

Another example of using longitudinal data to test hypotheses concerns early hospital admissions. The views of Bowlby (1951) on the emotional effects of admission to hospital in early childhood have recently been criticized (Clarke and Clarke, 1976). The modern view is that such emotional disturbances as occur are of short duration and associated with painful or distressing treatment rather than with the breaking of mother/infant bonds. There is, moreover, an assumption that improvements in the hospital care of small children have removed the main objections to hospital admission. Possibly owing to this there has been, over the last twenty-five years, an increase in the proportion of children under 5 admitted to hospital and in those admitted on two or more occasions.

The 1946 birth cohort provides strong and unexpected evidence that one admission to hospital of more than a week's duration or repeated admissions before the age of 5 years (in particular, between 6 months and 4 years) are associated with an increased risk of behavior disturbance and poor reading in adolescence (Douglas, 1975). Children who have experienced early admissions are more troublesome out of class, more likely to be delinquent, and more likely to show unstable job patterns than those not admitted in the first 5 years. The association of troublesome and socially difficult behavior with early admissions is explained neither by the initial selection of children for hospital nor by the physical disabilities they sometimes carry in later life. But the children who are most vulnerable to early admission appear to be those who are highly dependent on their mothers or who are under stress at home at the time of admission. Again against expectation, it is found that children who have been subjected to surgical procedures or have been admitted to hospital with accidental injury show no long-term behavior or learning problems. Indeed, such long-term effects are most marked in children admitted to hospital for reasons that could not easily be explained to them. These observations, of course, relate to children admitted to hospital at a time when little account was being taken of the psychological needs of children in these institutions. However, a later study by Quinton and Rutter (1976) on a different population and using different methods of assessment confirms to a remarkable degree the 1946 birth cohort findings and brings the present policy of admitting children to hospital for relatively minor conditions under question.

The next example is concerned with the long-term consequences of chest illness in childhood and its association with chronic cough in adult life. Chest illness before the age of 2 years was associated with chronic cough at both age 20 and age 25, and the strength of this association increased with age. At 20 years neither social class of origin nor the level of air pollution experienced in childhood showed a statistically significant association with chronic cough in adult life; at age 25 years the association with social class was statistically significant and that with air pollution nearly so. It could be that the association between family circumstances in childhood and cough in adult life merely reflected environmental disadvantages continuing throughout the 25-year span. Alternatively, children of smokers might be more likely to become heavy adult smokers, which in turn might lead to chronic cough. However, both these possibilities have been excluded because improvements in socioeconomic circumstances did not change the association between early events and later cough, and the association was found to hold for both nonsmokers and smokers (Colley, Douglas, and Reid, 1973; Kiernan et al., 1976).

We have also looked at the relationship between a variety of events and illnesses in childhood and illness in early adult life. Males who have committed sexual and violent crimes are known to have considerably greater likelihood than others of having experienced emotional disruption before their fifth birthday, particularly disruption caused by the divorce or separation of their parents. It was hypothesized that if the emotional experience itself (rather than any post hoc labeling effect) accounted for this association, then those boys who underwent the experience but who did not become delinquent should show some other outcome. Since it was already known that they differed in psychophysiological response to stress at 11 years (Wadsworth, 1976), other outcomes were sought in the incidence, up to age 26 years, of seven disorders often associated with stress. These were psoriasis, eczema, asthma, migraine, psychiatric disease other than mental deficiency, peptic ulcers, and colitis. Two kinds of disorder were associated with earlier emotional disruption; namely, reports of admission to psychiatric hospitals and reports of treatment for peptic ulcers and colitis. Among the population of boys who, on the basis of early emotional disruption, were picked out in a discriminant analysis as likely delinquents, the incidence of peptic ulcers and colitis was 21.3 per thousand as compared with 8.3 per thousand among those who had not had serious emotional disruption. Similarly the incidence of hospitalized psychiatric disorder was 26 per thousand among the disrupted group and 15.5 per thousand among the others (Wadsworth, 1979).

The relationship between age at puberty and age at marriage and first parenthood has been studied (Kiernan, 1977). Age at menarche was recorded for girls in the 1946 birth cohort, and the degree of sexual maturity for boys at age 14¾ was assessed at a medical examination. By age 25, 84 percent of the women were married and nearly 60 percent were mothers, while 70 percent of the men were married and just over 50 percent were fathers. For men there was a direct relationship between degree of sexual maturity at age 15 and age both at marriage and at parenthood; other things being equal, the sooner a boy became a man in the sexual sense, the sooner he was likely to be married and a father. The girls presented a more complex case. When there was no history of premarital conception or illegitimate birth, early-maturing women married sooner than their later-maturing peers; but they did not become mothers any sooner. If, however, pregnancy intervened between menarche and marriage, there was no evidence of association between age at menarche and age at marriage. The most striking observation was that the proportion of teenage brides pregnant at marriage noticeably increased with age at menarche, so that girls who experienced menarche after their fourteenth birthday were nearly twice as likely to be pregnant at marriage as girls with menarche before their twelfth birthday. Social class or environmental factors failed to explain this relationship. Alternative explanations need to be sought; it might be, for example, that early and late maturers differ in their adjustment to the somatic and psychological changes associated with adolescence, or there may be biological differences between early- and late-maturing girls. After menarche there is a period of adolescent subfecundity, and it appears that fecundity then increases gradually with age. Perhaps the late maturers are more fecund than early maturers during the teenage years or more fecund throughout their reproductive life span.

I have said enough to show the rich field to be harvested in relating early life histories to later health and development. I now wish to turn to the important problem of the extent of social class differences in ill health.

SOCIAL CLASS AND ILL HEALTH

Social class differences in mortality have persisted in the United Kingdom and many other Western countries in spite of improved medical services and a general fall in the death rate. All classes have benefited from this fall, but instead of narrowing, the relative gap between the classes has been maintained and in some instances increased. It is not clear, however, whether these social differences in mortality arise from higher morbidity among the poor, deficient care, or both. Deficient care could arise either from failure to use available services or from regional differences in the provision or quality of services.

In the 1946 birth cohort up to age 26, social class differences in *mortality* have persisted, but there is little evidence of social class differences in *morbidity*. In early childhood there were higher prevalences of burns and lower respiratory tract infection among children from poor families (Douglas and Blomfield, 1958), but apart from these relatively small differences, there was no evidence of social class differences in serious or chronic illness (Pless and Douglas, 1971). It was not until age 25 that social inequalities reappeared and then at only a low level for respiratory symptoms (Kiernan et al., 1976). It seems, then, that after a period in the early years when social class differences in illness are evident, there may be a latent period followed in the mid-twenties or later by a reemergence of differences that are linked more to social class of origin than to achieved social class.

The absence of substantial morbidity differences may be a consequence of defining ill health in terms of services (for example, hospital or family practitioner) used. By extending our definition to include illness, absence from school and work, and the answers to symptom inventories, social class differences might be revealed and emerge more clearly when the analysis is restricted to groups of illnesses that are suspected of showing a high social class gradient. The answers to this analysis should be available by the end of the year, but it seems unlikely that they will show any substantial social class differences in the prevalence of either physical or mental illness in the mid-twenties.

STUDIES OF MORBIDITY AND HABITS OF LIFE

Birth cohort studies should be a useful source for linking ill health with different lifestyles and life events. They should, moreover, by defining the characteristics of people showing different styles of life, suggest how these could be changed. So far we have looked at this only in relation to smoking.

Much of the social class difference in respiratory illness in the 1946 birth cohort is explained by differences in smoking habit, in the age at which smoking started, and in the amount of tobacco smoked per day. Cherry and Kiernan (1976) have related personality scores at 16 with smoking. The relation between smoking and personality is not confined to groups who are either extremely neurotic or extremely extroverted, and the percentage smoking increases both with increasing extroversion and increasing neuroticism. Extroverts in general were more likely to smoke, and to smoke heavily, than introverts. But among smokers, the deep inhalers were the most neurotic. It is of particular interest that personality scores have some power in predicting which men and women who are not smoking at a given age will be smoking at a later age. They also help in predicting which of those smoking at a particular age will give it up during subsequent years.

In another publication Cherry (1978) finds that nervous strain at work relates both to a predisposition to anxiety and to the features of the day-to-day job. Men in high-level jobs are more likely to report nervous strain than men in manual work. However, there is little evidence that stressful jobs are held by men with particularly high (or low) resilience to stress.

IDENTIFICATION OF CHILDREN AT RISK

A recent report on the British child health services (Dept. of Health and Social Security, 1976) suggests that it is possible to identify children at risk, and it has also been suggested that health visitors (community nurses) could do this. Wadsworth and Morris (1978) have used the 1946 cohort illness records to examine the proposition that health visitors' assessment of home circumstances, maternal care, and use of child welfare services would discriminate a group of children at risk of hospital admission for certain illnesses. They conclude that the maximum reduction of hospital costs by such identification would be little better than one-third, and there would be an unquantifiable but real stress imposed on families in which the children were wrongly identified as at risk.

CONCLUSION

Comparisons in illness and in the use of services by different birth cohorts will present many opportunities for intergenerational research. So far only a few comparisons have been made, though more are planned. Calnan, Douglas, and Goldstein (1978) compared tonsillectomy and circumcision in the 1946 and 1958 cohorts. The particular interest here is that the two cohorts spanned a period when informed criticisms of both operations were beginning to appear and had by 1958 become intense. Both types of operation were less prevalent in the 1958 cohort, tonsillectomy falling by one-fifth and circumcision by more than half. These falls, however, were confined to tonsillectomy before the age of 6 and circumcision under 1 year. Social class differences in tonsillectomy were found in both cohort studies, but the strong social class gradient in circumcision reported in the 1946 cohort had vanished in the 1958 cohort. There were also regional and birth rank differences for both types of operation, which have shown substantial changes over time.

I have already mentioned the changes in the frequency of hospital admissions of very young children between 1946 and the present. Our later information was obtained by comparing the admissions in parents born in the 1946 study with those of their children some twenty to twenty-five years later and also from information coming from the 1970 study. The next step, of course, is to look at the types of condition for which children in these studies were admitted to hospital.

Finally, we are making a series of comparisons among the 1946, 1958, and 1970 cohorts on accidents and on obesity.

19 SOME RECOMMENDATIONS FOR THE DESIGN AND CONDUCT OF LONGITUDINAL INVESTIGATIONS

Birgitte R. Mednick, Sarnoff A. Mednick, and John J. Griffith

The longitudinal research described in this volume represents many subject years of experience. In a number of these chapters, these experiences are translated into practical and conceptual advice to anyone whose foresight is so deficient that he or she would begin a twenty-year project. This brief concluding chapter attempts to summarize those suggestions.

Longitudinal research in general and high-risk strategies in particular continue to receive far less attention than their potential for enhancing our knowledge of important psychological and social problems would seem to warrant. We have, however, had sufficient experience with these methodologies in the past twenty years or so to begin to develop some guidelines and recommendations for future projects. The suggestions that follow are based in large part on the experiences of the researchers whose projects are described in the preceding chapters.

GENERAL STRATEGIES FOR SUBJECT SELECTION AND IDENTIFICATION OF ANTECEDENT VARIABLES

Implications of Age of Subjects for Data Collection

Age of subjects at the time of data collection and at planned follow-up ages is an important factor to consider in the choice of variables to be included in a longitudinal research project. The literature in developmental psychology has demonstrated that the degree to which successful prediction of short- or long-term outcomes of a given variable may be obtained is highly influenced by variations in subject age. In a prospective study initiated with subjects who have reached adolescence, a rather high degree of predictability can be expected between the adolescent measures of personality traits and cognitive ability and similar measures obtained later in adulthood. Measures obtained on children during elementary school ages show considerably less correlation with later measures (Thomas, Chess, and Birch, 1968; McCall, Appelbaum, and Hogarty, 1973). The lowest levels of successful long-term prediction have been obtained in prospective longitudinal studies begun during infancy and early preschool years (Sameroff, 1979).

The following summary of measures and main findings from prospective research with infants may be useful for researchers planning prospective research. The focus of the section is on description of (1) the relative predictive power of different variables and/or combination of variables in this area of research and (2) the effect of subject age at follow-up on observed predictability of the independent variables. Though the literature reviewed is concerned only with studies beginning in infancy, generalizations may be made to research starting with older subjects.

The literature on prospective studies of infants shows that the predictive variables employed in the vast majority of prospective studies of infants and preschoolers fall into one of three categories: (1) a series of physical-risk variables observed at birth or shortly thereafter — for example, prematurity, neonatal brain damage, and asphyxia; (2) static measures of the social environment — for example, SES and mother's marital status; and (3) the results of different types of infant assessment — for example, Brazelton's Neonatal Behavioral Assessment Scale (Brazelton, 1973).

Physical-Risk Birth Variables

As summarized by Sameroff (1979), the overall findings of the literature on physical-risk variables are that peri- and neonatal complications or deviance have a measurable impact on child development during the preschool years, but that this relationship ceases to be significant at the time of school entry. (Cases in which very severe organic damage is involved clearly constitute an exception.) Whether this disappearance of symptoms signifies a permanent recovery from the underlying physical condition or whether a sleeper effect may be operating is not yet a settled issue in the literature. Mednick (1978) reported that children with transient (lasting less than a week) neonatal signs of brain damage showed no significant impairment at 1 year but presented relatively high levels of intellectual and neurological problems at 12 years of age compared to matched controls. This finding, as well as the findings from a series of retrospective studies of adults who had suffered perinatal trauma (Pasamanick and Knobloch, 1966), tends to support the notion that although the observable effects of this category of infant measures may disappear for some years during mid-childhood, measurable effects of the original trauma may reappear at a later age when the mastery of more complex patterns of behavioral and cognitive functioning is demanded. Thus, the temporal issue related to prediction on the basis of peri- or neonatal events is still unresolved. It is, however, quite unequivocally shown that the amount of variance of later outcome variables accounted for by this category of predictor variables alone is not dramatic at any age after the infancy period (Sameroff, 1979; Mednick, 1978; Broman, Nichols, and Kennedy, 1975).

Perinatal Variables in Interaction with Environmental Conditions

Some researchers have examined the effects of interactions between peri- and neonatal variables and measures of the social environment. These studies are in agreement in showing that perinatal traumas are more quickly and more adequately compensated for in higher SES groups and under stable family situations than under less advantageous environmental conditions.

Drillien (1964) demonstrated this kind of significant interaction between SES and prematurity on IQ measures of Scottish children at age 4. Werner, Bierman, and French (1971), examining the cognitive development and physical health of a Hawaiian birth cohort at 20 months, observed similar patterns of interaction between physical and social vulnerability. Studies examining more long-term interactions between disadvantageous environments report parallel findings; that is, good or adequate social conditions tend to be associated with high rates of recovery from perinatal trauma, whereas less than optimal environmental conditions tend to enhance the severity of the negative long-term sequelae of this category of risk variables (Pasamanick, Knobloch, and Lilienfeld,

1956; McDonald, 1964; Birch and Gussow, 1970; Werner, Bierman, and French, 1971).

Implications of Perinatal and Neonatal Variables
for Data Collection

Perinatal and neonatal physical traumas have been shown to have a significant, though generally not strong, effect on developmental outcomes during early childhood. In addition, some evidence exists that a sleeper effect is operative in the long-term outcomes associated with this category of infant predictor variables. The cited research evidence seems to suggest that information regarding perinatal and neonatal events will have the greatest predictive value if the planned follow-up ages are during preschool years; follow-up during elementary school years is likely to show no significant main effects of perinatal variables.

The level of predictability of later outcomes on the basis of perinatal and neonatal constitutional data tends to be greatly improved by addition of data describing conditions of the developmental environment. Thus, obtaining such information should be assigned high priority in studies aimed at predicting toward long-term outcomes as a function of perinatal and neonatal events.

Social Environment Measures

The research literature examining the effects of static environmental or social variables (Sameroff, 1979; Bradley, Caldwell, and Elardo, 1979; Bronfenbrenner, 1974) suggests that this category of predictors has no measurable impact on development and behavior during the first year of life. Sometime during the second year, most often around 18 months of age, the negative effects of less optimal environmental conditions begin to appear, and from then on, the negative effect becomes progressively pervasive (Kagan, Lapidus, and Moore, 1978). Exceptions to the general finding of no environmental effect during the first 18 months are illustrated by instances where specific environmental changes involving intensive infant-adult interactions were instituted as part of a preventive intervention program for children judged to be vulnerable according to biological or social criteria (Scarr-Salapatek and Williams, 1973; Heber, 1975). In such cases, positive effects of the systematic intensive manipulation of the environment may be observed within the first year. Thus it appears that environmental variables involving the quality of the caretaker and the infant-adult interaction affect infant outcomes before the effect of static environmental variables such as SES can be observed. Further, it has been convincingly demonstrated that these kinds of qualitative environmental variables (caretaker characteristics and interactions) continue to have a strong independent effect on child outcomes after the effect of static measures (SES) becomes observable; that is, after the age of 2 years. Sameroff (1979) notes that whereas perinatal variables, static social measures (SES and mother's education), and 4-, 8-, and 12-month infant assessment data together accounted for 28 percent of the variance on IQ scores at 4 years of age in the American Collaborative Study (Broman, Nichols, and Kennedy, 1975), the Rochester longitudinal study succeeded in accounting for 50 percent of the variance in 30-month IQ scores by adding predictors such as the mother's characteristics and behavior toward the child.

Implications of Social Environment Measures for Data Collection

It seems clear that in addition to static measures of the social environment, measures describing the characteristics of the caretaker and of the caretaker-child interaction should be given the highest priority in prospective longitudinal research on infant samples for the following reasons:

1.   Inclusion of these categories of predictor variables has been shown to improve the predictability of early and later emotional and cognitive outcomes to a highly significant degree. The effect of these variables on child outcomes are observable before the impact of variations in static environmental measures such as SES may be observed. After the second year, when SES effects become increasingly more predominant, these qualitative environmental variables still continue to present a strong independent contribution to developmental outcomes.

2.   In addition to improving the general level of predictability attained in prospective studies of infants, inclusion of variables describing caretaker characteristics and interaction patterns offers an opportunity for gaining more insight into the factors that underlie the previously mentioned strong effect of SES on child outcomes after 2 years of age. SES is known to covary with qualitative measures of the developing environment. Low SES has been shown to be associated with certain types of caretaker characteristics, child-rearing practices, nutrition, parent education and values, and so on (Bronfenbrenner, 1974; Bernstein, 1961). It is clearly these correlates of the static variable SES that are mediating

the observed effect rather than SES membership per se. Thus the more data available on such SES covariates, the better the chance for uncovering the relative importance of these factors in determining the overall SES effect. Such knowledge would clearly not only have a theoretical interest but also be a highly valuable source of information in the development of preventive intervention programs for low SES children.

3. Inclusion of variables describing caretaker characteristics and interaction style must be seen as especially crucial in studies beginning in early infancy. At this point of development, observations of caretaker characteristics and infant interaction patterns present the possibility for determining, to some degree, the role played by each of the actors in forming the long-term interpersonal relationship. As first pointed out by Bell (1968), the pattern of interaction developing between a child and his caretaker is by no means developed through a unidirectional process; that is, through the infant's responding to the caretaker's behavior. Rather, the pattern of interaction developing in an infant-caretaker dyad depends to an equal degree on the characteristics and typical reactions of each member of the dyad. By observing an infant-caretaker dyad from earliest infancy, some insight into the etiology of the child-adult interaction observed at later ages may be obtained. In contrast, the etiological information to be obtained about the interactional pattern itself as well as its impact on concurrent child characteristics must be seen as limited if one studies the interaction of adolescents with their parents. As an example, watching parents of a juvenile delinquent interact with the youngster and observing an unloving parental style will not allow us to conclude that this parental characteristic might have a causal relationship to the delinquency. It is also possible that such a child has caused the parents an extraordinary amount of difficulty or trouble (perhaps starting in infancy) by possessing characteristics that made caring for and raising the child a very frustrating task. In such circumstances, the observed parental style could be interpreted more correctly as an effect rather than as a cause. Obviously, interaction patterns observable between a child and his or her parents may never actually be divided in such a simple fashion into causes and effects because they have all been formed through the continued interaction of parental and child characteristics.

Infant Assessment Measures

The results from the literature on prediction of shorter- and/or longer-term outcomes on the basis of infant assessments have uniformly shown such prediction to present a rather disappointing low level of success, particularly in the areas of cognitive functioning and personality traits (Thomas, Chess, and Birch, 1968; St. Claire, 1978; Rosenblith, 1964, 1973; Sameroff, Krafchuk, and Bakow, 1978; Kagan, Lapidus, and Moore, 1978; Horowitz, Sullivan, and Linn, 1978; Crano, 1977; Corah et al., 1965; Ucko, 1965; McCall, Hogarty, and Hurlburt, 1973; Sameroff and Chandler, 1975).

Any thorough discussion of why infant assessment data share this low degree of predictive power is beyond the scope of this chapter. This question has been analyzed in detail by several authors (Sameroff, 1978; Crano, 1977). It will suffice here to summarize the most frequently cited reasons for the low predictability. One common explanation suggests that the grossness of the measures that one might obtain on infants is the reason for the low predictability. Another explanation specifically relevant to prediction of later cognitive functioning and temperament suggests that the low predictability is caused by the qualitative discontinuity of what is defined as measures of cognitive performance or personality in infancy and later in life. For example, in the area of cognitive development, measures obtained at a time when cognitive functioning is confounded with motor functioning cannot logically be expected to predict very strongly to measures of cognitive functioning at a later time when age norms are defined in terms of high levels of abstract thinking. Sameroff and Chandler (1975) suggest that this discontinuity has led to the paradoxical finding that measures describing the caretaking environment in fact constitute better predictors of later cognitive outcomes than do "cognitive" measures obtained on the infant himself.

Implications of Infant Assessment Measures for Data Collection

The lack of predictability of later functioning from infant measures should not be interpreted to mean that infant assessment data are inappropriate for use in longitudinal research. It is, however, important to note that confining the selection of measures to those considered to be infant measures of the traits or areas of competence that are to be measured at later subject ages will yield disappointing results. The recommendation to be extracted from the cited research seems rather to be that the widest range of measures possible, including varied measures on the infant, the environment, and their interaction, shows greater promise for successful prediction.

It should be pointed out that the increasing level of predictability of measures obtained at later ages in childhood is very likely to be caused by the fact that such measures possess higher qualitative continuity with the final outcome measures studied. In young adulthood the measured characteristics cease to change in quality from test to test, thus resulting in a high stability of measures obtained from late adolescence onward.

CONCLUSIONS REGARDING GENERAL RESEARCH STRATEGY

As mentioned earlier, some of the conclusions made about infant research seem generalizable to research begun with older subjects. The following points seem among the more important to mention in this category:

1. The planned follow-up ages of the subjects have implications for the kinds of variables to be included and the level of prediction to be expected in longitudinal research.
2. The importance of physical measures in prediction is heightened if such measures are analyzed in interaction with environmental measures.
3. The predictive power of environmental measures as well as the possibility of gaining insight into the mechanisms through which environmental effects on development are mediated is dramatically improved by inclusion of nonstatic environmental data. Examples are data based on direct observation describing the characteristics of significant persons in the environment and of the patterns of interaction developed between the subject and these persons.

PRACTICAL SUGGESTIONS

In the section below we provide some suggestions that are designed to increase project stability and to maximize effective utilization of the data collected.

Data Collection and Analysis

In general, investigators should be as flexible as possible in the planning stages of a longitudinal project. It is important to remember that some of the outcomes that will be related to the antecedent factors in the project may not evidence themselves for twenty years. The investigators will be wise to formulate hypotheses in a very general form and admit, among their antecedent measures, variables other than those directly and specifically suggested by their own theoretical orientation. During the course of the study it is important to make use of opportunities that present themselves for gathering additional information on the subjects.

In order to understand the complex relationships that appear in our data, we must become familiar with more recent sophisticated statistical techniques. An example of such a technique is path analysis, a procedure that allows for hypothesized causal models to be formulated in mathematical form so that their agreement with observed covariances among our variables can be examined. For longitudinal analyses this method has the special advantage of allowing for the differentiation of direct and mediated effects in the data. The interested reader is encouraged to consult Jöreskog's chapter in this volume, his earlier publications (Jöreskog, 1970; Jöreskog and von Thillo, 1972), and a recent article by Bentler (1980).

Organization of Longitudinal Research

1. Whenever possible, longitudinal projects should be multipurpose. In this way, different, perhaps multidisciplinary, lines of inquiry can be occurring simultaneously or in sequence. A single study may be organized into a series of subprojects, each with its own principal investigator, thus eliminating the need for costly multiple efforts. This not only makes for more efficient use of the project's data base but also increases the likelihood of multi-agency funding.

2. It is extremely desirable for longitudinal projects to have a stable and continuing base of funding. Whenever possible, efforts should be made to obtain multi-agency funding that can be phase-scheduled over the duration of the project. It can be important in this connection to gain public or community support for a particular study.

3. Gruenberg and LeResche (1970) recommend that at the inception of every longitudinal project an advisory board of outside distinguished scientists be appointed to help the investigators. They suggest that the advisory board be independent of the grant-giving agency so that the exchanges between the scientists and the advisory board can be uninhibited by financial considerations. The advisory board should be cross-disciplinary, since, as we have said, any large longitudinal study should be considered multipurpose. The function of the cross-disciplinary ad-

visory board should be to provide expertise as well as professional contacts necessary to exploit multidisciplinary opportunities properly.

Administration and Utilization of Information

1.   It is important to allow for and encourage publications of results by the project's staff. If this does not occur, staff members' professional advancement may be jeopardized and their willingness to maintain their relationships with the project affected. Continuity of professional staff is extremely important; turnover can be expensive because of training costs and is likely to reduce the quality of technical output.

2.   More so than in probably any other type of research paradigm, accuracy and precision in data collection and storage are essential in longitudinal studies. In many instances it is not possible to regather or reconstruct data that have been lost or improperly collected in the first place. The principal investigator should institute procedures that allow for periodic evaluation and quality control of the data collection phase of the project.

3.   Because almost all longitudinal projects are funded by public sources, investigators should consider these data as a type of public property (in a limited sense). Of course, the investigators' aims and interests must first be taken into account; but whenever possible the investigator should be open to the exploitation of "his" data or "her" population by outside responsible scientists. Perhaps this volume will catalyze such productive interactions.

4.   There should be a central clearinghouse for all longitudinal studies. Such a mechanism would encourage utilization of project data (the data from most longitudinal studies have been severely *underutilized*) and could result in significant savings of resources by reducing the need in certain areas for entire new studies.

It should be emphasized that longitudinal data sets deserve special recognition as a part of the public record. The justification for this special status derives not only from the great heuristic potential of these data sets but also from their very nature as complex, evolving groupings of information that are not, strictly speaking, recreatable in other times or settings. The organic character of these data sets will become more apparent when (and if) the longitudinal methodology is expanded to transgenerational studies.

CONCLUSION

Longitudinal research projects have often been conducted by scientists isolated by their discipline affiliation. The survival of projects has been a credit to astounding tenacity, dedication, and endless hours of labor. If projects have enjoyed support, it has frequently been sporadic and short-lived.

These data files represent a precious world resource for understanding the nature of human beings and how they thrive or wither in interaction with their environment. These data files are unique in the sense that they are not recreatable.

Their potential importance has not been fully realized. Part of the reason for this has been the aforementioned isolation of projects from each other. A pediatrician and a psychologist may be conducting similar developmental projects from offices in neighboring university buildings and be unaware of each other's work. Isolation has also resulted from national and language barriers. This isolation hinders mutual education and support. It makes comparison of results and techniques impossible. Thus potential advances of human knowledge are not realized. No one, standing alone, takes his or her own results seriously enough to make forceful recommendations on public policy. Strengthened by replication of results in other cohorts, longitudinal projects should be a public resource sought after by social planners and politicians.

The time may be ripe for an international organization of longitudinal researchers. Perhaps such an organization would lessen the mutual isolation of researchers in this field.

REFERENCES

Acheson, E. D. 1967. *Medical Record Linkage.* New York: Oxford University Press.

Allardt, E. 1975. *Att ha att älska att vara.* Lund: Argos.

Anderson, S. B., and Maier, M. H. 1963. "34,000 Pupils and How They Grew." *Journal of Teacher Education* 14:212–16.

Angell, R. C., and Freedman, R. 1953. "The Use of Documents, Records, Census Materials, and Indices." In L. Festinger and D. Katz, eds., *Research Methods in the Behavioral Sciences.* New York: Dryden Press.

Atkins, E.; Cherry, N.; Douglas, J. W. B.; Kiernan, K. E.; and Wadsworth, M. E. J. 1980. "The 1946 British Birth Cohort: An Account of the Origins, Progress and Results of the National Survey of Health Development." In S. A. Mednick and A. E. Baert, eds., *Prospective Longitudinal Research.* New York: Oxford University Press.

Ax, A. F., and Bamford, J. L. 1970. "The GSR Recovery Limb in Chronic Schizophrenia." *Psychophysiology* 7:145–47.

Babigian, H. M.; Gardner, E. A.; Miles, H. C.; and Romano, J. 1965. "Diagnostic Consistency and Change in a Follow-Up Study of 1,215 Patients." *American Journal of Psychiatry* 121:895–901.

Baldwin, J. A.; Leff, J.; and Wing, J. K. 1976. "Confidentiality of Psychiatric Data in Medical Information Systems." *British Journal of Psychiatry* 128: 417–27.

297

Baltes, P. B., and Schaie, K. W., eds. 1973. *Life-Span Developmental Psychology: Personality and Socialization*. New York: Academic Press.

Bayley, N. 1955. "On the Growth of Intelligence." *American Psychologist* 10:805–18.

———. 1964. "Consistency of Maternal and Child Behaviours in the Berkeley Growth Study." *Vita Humana* 7:73–95.

Becker, H. S. 1963. *Outsiders*. New York: Free Press.

Bell, B.; Christie, M. J.; and Venables, P. H. 1975. "Psychophysiology of the Menstrual Cycle." In P. H. Venables and M. J. Christie, eds., *Research in Psychophysiology*. London: Wiley.

Bell, R. Q. 1968. "A Reinterpretation of the Direction of Effects in Studies of Socialization." *Psychological Review* 75:81–95.

Bentler, P. M. 1973. "Assessment of Development Factor Change at the Individual and Group Level." In J. R. Nesselroade and H. W. Reese, eds., *Life-Span Developmental Psychology: Methodological Issues*. New York: Academic Press.

———. 1980. "Multivariate Analysis with Latent Variables: Causal Modeling." *Annual Review of Psychology* 31.

Bergman, L. R. 1971. "Some Univariate Models in Studying Change." Reports from the Psychological Laboratories, Suppl. 10, University of Stockholm.

Bergman, L. R., and Magnusson, D. 1969. "Overachievement and Catecholamine Output in an Achievement Situation." *Psychosomatic Medicine* 41:181–88.

Berkson, J. 1955. "The Statistical Study of Association between Smoking and Lung Cancer." Proceedings of Staff Meetings, Mayo Clinic, pp. 319–48.

Bernstein, B. 1961. "Social Class and Linguistic Development: A Theory of Social Learning." In A. H. Halsey, J. Floud, and C. A. Anderson, eds., *Education, Economy and Society*. Glencoe, Ill.: Free Press.

Birch, H., and Gussow, J. 1970. *Disadvantaged Children: Health, Nutrition and School Failure*. New York: Harcourt, Brace & World.

Birch, H. G.; Riedchardson, S. A.; Baird, D.; Horobin, G.; and Illsley, R. 1970. *Mental Subnormality in the Community*. Baltimore, Md.: Williams & Wilkins.

Blalock, H. M. 1961. *Causal Inferences in Nonexperimental Research*. Chapel Hill: University of North Carolina Press.

Blau, P. M., and Duncan, O. D. 1967. *The American Occupational Structure*. New York: Wiley.

Block, J. 1971. *Lives through Time*. Berkeley, Calif.: Bancroft Books.

Block, J. H. 1973. "Conceptions of Sex Roles: Some Cross-Cultural and Longitudinal Perspectives." *American Psychologist* 28:512–29.

Bloom, B. S. 1964. *Stability and Change in Human Characteristics*. New York: Wiley.

Boalt, G. 1947. *Skolutbildning och skolresultat för barn i olika samhällsgrupper*. Stockholm: Norstedts.

Bohrnstedt, G. W. 1969. "Observations on the Measurement of Change." In E. F. Borgatta, ed., *Sociological Methodology: 1969*. San Francisco: Jossey-Bass.

Boudon, R. 1974. *Education, Opportunity and Social Inequality*. New York: Wiley.

Bowlby, J. 1951. *Maternal Care and Mental Health*. Monograph Series No. 2. Geneva: World Health Organization.

Bradley, H. R.; Caldwell, B. M.; and Elardo, R. 1979. "Home Environment and Cognitive Development in the First 2 Years: A Cross-Lagged Panel Analysis." *Developmental Psychology* 15(3):246–50.

Brazelton, T. 1973. *Neonatal Behavioral Assessment Scale*. Philadelphia: Lippincott.

Brener, J. 1967. "Heart Rate." In P. H. Venables and I. Martin, eds., *A Manual of Psychophysiological Methods*. Amsterdam: North-Holland.

Brim, O. G., and Kagan, J., eds. 1980. *Constancy and Change in Human Development*. Cambridge, Mass.: Harvard University Press.

Broman, S.; Nichols, P.; and Kennedy, W. 1975. *Preschool IQ: Prenatal and Early Developmental Correlates*. Hillsdale, N.J.: Erlbaum.

Bronfenbrenner, U. 1974. "A Report on Longitudinal Evaluations of Pre-School Programs." DHEW Publication No. (OHD) 75–125.

Buchsbaum, M. 1975. "Average Evoked Response, Augmenting/Reducing in Schizophrenia and Affective Disorders." In D. X. Freedman, ed., *Biology of the Major Psychoses*. New York: Raven Press.

———. 1976. "Self-Regulation of Stimulus Intensity." In G. E. Schwartz and D. Shapiro, eds., *Consciousness and Self-Regulation*. Vol. 1. New York: Plenum.

Buchsbaum, M.; Coursey, R. D.; and Murphy, D. L. 1976. "The Biochemical High-Risk Paradigm: Behavioral and Familial Correlates of Low Platelet Monoamine Oxidase Activity." *Science* 194:339–41.

Bühler, C.; Keith-Spiegel, P.; and Thomas, K. 1973. "Developmental Psychology." In B. B. Wolman, ed., *Handbook of General Psychology*. Englewood Cliffs, N.J.: Prentice-Hall.

Bull, K., and Lang, P. J. 1972. "Intensity Judgments and Physiological Response Amplitude." *Psychophysiology* 9:428–36.

Butler, N. R., and Alberman, E. D. 1969. *Perinatal Problems*. Edinburgh: Livingstone.

Callaway, E.; Tueting, P.; and Koslow, S. 1978. *Brain-Event Related Potentials in Man*. New York: Academic Press.

Calnan, M.; Douglas, J. W. B.; and Goldstein, H. 1978. "Tonsillectomy and Circumcision — Comparison of Two Cohorts." *International Journal of Epidemiology* 7:79–85.

Cannell, C. F., and Kahn, R. L. 1968. "Interviewing." In G. Lindzey and E. Aronson, eds., *Handbook of Social Psychology*, 2d ed. Vol. 2. Reading, Mass.: Addison-Wesley.

Carmichael, L. 1926. "The Development of Behavior in Vertebrates Experimentally Removed from the Influence of External Stimulation." *Psychological Review* 33:51–58.

———. 1927. "A Further Study of the Development of Behavior in Vertebrates

Experimentally Removed from the Influence of External Stimulation." *Psychological Review* 34:34–47.

Chamberlain, R.; Chamberlain, G.; Howlett, B.; and Claireaux, A. 1975. *British Births, 1970.* London: Heinemann.

Cherry, N. 1974. "Components of Occupational Interest." *British Journal of Educational Psychology* 44:22–30.

————. 1978. "Stress, Anxiety and Work: A Longitudinal Study." *Journal of Occupational Psychology* 51:259–70.

Cherry, N., and Kiernan, K. E. 1976. "Personality Scores and Smoking Behaviour." *British Journal of Preventive and Social Medicine* 30:123–31.

Clarke, A. M., and Clarke, A. D. B. 1976. *Early Experience: Myth and Evidence.* London: Open Books.

Classification of Occupations. 1951. London: Her Majesty's Stationery Office (HMSO).

Colley, J. R. T.; Douglas, J. W. B.; and Reid, D. D. 1973. "Respiratory Disease in Young Adults: Influence of Early Childhood Lower Respiratory Tract Illness, Social Class, Air Pollution and Smoking." *British Medical Journal* 11:195–98.

Commission of the European Communities. 1978. *Report on the Joint EEC/WHO Workshop on Physical Activity in Primary Prevention of Ischaemic Heart Disease.* Luxembourg, February 22–24, 1977.

Cooper, B., and Morgan, H. G. 1973. *Epidemiological Psychiatry.* Springfield, Ill.: Charles C Thomas.

Corah, N.; Anthony, E. J.; Painter, P.; Stern, J. A.; and Thurston, D. L. 1965. "Effects of Perinatal Anoxia after Seven Years." *Psychological Monographs* 79(3), No. 596.

Corballis, M. C. 1973. "A Factor Model for Analyzing Change." *British Journal of Mathematical and Statistical Psychology* 26:90–97.

Corballis, M. C., and Traub, R. E. 1970. "Longitudinal Factor Analysis." *Psychometrika* 35:79–98.

Crano, W. D. 1977. "What Do Infant Mental Tests Test? A Cross-Lagged Panel Analysis of Selected Data from the Berkeley Growth Study." *Child Development* 48:144–51.

Cronbach, L. J., and Furby, L. 1970. "How Should We Measure 'Change' — Or Should We?" *Psychological Bulletin* 75:68–80.

Crowell, D. H.; Blurton, L. B.; Kobayashi, L. R.; McFarland, J. L.; and Yang, R. K. 1976. "Studies in Early Infant Learning: Classical Conditioning of the Neonatal Heart Rate." *Developmental Psychology* 12:373–97.

Curtiss, S. 1977. *Genie.* New York: Academic Press.

Dallas, J. 1971. "Patient Follow-up in a Long-Term Study." *Johns Hopkins Medical Journal* 128:244.

Davies, P. A. 1976. "Outlook for the Low Birthweight Baby — Then and Now." *Archives of Diseases of Childhood* 51:817.

Delbetænkning om offentlige registre [Partial report about public registers]. 1976. Report No. 767. Copenhagen: Statens Trykningskontor.

Dentler, R. A., and Monroe, L. J. 1961. "Social Correlates of Early Adolescent Thefts." *American Sociological Review* 26:733–43.

Department of Health and Social Security. 1976. *Priorities for Health and Personal Social Services in England.* London: HMSO.

Dobbing, J. 1973. "The Later Development of the Central Nervous System and Its Vulnerability." In J. A. Davis and J. Dobbing, eds., *Scientific Foundations of Paediatrics.* London: Heinemann.

Dohrenwend, B. P.; Egri, G.; and Mendelsohn, F. 1971. "Psychiatric Disorder in General Populations: A Study of the Problem of Clinical Judgment." *American Journal of Psychiatry* 127:1304–12.

Dollard, J. 1949. *Criteria for the Life History.* New York: Peter Smith.

Douglas, J. W. B. 1964. *The Home and the School.* London: McGibbon and Kee.

———. 1975. "Early Hospital Admissions and Later Disturbances of Behaviour and Learning." *Developmental Medicine and Child Neurology* 17:456–80.

———. 1976. "The Use and Abuse of National Cohorts." In M. Shipman, ed., *The Organization and Impact of Social Research.* London: Routledge-Kegan Paul.

Douglas, J. W. B., and Blomfield, J. M. 1958. *Children under Five.* London: Allen and Unwin.

Douglas, J. W. B., and Cherry, N. 1977. "Sex and Qualifications." *Times Educational Supplement*, December 9.

Douglas, J. W. B.; Ross, J. M.; and Simpson, H. R. 1968. *All Our Future.* London: Peter Davies.

Douglas, J. W. B., and Rowntree, G. R. 1948. *Maternity in Great Britain.* London: Oxford University Press.

Drillien, C. M. 1964. *The Growth and Development of the Prematurely Born Infant.* Edinburgh and London: Livingstone.

Drohocki, Z. 1948. "L'integrateur de l'électro-production cérébrale par l'encephalographie quantitative." *Revue Neurologique (Paris)* 80:619–24.

Duncan, O. D. 1969. "Some Linear Models for Two-Wave, Two-Variable Panel Analysis." *Psychological Bulletin* 72:177–82.

———. 1972. "Unmeasured Variables in Linear Models for Panel Analysis." In H. L. Costner, ed., *Sociological Methodology: 1972.* San Francisco: Jossey-Bass.

———. 1975a. *Introduction to Structural Equation Models.* New York: Academic Press.

———. 1975b. "Some Linear Models for Two-Wave, Two-Variable Panel Analysis with One-Way Causation and Measurement Errors." In H. M. Blalock, ed., *Quantitative Sociology: International Perspectives on Mathematical and Statistical Modelling.* New York: Academic Press.

Dunér, A. 1978. "Problems and Designs in Research in Educational and Vocational Career." In A. Dunér, ed., *Research into Personal Development: Educational and Vocational Choice.* Amsterdam: Swets & Zeitlinger.

Dupont, A. 1975. "Mentally Retarded in Denmark." *Danish Medical Bulletin* 22:243–51.

————. 1979. "Psychiatric Case Register as a Basis for Estimation and Monitoring of Needs." In H. Häfner, ed., *Estimating Needs for Mental Health Care: A Contribution of Epidemiology*. New York: Springer.

Dupont, A.; Videbech, T.; and Weeke, A. 1974. "A Cumulative National Psychiatric Register: Its Structure and Application." *Acta Psychiatrica Scandinavica* 50:161–73.

Edelman, G. M. 1978. "Group Selection and Phasic Reentrant Signalling: A Theory of Higher Brain Function." In G. M. Edelman and V. B. Mountcastle, eds., *The Mindful Brain*. Cambridge, Mass.: MIT Press.

Ekehammar, B. 1977. "Test of a Psychological Cost-Benefit Model for Career Choice." *Journal of Vocational Behavior* 10:245–60.

————. 1978. "Psychological Cost-Benefit as an Intervening Construct in Career Choice Models." *Journal of Vocational Behavior* 12:279–89.

Ekström, K. 1972. *Gonorrhoea hos unge*. Copenhagen: Munksgaard.

Elmhorn, K. 1965. "Study in Self-Reported Delinquency among Schoolchildren in Stockholm." In K. O. Christiansen, ed., *Scandinavian Studies in Criminology*. Oslo: Universitetsforlaget.

Eme, R. F. 1979. "Sex Differences in Childhood Psychopathology: A Review." *Psychological Bulletin* 86:574–95.

Emerson, R. M. 1969. "Operant Psychology and Exchange Theory." In R. L. Burgess and D. Bushell, eds., *Behavioral Sociology*. New York: Columbia University Press.

Emmerich, W. 1968. "Personality Development and Concepts of Structure." *Child Development* 39: 671–90.

Endicott, J., and Spitzer, R. 1972. "Current and Past Psychopathology Scales (CAPPS)." *Archives of General Psychology* 27:678–87.

Endler, N. S., and Magnusson, D. 1976. "Toward an Interactional Psychology of Personality." *Psychological Bulletin* 83:956–74.

Fællesindhold for registrering af stationære patienter [Guidance for registration of long-stay patients]. 1976. Koordinationsgruppen for individbaseret patientregistrering. Copenhagen: Sundhedsstyrelsen.

Ferguson, M. 1918. *Social and Economic Factors in the Causation of Rickets*. MRC Special Report Series, No. 20.

Fitzhardinge, P. M., and Ramsey, M. 1973. "The Improving Outlook for the Small Prematurely Born Infant." *Developmental Medicine and Child Neurology* 15:447–59.

Flavell, J. H. 1972. "An Analysis of Cognitive Developmental Sequences." *Genetic Psychology Monographs* 86:279–350.

Flor-Henry, P. 1974. "Psychosis, Neurosis, and Epilepsy." *British Journal of Psychiatry* 124:144–50.

Forrest, A. D., and Hay, A. J. 1972. "The Influence of Sex on Schizophrenia." *Acta Psychiatrica Scandinavica* 48:49–58.

Francis-Williams, J. C., and Davies, P. A. 1974. "Very Low Birthweight and Later Intelligence." *Developmental Medicine and Child Neurology* 16:709.

Fredriksen, C. R., 1974. "Models for the Analysis of Alternative Sources of Growth in Correlated Stochastic Variables." *Psychometrika* 39:223–45.

Fremming, K. H. 1951. "The Expectation of Mental Infirmity in a Sample of the Danish Population." Papers on Eugenics, No. 7. London: Eugenics Society.

Friedman, M., and Rosenman, R. H. 1974. *Type-A Behavior and Your Heart.* New York: Knopf.

Gam, J. 1980. "A 5-Year Retrospective Investigation of All First-Admitted Schizophrenics to Danish Psychiatric Institutions in the Fiscal Year from April 1, 1970, to April 1, 1971." In E. Strömgren, A. Dupont, and J. Achton Nielsen, eds., *Epidemiological Research as Basis for the Organization of Extramural Psychiatry.* Copenhagen: Munksgaard. *Acta Psychiatrica Scandinavica* 62, suppl. 285.

Garber, H., and Heber, F. R. 1977. "The Milwaukee Project: Indications of the Effectiveness of Early Intervention in Preventing Mental Retardation." In P. Mittler, ed., *Research to Practice in Mental Retardation: Care and Intervention.* Vol. 1, pp. 119–27.

Gardner, E. A.; Miles, H. C.; Iker, H. P.; and Romano, J. 1963. "A Cumulative Register of Psychiatric Services in a Community." *American Journal of Public Health* 53:1269–77.

Gardner, G. G. 1967. "Role of Maternal Psychopathology in Male and Female Schizophrenics." *Journal of Consulting Psychology* 31:411–13.

Gatchel, R. J., and Lang, P. J. 1973. "Accuracy of Psychophysical Judgments and Physiological Response Amplitude." *Journal of Experimental Psychology* 98:175–83.

Goldberger, A. S. 1972. "Structual Equation Methods in the Social Sciences." *Econometrica* 40:979–1001.

Goldstein, L.; Murphree, H. B.; Sugerman, A. A.; Pfeiffer, C. C.; and Jenney, E. H. 1963. "Quantitative Electroencephalographic Analysis of Naturally Occurring (Schizophrenic) and Drug-Induced Psychotic States in Human Males." *Clinical Pharmacology and Therapeutics* 4:10–21.

Goldstein, L.; Sugerman, A. A.; Stolberg, H.; Murphree, H. B.; and Pfeiffer, C. C. 1965. "Electro-cerebral Activity in Schizophrenics and Non-psychotic Subjects: Quantitative EEG Amplitude Analysis." *EEG and Clinical Neurophysiology* 19:350–61.

Goodman, L. 1970. "The Multivariate Analysis of Qualitative Data: Interactions among Multiple Classifications." *Journal of the American Statistical Association* 65 (329):226–56.

Goodwin, D. W.; Schulsinger, F.; Hermansen, L.; Guze, S. B.; and Winokur, G. 1973. "Alcohol Problems in Adoptees Raised Apart from Alcoholic Biological Parents." *Archives of General Psychiatry* 28:238–43.

Goodwin, D. W.; Schulsinger, F.; Knop, J.; Mednick, S. A.; and Guze, S. B. 1977. "Alcoholism and Depression in Adopted-out Daughters of Alcoholics." *Archives of General Psychiatry* 34:751–55.

Goodwin, D. W.; Schulsinger, F.; Møller, N.; Hermansen, L.; Winokur, G.; and

Guze, S. B. 1974. "Drinking Problems in Adopted and Nonadopted Sons of Alcoholics." *Archives of General Psychiatry* 31:164–69.

Gordon, R., and Jacobson, A. G. 1978. "The Shaping of Tissues in Embryos." *Scientific American* 238 (6):106–13.

Gottesman, I. I., and Shields, J. 1972. *Schizophrenia and Genetics: A Twin Study Vantage Point.* New York: Academic Press.

———. 1976. "Rejoinder: Toward Optimal Arousal and Away from Original Sin." *Schizophrenia Bulletin* 2:447–53.

Gouldner, A. W., and Peterson, R. A. 1964. *Notes on Technology and the Moral Order.* Indianapolis, Ind.: Bobbs-Merrill.

Graham, F. K. 1978. "Constraints on Measuring Heart Rate and Period Sequentially through Real and Cardiac Time. *Psychophysiology* 15:492–95.

Graham, F. K.; Ernhart, C. B.; Thurstone, D.; and Crafft, M. 1962. "Development Three Years after Perinatal Anoxia and after Potentially Damaging Newborn Experiences." *Psychological Monographs* 76:522.

Graham, P. J., ed. 1977. *Epidemiological Approaches in Child Psychiatry.* New York: Academic Press.

Griffith, J. J.; Mednick, S. A.; Schulsinger, F.; and Diderichsen, B. 1980. "Verbal Associative Disturbances in Children at High Risk for Schizophrenia." *Journal of Abnormal Psychology* 89:125–31.

Gruenberg, E. M. 1976. "The Future of Community Medicine." *Lancet* 2:262.

Gruenberg, E. M., and LeResche, L. 1970. "Reaction: The Future of Longitudinal Studies." In *Research Bulletin 70–54.* Princeton, N.J.: Educational Testing Service.

Gruzelier, J. H. 1973. "Bilateral Asymmetry of Skin Conductance Activity and Levels in Schizophrenics." *Biological Psychology* 1:21–42.

Gruzelier, J. H., and Venables, P. H. 1974. "Bimodality and Lateral Asymmetry of Skin Conductance Orienting Activity in Schizophrenics: Replication and Evidence of Lateral Asymmetry in Patients with Depression and Disorders of Personality." *Biological Psychiatry* 8:55–73.

Hagnell, O. 1966. *A Prospective Study of the Incidence of Mental Disorder.* Lund: Scandinavian University Books.

———. 1980. "The Lundby Study." In S. A. Mednick and A. E. Baert, eds., *Prospective Longitudinal Research.* New York: Oxford University Press.

Hagnell, O., and Kreitman, N. 1974. "Mental Illness in Married Pairs in a Total Population." *British Journal of Psychiatry* 125:293–302.

Hagnell, O., and Rorsman, B. 1978. "Suicide and Endogenous Depression with Somatic Symptoms in the Lundby Study." *Neuropsychobiology* 4:180–87.

Hare, R. D. 1978. "Electrodermal and Cardiovascular Correlates of Psychopathy." In R. D. Hare and D. Schalling, eds., *Psychopathic Behaviour.* London: Wiley.

Härnqvist, K. 1968. "Relative Changes in Intelligence from 13 to 18." *Scandinavian Journal of Psychology* 9:50–82.

Härnquist, K., and Svensson, A. 1967. "Milieu social, rendement des élèves et orientation scolaire." *Bulletin de Psychologie* 257(20):10–15.

Harris, C. W. 1963. "Canonical Factor Models for the Description of Change." In C. W. Harris, ed., *Problems in Measuring Change*. Madison: University of Wisconsin Press.

Hatton, H. M.; Berg, W. K.; and Graham, F. K. 1970. "Effects of Acoustic Rise Time on Heart Rate Response." *Psychonomic Science* 19:101–03.

Hauge, M. 1980. "The Danish Twin Register." In S. A. Mednick and A. E. Baert, eds., *Prospective Longitudinal Research*. New York: Oxford University Press.

Heber, R. 1975. "Intensive Intervention Program Prevents Retardation." *APA Monitor* 7:9–10.

Heise, D. R. 1969. "Separating Reliability and Stability in Test-Retest Correlations." *American Sociological Review* 34:93–101.

―――. 1970. "Causal Inference from Panel Data." In E. F. Borgatta and G. W. Borhnstedt, eds., *Sociological Methodology*. San Francisco: Jossey-Bass.

―――. 1975. *Causal Analysis*. New York: Wiley.

Helgason, T. 1961. "The Frequency of Depressive States in Iceland as Compared with the Other Scandinavian Countries." *Acta Psychiatrica Scandinavica* (suppl.) 162:81–90.

―――. 1964. "The Epidemiology of Mental Disorder in Iceland." *Acta Psychiatrica Scandinavica* (suppl.) 173.

―――. 1970. "Neurosernes og alkoholismens epidemiologi." *Nordisk Psykiatrisk Tidsskrift* 24:28–44.

―――. 1973. "Epidemiology of Mental Disorders in Iceland: A Geriatric Follow-up (Preliminary Report)." In R. de la Fuente and M. N. Weisman, eds., *Psychiatry*. Part 1. Proceedings of the V World Congress of Psychiatry. Excerpta Medica International Congress Series No. 274, Amsterdam.

―――. 1979. "Epidemiological Investigations concerning Affective Disorders." In M. Schou and E. Strömgren, eds., *Origin, Prevention and Treatment of Affective Disorders*. London: Academic Press.

―――. 1980. "Epidemiological Follow-up Research within a Geographically Stable Population." In G. W. Schimmelpenning, ed., *Ziele Methoden und Ergebnisse der psychiatrischen Verlaufsforsuchung*. Bern: Verlag Hans Huber.

Henricson, M. 1973. *The Norms and Norm Climate of Teenagers*. Stockholm: Utbildningsförlaget. (In Swedish with an English summary.)

Henry, L. 1976. *Population Analysis and Models*. London: Edward Arnold.

Herrmann, E. 1973. "Long-Range Effects of Early Parental Separation Experiences in Children with High and Low Risk for Schizophrenia." Ph.D. dissertation. New School for Social Research, New York.

Hill, R. 1970. *Family Development in Three Generations*. Cambridge, Mass.: Schenkman.

Hindelang, M. J. 1978. "Race and Involvement in Common Law Personal Crimes." *American Sociological Review* 43:93–109.

Hindelang, M. J.; Hirschi, T.; and Weis, J. G. 1979. "Correlates of Delinquency." *American Sociological Review* 44:995–1014.

Hirschi, T. 1969. *Causes of Delinquency*. Berkeley: University of California Press.

———. "Labelling Theory and Juvenile Delinquency: An Assessment of the Evidence." In W. R. Gove, ed., *The Labelling of Deviance*. New York: Sage.

Holland, W. W., and Gilderdale, S., eds. 1977. *Epidemiology and Health*. London: Henry Kimpton.

Holzman, P. S.; Kringlen, E.; Levy, D. L.; Proctor, L. R.; Haberman, S. J.; and Yasillo, N. J. 1977. "Abnormal-Pursuit Eye Movements in Schizophrenia." *Archives of General Psychiatry* 34:802–05.

Holzman, P. S.; Levy, D. L.; and Proctor, L. R. 1976. "Smooth-Pursuit Eye Movements, Attention and Schizophrenia." *Archives of General Psychiatry* 33:1415–20.

Horowitz, F. D.; Sullivan, J. W.; and Linn, P. 1978. "Stability and Instability in the Newborn Infant: The Quest for Elusive Threads." In A. Sameroff, ed., *Organization and Stability of Newborn Behavior: A Commentary on the Brazelton Neonatal Behavior Assessment Scale*. Monograph of the Society for Research in Child Development, Vol. 43(5–6).

Huisjes, H. J.; Okken, A.; Prechtl, H. F. R.; and Touwen, B. C. L. 1975. "Neurological and Paediatric Findings in Newborns of Mothers with Hypertensive Disease in Pregnancy." In Z. K. Stembera, K. Polácek, and U. Sabata, eds., *Perinatal Medicine*. Stuttgart: Thieme.

Huisjes, H. J.; Touwen, B. C. L.; Hoekstra, J.; van Woerden-Blanksma, J. T.; Bierman-van Eendenburg, M. E. C.; Jurgens-van der Zee, A. D.; and Olinga, A. A. 1980. "Obstetrical-Neonatal Neurological Relationship: A Replication Study." *European Journal of Obstetric and Gynecological Reproductive Biology* 10(4):247.

Hutchings, B., and Mednick, S. A. 1974. "Registered Criminality in the Adoptive and Biological Parents of Registered Male Adoptees." In S. A. Mednick, F. Schulsinger, J. Higgins, and B. Bell, eds., *Genetics, Environment and Psychopathology*. Amsterdam: North-Holland–American Elsevier.

Inghe, G. 1960. *Fattiga i folkhemmet*. Monografier utgivna av Stockholms kommunalförvaltning. Stockholm: Almquist & Wiksell.

Itil, T. M.; Hsu, M. S.; Saletu, B.; and Mednick, S. 1974. "Computer EEG and Auditory Evoked Potential Investigations in Children at High Risk for Schizophrenia." *American Journal of Psychiatry* 131:892–900.

Itil, T. M.; Saletu, B.; and Davis, S. 1972. "EEG Findings in Chronic Schizophrenics Based on Digital Computer Period Analysis and Analog Power Spectra." *Biological Psychiatry* 5:1–13.

Itil, T. M.; Simeon, J.; and Coffin, C. 1976. "Qualitative and Quantitative EEG in Psychotic Children." *Diseases of the Nervous System* 37:247–52.

Janes, C. L., and Stern, J. A. 1976. "Electrodermal Response Configuration as a Function of Rated Psychopathology in Children." *Journal of Nervous and Mental Disease* 162:184–94.

Janson, C-G. 1968. "Brott och sociala strata." C-G. Janson, ed., *Det differentierade samhället*. Stockholm: Prisma.

————. 1975. *Project Metropolitan — A Presentation*. Stockholm: Project Metropolitan Research Report No. 1.

————. 1977. *The Handling of Juvenile Delinquency Cases*. Stockholm: Project Metropolitan Research Report No. 7.

————. 1978. *The Longitudinal Approach*. Stockholm: Project Metropolitan Research Report No. 9.

Janson, C-G., and Jonsson, E. 1965. "Metodproblem vid studier av konsumentbeteende." In C. Boalt and E. Jonsson, eds., *Konsumtionen i sociologisk belysning*. Stockholm: Svenska bokförlaget.

Jasper, H. H. 1958. "The Ten-Twenty Electrode System of the International Federation." *EEG and Clinical Neurophysiology* 10:371–75.

Jennings, J. R.; Stringfellow, J. C.; and Graham, M. 1974. "A Comparison of Statistical Distributions of Beat-by-Beat Heart Rate and Heart Period." *Psychophysiology* 11:207–10.

Johansson, S. 1970. *Om levnadsnivåundersökningen*. Stockholm: Allmänna Förlaget.

John, E. R.; Karmel, B. Z.; Corning, W. C.; Easton, P.; Brown, D.; Ahn, H.; John, M.; Harmony, T.; Prichep, L.; Toro, A.; Gerson, I.; Bartlett, F.; Thatcher, R.; Kaye, H.; Valdes, P.; and Schnartz, E. 1977. "Neurometrics." *Science* 196:1393–1410.

Jones, R. H.; Crowell, D. H.; and Kapuniai, L. E. 1969. "Change Detection Model for Serially Correlated Data." *Psychological Bulletin* 71:352–58.

Jöreskog, K. G. 1970. "A General Method for Estimating a Linear Structural Equation System." *Research Bulletin 70–54*, Princeton, N.J.: Educational Testing Service.

————. 1970. "Factoring the Multitest-Multioccasion Correlation Matrix." In C. E. Lunneborg, ed., *Current Problems and Techniques in Multivariate Psychology*. Proceedings of a conference honoring Professor Paul Horst. Seattle: University of Washington.

————. 1979. "Statistical Estimation of Structural Models in Longitudinal Developmental Investigations." In J. R. Nesselroade and P. B. Baltes, eds., *Longitudinal Research in the Study of Behavior and Development*. New York: Academic Press.

Jöreskog, K. G., and Sörbom, D. 1976. "Statistical Models and Methods for Test-Retest Situations." In D. N. M. de Gruijter and L. J. and T. van der Kamp, eds., *Advances in Psychological and Educational Measurement*. London: Wiley.

————. 1977. "Statistical Models and Methods for Analysis of Longitudinal Data." In D. J. Aigner and A. S. Goldberger, eds., *Latent Variables in Socioeconomic Models*. Amsterdam: North-Holland.

Jöreskog, K. G., and von Thillo, M. 1972. "LISREL: A General Computer Program for Estimating a Linear Standard Equation System Involving Multiple Indicators of Unmeasured Variables." *Research Bulletin 72–56*, Princeton, N.J.: Educational Testing Service.

Jurgens-van der Zee, A. D.; Bierman-van Eendenburg; Fidler, V. J.; Olinga, A.

A.; Visch, J. H.; Touwen, B. C. L.; and Huisjes, H. J. 1979. "Preterm Birth, Growth Retardation and Acidemia in Relation to Neurological Abnormality of the Newborn." *Early Human Development* 3(2):141.

Kaad, U., and Hesselholdt, S. 1976. "113 danske familiers bidrag til belysning af de socialt betingede opdragelsesforskelle og hvad de betyder for skolen." In J. Gregersen and O. Varming, eds., *Pædagogisk psykologi, undervisningspsykologi*. Copenhagen: Busck.

Kagan, J. 1976. "Emergent Themes in Human Development." *American Scientist* 64:186–96.

Kagan, J.; Kearsley, R.; and Zelazo, P. 1978. *Infancy: Its Place in Human Development*. Cambridge, Mass.: Harvard University Press.

Kagan, J.; Lapidus, D. R.; and Moore, M. 1978. "Infant Antecedents of Cognitive Development: A Longitudinal Study." *Child Development* 49:1005–23.

Karlsson, G. 1961a. "Inledning." In G. Karlsson, ed., *Sociologiska metoder*. Stockholm: Scandinavian University Books.

———. 1961b. "Om teorier och teoretiserande." In G. Karlsson, ed., *Sociologiska metoder*. Stockholm: Scandinavian University Books.

Kastrup, M.; Dupont, A.; Bille, M.; and Lund, H. 1977. "Traffic Accidents Involving Psychiatric Patients: Description of the Material and General Results." *Acta Psychiatrica Scandinavica* 55:355–68.

Kastrup, M.; Nakane, Y.; Dupont, A.; and Bille, M. 1976. "Psychiatric Treatment in a Delimited Population — With Particular Reference to Out-Patients." *Acta Psychiatrica Scandinavica* 53:35–50.

Kessner, D. M.; Singer, J.; Kalk, C. E.; and Schlesinger, E. R. 1973. *Infant Death: An Analysis by Maternal Risk and Health Care. (Contrasts in Health Status.)* Vol. 1. Washington, D.C.: National Academy of Sciences.

Kety, S. S.; Rosenthal, D.; Wender, P. H.; Schulsinger, F.; and Jacobsen, B. 1975. "Mental Illness in the Biological and Adoptive Relatives of Adopted Individuals Who Became Schizophrenic." In R. Fieve, D. Rosenthal, and H. Brill, eds., *Genetic Research in Psychiatry*. Baltimore, Md.: Johns Hopkins University Press.

Keyfitz, N., and Flieger, W. 1968. *World Population: An Analysis of Vital Data*. Chicago: University of Chicago Press.

Kiernan, K. E. 1977. "Age at Puberty in Relation to Age at Marriage and Parenthood: A National Longitudinal Study." *Annals of Human Biology* 4:301–08.

Kiernan, K. E.; Colley, J. R. T.; Douglas, J. W. B.; and Reid, D. D. 1976. "Chronic Cough in Young Adults in Relation to Smoking Habits, Childhood Environment and Chest Illness." *Respiration* 33:236–44.

Kirkegaard-Sørensen, L., and Mednick, S. A. 1975. "Registered Criminality with Children at High Risk for Schizophrenia." *Journal of Abnormal Psychology* 84:197–204.

Klemperer, J. 1933. "Zur Belastungsstatistik der Durchschnittsbevölkerung: Psychosenhäufigkeit unter 1000 stichprobenmässig ausgelesenen Probanden." *Z. ges. Neurol. Psychiat.* 146:277–316.

Kruse, E.; Zachau-Christiansen, B.; Hansen, M.; Hesselholdt, S.; and Fordrup, S. 1975. *Lav fødselsvaegt — et risikomoment?* Elsinore: Skolepsykologi.

Kyng, B. 1974. *Opvaekstvilkar og udvikling.* Copenhagen: Gyldendal.

Landau, S. G.; Buchsbaum, M. S.; Carpenter, W.; Strauss, J.; and Sacks, M. 1975. "Schizophrenia and Stimulus Intensity Control." *Archives of General Psychiatry* 32:1239–45.

Lenski, G. 1966. *Power and Privilege.* New York: McGraw-Hill.

Levnadsnivåundersökningen 1974. 1977. "Codebook." Stockholm: Institute of Social Studies (stencil).

Lewis, D. O.; Balla, D.; Shanok, S.; and Snell, L. 1976. "Delinquency, Parental Psychopathology and Parental Criminality." *Journal of Child Psychiatry* 15:665–78.

Lier, L., and Michelsen, N. 1978. "Fumlere og tumlere." Ph.D. dissertation. Copenhagen University, Institute of Social Medicine.

Lilienfeld, A. M., and Pasmanick, B. 1955. "The Association of Maternal and Fetal Factors with Development of Cerebral Palsy and Epilepsy." *American Journal of Obstetrics and Gynecology* 70:93.

Lobstein, T. 1978. "Detection of Transient Responses in Adult Heart Rate." *Psychophysiology* 15:380–81.

Longitudinell Problematik II. 1974. *Proceedings of the Conference on Longitudinal Research.* Department of Psychology, University of Stockholm (stencil).

Lord, F. M. 1963. "Elementary Models for Measuring Change." In C. W. Harris, ed., *Problems in Measuring Change.* Madison: University of Wisconsin Press.

Lowe, C. R., and Lwanga, S. K., eds. 1978. *Health Statistics.* Manual for teachers of medical students, sponsored by the IEA and WHO. Oxford: Oxford University Press.

Lowry, R. 1977. "Active Circuits for Direct Linear Measurement of Skin Resistance and Conductance." *Psychophysiology* 14:329–31.

Lykken, D. T., and Venables, P. H. 1971. "Direct Measurement of Skin Conductance: A Proposal for Standardization." *Psychophysiology* 8:656–72.

Maccoby, E. E., and Jacklin, C. N. 1974. *The Psychology of Sex Differences.* Stanford, Calif.: Stanford University Press.

MacMullen, R. 1977. "Review of F. Millar: The Emperor in the Roman World." *Times Literary Supplement,* April 8, p. 418.

Magnusson, D. 1976a. "Overachievement as a Person Characteristic and Its Relation to Physiological Reactions." Reports from the Department of Psychology, University of Stockholm, No. 493.

————. 1976b. "The Person and the Situation in an Interactional Model of Behavior." *Scandinavian Journal of Psychology* 17:81–96.

————. 1978. "Achievement, Overachievement and Physiological Reactions among Males and Females." Invited lecture at the annual meeting of the Western Psychological Association, San Francisco, April 19–22.

Magnusson, D., and Backteman, G. 1977a. "Longitudinal Stability of Person Characteristics: Intelligence and Creativity." Reports from the Department of Psychology, University of Stockholm. No. 511.

————. 1977b. "Longitudinal Stability of Person Characteristics: Personality Trait Rating." Manuscript. Stockholm.

Magnusson, D., and Dunér, A. 1980. "The Örebro Project: A Longitudinal Study of Individual Development and Adjustment." In S. A. Mednick and A. E. Baert, eds., *Prospective Longitudinal Research*. New York: Oxford University Press.

Magnusson, D.; Dunér, A.; and Zetterblom; G. 1975. *Adjustment: A Longitudinal Study*. New York: Wiley.

Magnusson, D., and Endler, N. S. 1977. *Personality at the Crossroads: Current Issues in Interactional Psychology*. Hillsdale, N.J.: Lawrence Erlbaum Assoc.

Malmquist, E. 1973. *Läs-och skrivsvårigheter hos barn*. Lund: Gleerup.

Mårdberg, B. 1973. "A Model for Selection and Classification in Industrial Psychology." Reports from the Psychological Laboratories, University of Stockholm, Suppl. 19.

Maricq, H. R., and Edelberg, R. 1975. "Electrodermal Recovery Rate in a Schizophrenic Population." *Psychophysiology* 55:316–27.

Mason, W. M.; Winsborough, H. H.; and Poole, W. K. 1973. "Some Methodological Issues in Cohort Analysis of Archival Data." *American Sociological Review* 38(2):242–57.

Mausner, J. S., and Bahn, A. K. 1974. *Epidemiology: An Introductory Text*. Philadelphia: Saunders.

McCall, R. B. 1977. "Challenges to a Science of Developmental Psychology." *Child Development* 48:333–44.

McCall, R. B.; Appelbaum, M. I.; and Hogarty, P. S. 1973. "Developmental Changes in Mental Performance." Monograph, Society for Research in Child Development, Vol. 38(3).

McCall, R. B.; Hogarty, P. S.; and Hurlburt, N. 1973. "Transitions in Infant Sensorimotor Development and the Prediction of Childhood IQ." *American Psychologist* 27:728–48.

McDevitt, H. O., and Bodmer, W. F. 1974. "HL-A: Immune Response Genes and Disease." *Lancet* 1:1269–75.

McDonald, R. L. 1964. "Intelligence in Children of Very Low Birthweight." *British Journal of Preventive and Social Medicine* 18:59–74.

Mednick, B. 1977. "'Intellectual and Behavioral Functioning of Ten- to Twelve-Year-Old Children Who Showed Certain Transient Symptoms in the Neonatal Period." *Child Development* 48:844–53.

————. 1978. "Intellectual and Behavioral Functioning of 10–11-Year-Old Children Who Showed Certain Transient Neurological Symptoms in the Neonatal Period." In S. Chess and A. Thomas, eds., *Annual Progress in Child Psychiatry and Child Development*. New York: Brunner/Mazel.

Mednick, B.; Baker, R.; and Sutton-Smith, B. 1979. "Teenage Pregnancy and Perinatal Mortality." *Journal of Youth and Adolescence* 8:343–57.

Mednick, B., and Michelsen, N. 1972. "Neurological and Motor Functioning of 10–11-Year-Old Children Who Showed Certain Transient Neurological Symptoms in the First Five Days of Life." *Acta Neurologica Scandinavica* 56:70–78.

Mednick, S. A. 1958. "A Learning Theory Approach to Research in Schizophrenia." *Psychological Bulletin* 55:316–26.

———. 1960. "The Early and Advanced Schizophrenic." In S. A. Mednick and J. Higgins, eds., *Current Research in Schizophrenia*. Ann Arbor, Mich.: Edwards.

———. 1970. "Breakdown in Individuals at High Risk for Schizophrenia: Possible Predispositional Perinatal Factors." *Mental Hygiene* 54:50–63.

———. 1978. "Berkson's Fallacy and High-Risk Research." In L. C. Wynne, R. L. Cromwell, and S. Mathysse, eds., *The Nature of Schizophrenia*. New York: Wiley.

Mednick, S. A., and Baert, A. E. 1981. *Prospective Longitudinal Research: An Empirical Basis for Primary Prevention of Psychosocial Disorders*. Oxford: Oxford University Press. (Published on behalf of the WHO Regional Office for Europe.)

Mednick, S. A., and Lanoil, G. 1977. "Intervention in Children at High Risk for Schizophrenia." In G. W. Albee and J. M. Joffe, eds., *Primary Prevention in Psychopathology*. Hanover, N.H.: University Press of New England.

Mednick, S. A., and McNeil, T. F. 1968. "Current Methodology in Research on the Etiology of Schizophrenia." *Psychological Bulletin* 70:681–93.

Mednick, S. A.; Mura, E.; Schulsinger, F.; and Mednick, B. 1971. "Perinatal Conditions and Infant Development in Children with Schizophrenic Parents." *Social Biology* 18:103–13.

Mednick, S. A., and Schulsinger, F. 1968. "Some Pre-Morbid Characteristics Related to Breakdown in Children with Schizophrenic Mothers." In D. Rosenthal and S. S. Kety, eds., *The Transmission of Schizophrenia*. New York: Pergamon Press.

Mednick, S. A.; Schulsinger, F.; Higgins, J.; and Bell, B., eds. 1974. *Genetics, Environment and Psychopathology*. Amsterdam: North-Holland.

Mednick, S. A.; Schulsinger, H.; and Schulsinger, F. 1975. "Schizophrenia in Children of Schizophrenic Mothers." In A. Davids, ed., *Childhood Personality and Psychopathology: Current Topics*. New York: Wiley.

Mednick, S. A.; Schulsinger, F.; Teasdale, T. W.; Schulsinger, H.; Venables, P. H.; and Rock, D. R. 1978. "Schizophrenia in High-Risk Children: Sex Differences in Pre-Disposing Factors." In G. Serban, ed., *Cognitive Defects in the Development of Mental Illness*. New York: Brunner/Mazel.

Menkes, J. H. 1977. "Early Feeding History of Children with Learning Disorders." *Developmental Medicine and Child Neurology* 19:169–74.

Merritt, R. L., and Rokkan, S., eds. 1966. *Comparing Nations*. New Haven, Conn.: Yale University Press.

Merton, R. K. 1945. "Sociological Theory." *American Journal of Sociology* 50:462–73. See also Merton, 1957, chap. 2, pp. 85–101.

———. 1948. "The Bearing of Empirical Research upon the Development of

Social Theory." *American Sociological Review* 13:505–15. See also Merton, 1957, chap. 3, pp. 102–17.

———. 1957. *Social Theory and Structure,* rev. and enl. ed. Glencoe, Ill.: Free Press.

Mirdal, G.; Mednick, S. A.; Schulsinger, F.; and Fuchs, F. 1974. "Perinatal Complications in Children of Schizophrenic Mothers." *Acta Psychiatrica Scandinavica* 50:553–68.

Mombour, W. 1975. "Klassifikation, Patientenstatistik, Register." In K. P. Kisker, J.-E. Meyer, C. Müller, and E. Strömgren, eds., *Psychiatrie der Gegenwart: Forschung und Praxis,* 3d ed. New York: Springer.

Mood, A. M. 1950. *Introduction to the Theory of Statistics.* New York: McGraw-Hill.

Morris, J. N. 1975. *Uses of Epidemiology.* London: Churchill Livingstone.

Murdock, G. P. 1949. *Social Structure.* New York: Macmillan.

Murphy, D. L.; Donnelly, C. H.; Miller, L.; and Wyatt, R. J. 1976. "Platelet Monoamine Oxidase in Chronic Schizophrenia." *Archives of General Psychiatry* 33:1377–81.

Myslobodsky, M. S., and Horesh, N. 1978. "Bilateral Electrodermal Activity in Depressive Patients." *Biological Psychology* 6:111–20.

Nelson, E. E., and Starr, B. C. 1972. "Interpretation of Research on Age." In M. W. Riley et al., eds., *Aging and Society.* Vol. 3. New York: Russell Sage Foundation.

Nesselroade, J. R. 1972. "Note on the 'Longitudinal Factor Analysis' Model." *Psychometrika* 37:187–91.

Nesselroade, J. R., and Baltes, P. B. 1978. *Longitudinal Research in Human Development: Design and Analysis.* New York: Academic Press.

Nies, A.; Robinson, D. S.; Lamborn, K. R.; and Lampert, R. P. 1973. "Genetic Control of Platelet and Plasma Monoamine Oxidase Activity." *Archives of General Psychiatry* 28:834–38.

Niswander, K. R., and Gordon, M. 1972. *The Women and Their Pregnancies: The Collaborative Perinatal Study of the National Institute of Neurological Diseases and Stroke.* Philadelphia: Saunders.

Norlén, U. 1977. "Response Errors in the Answers to Retrospective Questions." *Statistisk Tidskrift* 4:331–41.

Nye, F. I. 1958. *Family Relationships and Delinquent Behavior.* New York: Wiley.

Olofsson, B. 1971. *What Did We Say? On Criminal and Conformist Behavior among Teenagers.* Stockholm: Utbildningsförlaget. (In Swedish with English summary.)

Olsson, U., and Bergman, L. R. 1977. "A Longitudinal Factor Model for Studying Change in Ability Structure." *Multivariate Behavioral Research* 12:221–42.

Orvaschel, H. 1976. "An Examination of Children at Risk for Schizophrenia as a Function of the Sex of the Sick Parent and the Sex of the Child." Ph.D. dissertation. New School for Social Research, New York.

Packham, J. 1975. *The Child's Generation: Child Care Policy from Curtis to Houghton*. London: Basil Blackwell and Martin Robertson.

Pasamanick, B., and Knobloch, H. 1966. "Retrospective Studies on the Epidemiology of Reproductive Casualty: Old and New." *Merrill-Palmer Quarterly* 12:7–26.

Pasamanick, B.; Knobloch, H.; and Lilienfeld, A. M. 1956. "Socio-economic Status and Some Precursors of Neuropsychiatric Disorders." *American Journal of Orthopsychiatry* 26:594–601.

Patterson, P. H.; Potter, D. D.; and Furshpan, E. J. 1978. "The Chemical Differentiation of Nerve Cells." *Scientific American* 239 (1):50–59.

Pharoah, P. 1976. "Obstetric and Neonatal Care Related to Outcome: A Comparison of Two Maternity Hospitals." *British Journal of Preventive Social Medicine* 30:257–61.

Phillips, D. L. 1971. *Knowledge from What?* Chicago: Rand McNally.

Piaget, J. 1971. *Biology and Knowledge*. Trans. by Beatrix Walsh. Chicago: University of Chicago Press.

Pless, I. B., and Douglas, J. W. B. 1971. "Chronic Illness in Childhood — Part 1: Epidemiological and Clinical Characteristics." *Pediatrics* 47:405.

Pollin, W., and Stabenau, J. R. 1968. "Biological, Psychological, and Historical Differences in a Series of Monozygotic Twins Discordant for Schizophrenia." *Journal of Psychiatric Research* 6 (Suppl. 1):317–32.

Prechtl, H. F. R. 1968. "Neurological Findings in Newborn Infants after Pre- and Perinatal Complications." In H. H. P. Jonxis, H. K. A. Visser, and J. A. Troelstra, eds., *Effects of Prematurity and Dysmaturity*. Leiden: Stenfert Kroese.

————. 1977. "The Neurological Examination of the Full-Term Newborn Infant," 2d ed. *Clinics in Developmental Medicine*, No. 63, London.

Prioritering i sundhedsvæsenet [Priority of activities in health organization and health systems]. 1977. Report No. 809. Copenhagen: Statens Trykningskontor.

Project Metropolitan. 1975a. *The School Study — A Code Book*. Stockholm: Project Metropolitan Research Report No. 3.

————. 1975b. *The Family Study — A Code Book*. Stockholm: Project Metropolitan Research Report No. 4.

Prokasy, W. F., and Kumpfer, K. L. 1973. "Classical Conditioning." In W. F. Prokasy and D. C. Raskin, eds., *Electrodermal Activity in Psychological Research*. New York: Academic Press.

Quinton, D., and Rutter, M. 1976. "Early Hospital Admissions and Later Disturbances of Behaviour: An Attempted Replication of Douglas' Findings." *Developmental Medicine and Child Neurology* 18:447–53.

Ramsøy, N. R. 1977. *Sosial mobilitet i Norge*. Oslo: Tiden.

Rawlings, G.; Reynolds, E.; Stewart, A.; and Strange, L. 1971. "Changing Prognosis for Infants of Very Low Birth Weight." *Lancet* 1:516.

Reisby, N. 1967. "Psychoses in Children of Schizophrenic Mothers." *Acta Psychiatrica Scandinavica* 43:8–20.

Reiss, A. J., and Rhodes, A. L. 1961. "The Distribution of Juvenile Delinquency in the Social Structure." *American Sociological Review* 26:720–32.

Rémond, A., ed. 1977. *EEG Informatics: A Didactic Review of Methods and Applications of EEG Data Processing.* Amsterdam: Elsevier.

Riley, M. W. 1963. *Sociological Research I: A Case Approach.* New York: Harcourt, Brace & World.

Riley, M. W., and Foner, A. 1968. *Aging and Society.* Vol. 1. New York: Russell Sage Foundation.

Riley, M. W.; Johnson, M.; and Foner, A., eds. 1972. *Aging and Society.* Vol. 3. New York: Russell Sage Foundation.

Rodgers, B. 1978. "Feeding in Infancy and Later Ability and Attainment: A Longitudinal Study." *Developmental Medicine and Child Neurology* 20:421–26.

Rogers, A. 1975. *Introduction to Multiregional Mathematical Demography.* New York: Wiley.

Rogoff, B. 1977. "A Study of Memory." Unpublished Ph.D. dissertation. Harvard University, Cambridge, Mass.

Rosenblith, J. 1964. "Prognostic Value of Behavioral Assessments of Neonates." *Biologia Neonatorum* 6:76–103.

———. 1973. "Relations between Neonatal Behaviors and Those at Eight Months." *Developmental Psychology* 10:779–92.

Rosenthal, D. 1962. "Familial Concordance by Sex with Respect to Schizophrenia." *Psychological Bulletin* 59:401–21.

———. 1971. "A Program of Research on Heredity in Schizophrenia." *Behavioral Science* 16:191–201.

———. 1974. "The Concept of Sub-Schizophrenic Disorders." In S. A. Mednick, F. Schulsinger, J. Higgins, and B. Bell, eds., *Genetics, Environment and Psychopathology.* Amsterdam: North-Holland–American Elsevier.

Rosenthal, D.; Wender, P. H.; Kety, S. S.; Schulsinger, F.; Welner, J.; and Østergaard, L. 1968. "Schizophrenics' Offspring Reared in Adoption Homes." In D. Rosenthal and S. S. Kety, eds., *The Transmission of Schizophrenia.* London: Pergamon Press.

Rutter, M. 1970. "Sex Differences in Children's Responses to Family Stress." In E. Anthony and C. Koupernki, eds., *The Child in His Family.* New York: Wiley.

Rutter, M., and Madge, N. 1976. *Cycles of Disadvantage.* London: Heinemann.

Rutter, M.; Yule, W.; Tizard, J.; and Graham, P. 1966. *Severe Reading Retardation: Its Relationship to Maladjustment, Epilepsy and Neurological Disorders.* Middlesex, Eng.: Association for Special Education.

Sameroff, A. 1975. "Early Influences on Development: Fact or Fancy?" *Merrill-Palmer Quarterly* 21(4):267–93.

———. 1978. "Summary and Conclusions: The Future of Newborn Assessment." In A. Sameroff, ed., *Organization and Stability of Newborn Behavior: A Commentary on the Brazelton Neonatal Behavior Assessment Scale.* Monograph of the Society for Research in Child Development, Vol. 43(5–6).

———. 1979. "The Etiology of Cognitive Competence: A Systems Perspective." In R. Kearsley and I. Siegel, eds., *Infants at Risk: Assessment of Cognitive Functioning*. New York: Wiley.

Sameroff, A., and Chandler, M. 1974. "Reproductive Risk and the Continuum of Caretaking Casualty." *Review of Child Development Research*:187–244.

Sameroff, A.; Krafchuk, E. E.; and Bakow, H. A. 1978. "Issues in Grouping Items from the Neonatal Behavioral Assessment Scale." In A. Sameroff, ed., *Organization and Stability of Newborn Behavior: A Commentary on the Brazelton Neonatal Behavior Assessment Scale*. Monograph of the Society for Research in Child Development, Vol. 43(5–6).

Scarr-Salapatek, S., and Williams, M. L. 1973. "The Effects of Early Stimulation on Low Birthweight Infants." *Child Development* 44:94–101.

Schaie, K. W. 1965. "A General Model for the Study of Developmental Problems." *Psychological Bulletin* 64:92–107.

Schildkraut, J. J.; Herzog, J. M.; Orsular, P. J.; Edelman, S. E.; Schein, H. M.; and Frazier, S. H. 1976. "Reduced Platelet Monoamine Oxidase Activity in a Sub-group of Schizophrenic Patients." *American Journal of Psychiatry* 133:438–40.

Schulsinger, F. 1972. "Psychopathy: Heredity and Environment." *International Journal of Mental Health* 1:190–206.

Schulsinger, F.; Kety, S. S.; Rosenthal, D.; and Wender, P. H. 1979. "A Family Study of Suicide." In M. Schou and E. Strömgren, eds., *Origin, Prevention, and Treatment of Affective Disorders*. London: Academic Press.

Schulsinger, F.; Mednick, S. A.; Venables, P. H.; Raman, A. C.; and Bell, B. 1975. "Early Detection and Prevention of Mental Illness: The Mauritius Project. (A Preliminary Report.)" *Neuropsychobiology* 1:166–79.

Schulsinger, H. 1976. "A Ten-Year Follow-up of Children of Schizophrenic Mothers: Clinical Assessment." *Acta Psychiatrica Scandinavica* 53:371–86.

Schyberger, B. W. 1965. *Methods of Readership Research*. Lund Business Studies. Lund: Gleerup.

Sellers, M. J. 1979. "The Effects of Motivation and Strategy Instruction on Recall Memory." Unpublished Ph.D. dissertation. Harvard University, Cambridge, Mass.

Selltiz, C.; Wrightsman, L. S.; and Cook, S. W. 1976. *Research Methods in Social Relations*, 3d ed. Appendix B: A. Kornhauser and P. B. Sheatsley, "Questionnaire Construction and Interview Procedure." New York: Holt, Rinehart & Winston.

Sewell, W. H.; Haller, A. O.; and Portes, A. 1969. "The Educational and Early Occupational Attainment Process." *American Sociological Review* 34(1):82–92.

Shagass, C.; Roemer, R. A.; and Amadeo, M. 1976. "Eye-Tracking Performance and Engagement of Attention." *Archives of General Psychiatry* 33:121–25.

Siddle, D. A. T. 1977. "Electrodermal Activity and Psychopathy." In S. A. Mednick and K. O. Christiansen, eds., *Biosocial Bases of Criminal Behavior*. New York: Gardner.

Silverman, J. 1964. "Scanning-Control Mechanism and Cognitive Filtering in Paranoid and Nonparanoid Schizophrenics." *Journal of Consulting Psychology* 28:385–93.

Silverman, J.; Berg, P. S.; and Kantor, R. 1966. "Some Perceptual Correlates of Institutionalization." *Journal of Nervous and Mental Disorders* 141:651–57.

Sobel, D. E. 1961. "Children of Schizophrenic Patients: Preliminary Observations on Early Development." *American Journal of Psychiatry* 118:512–17.

Socialforskningsinstituttets Publikationer nr. 34. 1968. *Børns opvækstvilkàr.* Copenhagen: Teknisk Forlag.

Sörbom, D., and Jöreskog, K. G. 1981. "The Use of Structural Equation Models in Evaluation Research." Paper presented at the Conference on Experimental Research in the Social Sciences, Gainesville, Florida, January 8–10.

St. Clair, K. 1978. "Neonatal Assessment Procedures: A Historical Review." *Child Development* 49:280–92.

Stahl, S. M. 1977. "The Human Platelet." *Archives of General Psychiatry* 34:509–16.

Stern, S.; Mednick, S. A.; and Schulsinger, F. 1974. "Social Class, Institutionalization and Schizophrenia." In S. A. Mednick et al., eds., *Genetics, Environment and Psychopathology.* Amsterdam: North-Holland–Elsevier.

Stjórnartíoindi 1896–1898, c-deild. Mannfjöldi, 1895–1897. (Population in Reykjavik, Iceland.)

Sutherland, E. H., and Cressey, D. R. 1960. *Principles of Criminology,* 6th ed. Chicago: Lippincott.

Svalastoga, K. 1959. *Prestige, Class and Mobility.* Copenhagen: Gyldendal.

———. 1976. *Analytic Strategy in Sequential Research.* Stockholm: Project Metropolitan Research Report No. 6.

Svensson, A. 1971. *Relative Achievement.* Stockholm: Almquist & Wiksell.

Swedner, H. 1968. "Brottligheten i Sverige." In J. Israel, ed., *Sociala avvikelser och social kontroll,* 2d ed. Stockholm: Almquist & Wiksell.

Tahmoush, A. J.; Jennings, J. R.; Lee, A. L.; Camp, S.; and Weber, F. 1976. "Characteristics of a Light Emitting Diode-Transistor Photoplethysmograph." *Psychophysiology* 13:357–62.

Talovic, S. A.; Mednick, S. A.; Schulsinger, F.; and Falloon, I. R. H. 1980. "Schizophrenia in High-Risk Subjects: Prognostic Maternal Characteristics." *Journal of Abnormal Psychology* 89:501–04.

Theodorson, G. A., and Theodorson, A. G. 1969. *A Modern Dictionary of Sociology.* New York: T.Y. Crowell.

Thomae, H. 1980. "The Bonn Longitudinal Study of Aging (BLSA): An Approach to Differential Gerontology." In S. A. Mednick and A. E. Baert, eds., *Prospective Longitudinal Research.* New York: Oxford University Press.

Thomas, A.; Chess, S.; and Birch, H. 1968. *Temperament and Behavior Disorders in Children.* New York: New York University Press.

Thorndike, R. L. 1966. "Intellectual Status and Intellectual Growth." *Journal of Educational Psychology* 57:121–27.

Tittle, C. R.; Villemez, W. J.; and Smith, D. A. 1978. "The Myth of Social Class and Criminality: An Empirical Assessment of the Empirical Evidence." *American Sociological Review* 43:643–56.

Torgerson, W. S. 1958. *Theory and Methods of Scaling*. New York: Wiley.

Touwen, B. C. L. 1976. "Neurological Development in Infancy." *Clinics in Developmental Medicine,* No. 58, London.

Touwen, B. C. L.; Huisjes, H. J.; Jurgens-v.d. Zee, A. D.; Bierman-van Eendenburg, M. E. C.; Smrikovsky, M.; and Olinga, A. A. 1980. "Obstetrical Condition and Neonatal Neurological Morbidity: An Analysis with the Help of the Optimality Concept." *Early Human Development* 4(3):207.

Treiman, D. J. 1977. *Occupational Prestige in Comparative Perspective*. New York: Academic Press.

Ucko, L. E. 1965. "A Comparative Study of Asphyxiated and Non-Asphyxiated Boys from Birth to Five Years." *Developmental Medicine and Child Neurology* 7(6):643–57.

Venables, P. H. 1978. "Psychophysiology and Psychometrics." *Psychophysiology* 15:302–15.

Venables, P. H., and Christie, M. J. 1973. "Mechanisms, Instrumentation, Recording Techniques and Quantification of Responses." In W. F. Prokasy and D. C. Raskin, eds., *Electrodermal Activity in Psychological Research*. New York: Academic Press.

———. 1980. "Electrodermal Activity." In I. Martin and P. H. Venables, eds., *Techniques in Psychophysiology*. Chicester, Eng.: Wiley.

Venables, P. H.; Fletcher, R. P.; Mednick, S. A.; Schulsinger, F.; and Cheeneebash, R. In press. "Aspects of Development of Electrodermal and Cardiac Activity between 5 and 25 years."

Venables, P. H.; Mednick, S. A.; Schulsinger, F.; Raman, A. C.; Bell, B.; Dalais, J. C.; and Fletcher, R. P. 1978. "Screening for Risk of Mental Illness." In G. Serban, ed., *Cognitive Defects in the Development of Mental Illness*. New York: Brunner/Mazel.

Videbech, T.; Weeke, A.; and Dupont, A. 1974. "Endogenous Psychoses and Season of Birth." *Acta Psychiatrica Scandinavica* 50:202–18.

Voorhees-Rosen, D., and Rosen, D. 1980. "Shetland: The Effects of Rapid Social Change on Mental Health." In S. A. Mednick and A. E. Baert, eds., *Prospective Longitudinal Research*. New York: Oxford University Press.

Wadsworth, M. E. J. 1976. "Delinquency, Pulse Rates and Early Emotional Deprivation." *British Journal of Criminology* 16:245–56.

———. 1979. *Roots of Delinquency: Infancy, Adolescence and Crime*. Oxford: Martin Robertson; New York: Barnes & Noble.

Wadsworth, M. E. J., and Morris, S. 1978. "Assessing Chances of Hospital Admission in Pre-School Children: A Critical Evaluation." *Archives of Disease in Childhood* 53:159–63.

Walker, E. F.; Cudeck, R.; Mednick, S. A.; and Schulsinger, F. 1980. "Effects of Parental Absence and Institutionalization on the Development of Clinical Symptoms in High-Risk Children." *Acta Psychiatrica Scandinavica*.

Wall, W. D., and Williams, H. L. 1970. *Longitudinal Studies and the Social Sciences*. London: Heinemann.

Walldén, M. 1974. *Individers aktivitetsmönster*. Part I. Stockholm: Byggforskningen R 11.

Wallerstein, J. S., and Wyle, C. J. 1947. "Our Law-Abiding Law-Breakers." *Probation* 25:107–12. Quoted by Swedner, 1968, p. 191.

Watt, N. F.; Stolorow, R. D.; Lubensky, A. W.; and McClelland, D. C. 1970. "School Adjustment and Social Behavior of Children Hospitalized for Schizophrenia as Adults." *American Journal of Orthopsychiatry* 40:637–57.

Weeke, A.; Kastrup, M.; and Dupont, A. 1979. "Long-stay Patients in Danish Psychiatric Hospitals." *Psychological Medicine* 9:551–66.

Weeke, A., and Strömgren, E. 1978. "Fifteen Years Later: A Comparison of Patients in Danish Psychiatric Institutions in 1957, 1962, 1967, and 1972." *Acta Psychiatrica Scandinavica* 57:129–44.

Wender, P. H.; Rosenthal, D.; Kety, S. S.; Schulsinger, F.; and Welner, J. 1974. "Crossfostering." *Archives of General Psychiatry* 30:121–28.

Werner, E. E.; Bierman, J. M.; and French, F. E. 1971. *The Children of Kauai*. Honolulu: University of Hawaii Press.

Werts, C. E.; Linn, R. L.; and Jöreskog, K. G. 1971. "Estimating the Parameters of Path Models Involving Unmeasured Variables." In H. M. Blalock, ed., *Causal Models in the Social Sciences*. Chicago and New York: Aldine and Atherton.

West, D. J., and Farrington, D. P. 1977. *The Delinquent Way of Life*. London: Heinemann.

Westergaard, H. 1928. "Some Remarks on the Service of Statistics in Anthropological Investigations," *Meddelelser om Danmarks Antropologi*. Vol. 2. Copenhagen: G. E. C. Gads Forlag, pp. 162–63.

White, H. 1973. *Metahistory: The Historical Imagination in 19th-Century Europe*. Baltimore, Md.: Johns Hopkins University Press.

White, K. L., and Henderson, M. M., eds. 1976. *Epidemiology as a Fundamental Science: Its Uses in Health Services Planning, Administration and Evaluation*. New York: Oxford University Press.

Wicksell, S. D. 1920. *Elementen av statistikens teori*. Lund: Svenska försäkringsföreningen.

Wiley, D. E., and Harnischfeger, A. 1973. "Post Hoc, Ergo Propter Hoc: Problems in the Attribution of Change." Report No 7. University of Chicago: Studies of Educative Processes.

Wilson, R. S. 1974. "CARDIVAR: The Statistical Analysis of Heart Rate Data." *Psychophysiology* 11:76–85.

Wing, J. K. 1975. "Epidemiological Methods and the Clinical Psychiatrist." In P. Sainsbury and N. Kreitman, eds., *Methods of Psychiatric Research*, 2d ed. London: Oxford University Press.

Wing, L.; Bramley, C.; Hailey, A.; and Wing, J. K. 1968. "Camberwell Cumulative Psychiatric Case Register. Part I: Aims and Methods." *Social Psychiatry* 3:116–23.

Wing, J. K.; Cooper, J. E.; and Sartorius, N. 1974. *The Measurement and Classification of Psychiatric Symptoms.* Cambridge: Cambridge University Press.

Wing, J. K.; Mann, S. A.; Leff, J. P.; and Nixon, J. M. 1978. "The Concept of a Case in Psychiatric Population Surveys." *Psychological Medicine* 8:203–17.

Wing, L.; Wing, J. K.; Hailey, A.; Bahn, A. K.; Smith, H. E.; and Baldwin, J. A. 1967. "The Use of Psychiatric Services in Three Urban Areas: An International Case Register Study." *Social Psychiatry* 2:158–67.

Wohlwill, J. F. 1973. *The Study of Behavioral Development.* New York: Academic Press.

Woods, G. E. 1976. "The Incidence of Handicapping Conditions in Childhood Resulting from Perinatal Morbidity." *Developmental Medicine and Child Neurology* 18:394.

World Health Organization (WHO). 1967. *Manual of the International Statistical Classification of Diseases, Injuries, and Causes of Death,* 8th rev. ed. Vol. 1. Geneva.

―――. 1968. "Neurophysiological and Behavioral Research in Psychiatry." Technical Report No. 381. Geneva.

Yarrow, M. R.; Campbell, J. D.; and Berton, R. V. 1970. "Recollections of Childhood: A Study of the Retrospective Method." Monograph of the Society for Research and Child Development, Vol. 35 (138).

Yolles, S., and Kramer, M. 1969. "Vital Statistics." In L. Bellak and L. Loeb, eds., *The Schizophrenic Syndrome.* New York: Grune & Stratton.

Zachau-Christiansen, B. 1972. *The Influence of Prenatal and Perinatal Factors on Development during the First Year of Life with Special Reference to the Development of Signs of Cerebral Dysfunction: A Prospective Study of 9006 Pregnancies.* Helsingør: Poul A. Andersens Forlag.

Zachau-Christiansen, B., and Ross, E. M. 1975. *Babies: Human Development during the First Year.* London: Wiley.

Zetterberg, H. L. 1963. *On Theory and Verification in Sociology,* 2d ed. Totowa, N.J.: Bedminster.

Zettergren, P. 1977. "Utstötta och isolerade barns livssituation" [The life situation of socially rejected and isolated children]. Report no. 19, Department of Psychology, University of Stockholm.

―――. 1980. "Social Situation och utveckling. En studie av utstötta och isolerade barn" [Social situation and development. A study of rejected and isolated children]. Report no. 36, Department of Psychology, University of Stockholm.

INDEX

LIST OF CONTRIBUTORS

ANDRÉ E. BAERT, M.D., Chief, Mental Health Office, WHO, Regional Office for Europe, Copenhagen, Denmark

CYRIL DALAIS, M.Phil., Academic Director, Joint Child Health and Education Project, Quatre Bornes, Mauritius

J. W. B. DOUGLAS, M.D., Head of Medical Research Unit on Environmental Factors in Mental and Physical Illness, London School of Economics, England

ANNALISE DUPONT, M.D., Head of Institute of Psychiatric Demography, Psychiatric Hospital, near Arhus, Denmark

JOHN J. GRIFFITH, Ph.D., Social Science Research Institute, University of Southern California, Los Angeles, California, U.S.A.

TÓMAS HELGASON, M.D., Professor of Psychiatry, University of Reykjavik, Iceland

HENK J. HUISJES, M.D., Professor of Obstetrics and Gynecology, University Hospital, Groningen, The Netherlands

JOHANNES IPSEN, M.D., Professor of Epidemiology and Medical Statistics, University of Arhus, Denmark

CARL-GUNNAR JANSON, Ph.D., Professor of Sociology, University of Stockholm, Sweden

KARL G. JÖRESKOG, Ph.D., Professor of Statistics, University of Uppsala, Sweden

JEROME KAGAN, Ph.D., Professor of Psychology, Harvard University, Cambridge, Massachusetts, U.S.A.

DAVID MAGNUSSON, Ph.D., Professor of Psychology, University of Stockholm, Sweden

BIRGITTE R. MEDNICK, Ph.D., Educational Psychology, University of Southern California, Los Angeles, California, U.S.A.

SARNOFF A. MEDNICK, Ph.D., Dr.Med., Professor of Psychology, University of Southern California, Los Angeles, California, U.S.A., and Director of Psykologisk Institut, Kommunehospitalet, Copenhagen, Denmark

FINI SCHULSINGER, M.D., Professor of Psychiatry, University of Copenhagen, and Director of Psykologisk Institut, Kommunehospitalet, Copenhagen, Denmark

HANNE SCHULSINGER, Senior Lecturer, Department of Psychology, University of Copenhagen, Denmark

KAARE SVALASTOGA, Ph.D., Professor of Sociology, University of Copenhagen, Denmark

PETER H. VENABLES, Ph.D., Professor and Chairman of Psychology, University of York, England

CHARLES YIP TONG, M.D., Senior Consultant, Brown-Sequard Hospital, Beau Bassin, Mauritius

BENGT ZACHAU-CHRISTIANSEN, M.D., Professor of Pediatrics, University of Copenhagen, Denmark